TRUE

- Most of the big box-office names are either nymphomaniacs or homosexuals.

- The most famous tough men are notorious cowards.

- The only road to success is lined with gangsters and sugar daddies.

- The more famous a star, the more likely he is to be a drug addict or an alcoholic.

- If you kicked all the psychoanalysts out of Hollywood the streets would be littered with the corpses of suicides and murders.

Sound incredible? Before you make judgment, jot down your answers and then read this book. Pass or fail, you're in for a jolt. For here, in all its stunning irreverence, is a side of Hollywood you've never seen before . . .

HOLLYWOOD CONFIDENTIAL

HOLLYWOOD CONFIDENTIAL

PHIL HIRSCH, Editor

PYRAMID BOOKS • NEW YORK

HOLLYWOOD CONFIDENTIAL

A PYRAMID BOOK
First printing March, 1967

ACKNOWLEDGMENTS

These articles appeared in Man's Magazine, copyright © 1962, by Almat Publishing Corp., copyright © 1964, 1965, 1966 by Pyramid Publications, Inc. Permission to reprint them is gratefully acknowledged.

Printed in the United States of America

PYRAMID BOOKS are published by Pyramid Publications, Inc.
444 Madison Avenue, New York, New York 10022, U.S.A.

CONTENTS

HOLLYWOOD BUM

● *SY RIBAKOVE*

The skinny, ferret-faced kid rested his pickax on the parched Georgia roadbed and leaned down to finger his blistered ankle. The iron manacle, symbol of the chain gang, had worn the kid's skin raw in several places. Suddenly he looked up. Two guards, rifles slung lazily across their crooked elbows, were bringing a new prisoner to the sweating road crew. Squinting, the kid studied the new man. Big—but not as big as the Creole, he decided. Good. He brushed his matted hair out of his eyes, and hefted the ax again.

By lunchtime, the kid's scrawny, 16-year-old frame was aching, but he edged over to the new con before letting himself sink down into the soft dirt by the side of the road. He waited, silent, while a burly guard shackled him to the chain. Then he spoke:

"What they get ya for?"

"Assault," the new con said. "You?"

The kid shrugged. "Vagrancy." He moved in closer, his voice dropping to a confidential whisper. "Listen," he said, "we're short of straw ticks here."

"Yeah? So?"

"Well, I don't do it for everybody, but you're all right. For two bits I'll see you get a nice soft one tonight. A man can get dog weary around here. . . ."

By the time the gang was prodded back to work, the kid had a silver quarter stashed in his shoe.

At sundown the guards marched the gang back to the lockup and the prisoners fell exhausted onto their bunks; all but the new man, who sat on his bare bunk and looked questioningly at the kid. Snickering, the kid lay back on his mattress, shutting his eyes as he slowly stretched out.

7

"Damnyankee punk!" the new con hissed, realizing that he'd been taken. He rose menacingly. "I'm gonna break your lousy—"

But the kid was ready for him. "Easy, friend," he said softly. "You better meet my pardner first."

At which point, a hulking figure with fists like mallets and a glint in his eye that matched his reputation as a killer, rose from the next bunk. It was the Creole.

The new con took a step backward.

"So?" the kid taunted. "You got a complaint?"

"Forget it," the con said. "A mistake." He backed away, muttering helplessly.

For nearly a week the kid and the Creole worked their "con game" on each new arrival. Finally the kid had a couple of bucks stashed away, enough to take care of him on a planned escape. The next night the gang worked long past dark and the kid, noticing the guards momentarily distracted, split for the woods.

Two slugs slammed into the dry ground at his feet as he ran. The kid put his head down and ran faster, zig-zagging wildly. Once in the trees he'd be home free—the Cracker guards wouldn't waste time searching for him; too many other patsies were waiting in the Savannah lockup.

Before sunrise the next morning, Robert Charles Mitchum was on a freight, nursing his sore ankle, heading for parts unknown. . . .

Years later, with fame and fortune beckoning, Mitchum sat down in a movie studio commissary for his first Hollywood interview. "Tell me something about your early years, Bob," began the reporter.

"Sure," said Mitchum genially. "I once did time on a Georgia chain gang, and—"

The studio flack almost fell off his chair aiming an under-the-table kick, but Mitchum would not be silenced. He not only finished the story, but in the months that followed, he told it at interview after interview, much to the dismay of his studio bosses. Occasionally, when the mood was on him, he embroidered it with a sequel.

After his escape, Mitchum said, he discovered that the ankle had become gangrenous. Told it would have to be amputated, he escaped from the hospital, and limped home to his mother—who restored the foot to health by binding it up with an herb-and-unguent poultice she had learned as a child in the South.

There were other sequels as well—much more credible, but all of them the kind of story any actor trying to make a name for himself in Hollywood would have paid a fortune to keep out of print. Not Mitchum. He told his tales of barroom brawls, cross-country wanderings, brushes with the law, and he told them lovingly—and with relish. He was what he was—in his own words, "a bum, just a bum," and, oddly enough, the disreputable image didn't wreck his career. In fact, it saved it.

When a major scandal broke over his head in 1948, Mitchum was sentenced to two months in the Los Angeles County Jail. He emerged bigger than ever, his fan following intact. How did he survive? Because of the image he had fashioned for himself—on and off screen. No one was really shocked. Not the girls and women who, in the safety of dark movie houses, lost themselves in brutal fantasies of what it might be like to be alone with him; not the boys and men who saw in him the idealized portrait of a male figure who was damn good at being bad. Mitchum in jail was just what everybody expected.

Today Mitchum still maintains he is a bum (despite an income that approaches a cool million a year), laying claim to seven jail sentences, three of which are well documented. He moseys around his 300-acre Maryland farm in an old hunting jacket and a battered straw hat, insisting that his sole ambition is to retire and spend the rest of his days in a porch rocker.

His command of the seamier side of the English language is notorious. Lady reporters usually leave a Mitchum interview purple around the ears. (One Hollywood butterfly, hoping to cash in on a five minutes' acquaintance with Mitchum, asked for an autographed picture that was "a little different." "Certainly, ma'am," drawled Mitchum, and inscribed the photo: "To Beatrice: S–t! Love, Bob.")

Mitchum will take on anybody or anything: He stunned a contribution-seeking lady from the ASPCA by asking her if she didn't think all dogs should be shot (though he owns several himself), and alienated the United States Army during filming of the Normandy beachhead scenes of *The Longest Day* when he passed a remark regarding the fitness of the 250 GI's on loan to 20th-Century Fox. Mitchum later denied casting any aspersions on the armed forces, but the episode had repercussions all the way up to the General Staff and the Cabinet.

Mitchum also periodically disappears from home for

days at a time, only to be discovered tramping down some desolate rural road, or holed up with a country family in a Southern backwash. He maintains he never made a pass at an actress he worked with, but his name has been linked with several, most recently Shirley MacLaine (his co-star in *Two for the Seesaw* and *What a Way to Go*), who flew all the way to Kenya to watch the Mitchum muscle ripple on location for his newest film, *Mr. Moses.*

Despite these shenanigans—or maybe because of them—Mitchum is one of the half-dozen top male stars in Hollywood today. Unlike his only box-office rivals (Cary Grant, Gregory Peck, Bill Holden), Mitchum is short on looks ("I'm the ugliest actor in pictures. . . .") and shorter on charm (Off-screen, he can't be bothered with such social amenities as saying hello and goodby; on-screen his most memorable performances have been portrayals of the criminally deranged in such films as *Night of the Hunter* and *Cape Fear*.).

What he has, of course, is talent—plus a quality that a female moviegoer once described as follows: "Oh," she gasped, "he's got the most immoral face I ever saw. He's—you know—sexy in this *evil* kind of way."

Mitchum prefers to ignore such talk. "Hell," he says, "the only difference between me and other actors is that I've been in jail more than they have. Anyway, I'm just here between trains."

Mitchum has been "between trains" most of his 49 years. Born on August 16, 1917 in Bridgeport, Connecticut, of a mixed background (his mother was Norwegian, his father part Blackfoot Indian), he grew up in trouble all the way. Before he was two, his father, a railroad worker, was killed in a switching-yard accident, leaving Bob, his older sister and infant brother to fend for themselves while their mother worked.

Mitchum was a scrawny, fast-fisted kid whom the neighbors regarded as "some kind of degenerate." Sent to live with his grandmother in Fenton, Delaware, he got kicked out of school and eventually out of town; and when, at the age of twelve, he accidentally shot a friend in the hip with a shotgun, he came home and announced that everyone ought to be satisfied now—he was turning out to be the criminal they'd all predicted.

Mitchum's mother eventually remarried, but her older son Bob didn't care for the life-with-father bit any more. When he was fourteen, Mitchum decided to go on his own.

He lied his way into a job on a salvage ship, which lasted until the owners discovered his age and put him ashore. Then he headed west, hopping freights, doing odd jobs and spending a short time as a California beach bum, rolling drunks for lunch money ("I didn't know any better"). On his way back east, where his family had settled, he found a job in a Pennsylvania coal mine. On his first day in the pit, Mitchum discovered he had claustrophobia.

Shouting, "Lemme outa here!" he headed for the shaft elevator. But his way was blocked by a mountainous Polish foreman hefting a breakthrough hammer.

"You no quit!" the foreman ordered, swinging the hammer.

So Mitchum stayed a few terror-filled weeks before taking off . . . but to this day he gets the shakes in crowded elevators.

During the Depression days of the Thirties, thousands of homeless youths wandered across the face of America. Bob Mitchum stood out for two reasons. First, he wrote poetry —often sensitive, always pungent; the postcards he sent home to let his mother know he was still alive were frequently in verse. Second, his skinny frame was beginning to fill out and show signs of the powerful but sleepy-eyed giant he was to become; and anyone who cracked wise about his penchant for poetry found trouble.

From time to time Mitchum and his hobo buddies would drop off the freights to pick up a few bucks washing dishes or sweeping floors. But he was alone the night he soft-footed it off a slow-moving freight in Savannah, Georgia. It was his misfortune to land right in the path of a prowling cop. Even before he saw the "fuzz," Mitchum felt his beefy hand on his shoulder. The next thing he knew, he was being placed under arrest.

"What for?" he asked.

"Vagrancy, what the hell you think, boy?"

"Not me," Mitchum said. He fished into his jeans and pulled out his wad—thirty-eight hard-earned bucks.

The cop stared, then let Mitchum go. "Wise guy," he muttered, and deliberately hit Mitchum so hard with his billy that the kid sprawled to the ground. Then the cop hauled him to the lockup, and left him there in a cell with eight other men.

Five days later, not unduly worried, Mitchum found himself in court. He was sure that, with nearly a week in jail behind him, the judge would probably turn him loose with a lecture and an order to get out of town. He watched without interest when he heard his name called. Then suddenly he jerked erect. The testimony wasn't about "vagrancy." Two cops were telling the judge that a kid fitting Mitchum's description had robbed a local shoe store of forty bucks, and that Mitchum had approximately that amount on him when he was picked up.

Fighting his panic, Mitchum struggled to make sense out of what he was hearing. A cold fear gnawed at his belly, but when the judge gave him his chance to speak, he was ready.

"Your Honor, when was this robbery committed?"

The judge studied his notes. "Wednesday."

Mitchum grinned. "I spent last Wednesday all cozy in your own jail. Hell, Your Honor, I been there since Sunday!"

The judge blanched, shuffled through his papers, then glared. "Aw right," he said finally. "So you didn't do it. But I can still give you a little time for vagrancy!"

And that is how Bob Mitchum found himself on the Chatham County chain gang, from which he ultimately escaped. . . .

When he rejoined his family in Delaware, he found them in desperate financial trouble. Mitchum, who had considered going back to high school, took a job instead as an auto mechanic. (He still enjoys taking motors apart, and once bought a garage so he and his sons could tinker at will.) One night, his kid brother John introduced him to his date, a pretty fourteen-year-old girl named Dorothy Spence. By the time the evening was over, Dorothy was hooked on big brother Bob, and he was so impressed with the dark-haired girl that he stayed home until the entire Mitchum family moved to California some eight months later.

To save money, Mitchum bummed his way west, finally joining the family in Long Beach—where eight people jammed into a three-room house. To contribute to the family income, he went to work at his usual series of odd jobs, hitchhiking east every summer to make sure Dorothy was as good-looking as he remembered her.

After five years of getting nowhere financially, Mitchum fell in with a traveling astrologer named Carrol Righter, who hired him as advance man.

Setting up dates for Righter to do his stuff at high society parties gave Mitchum his first taste of a new kind of traveling—on passenger trains—and he stuck with the job for almost two years. It ended shortly after Mitchum got himself and Righter tossed out of a Philadelphia mansion for trying to sneak off with a couple of fifths of rye whiskey.

He was on his own again, he had $100 saved, and he decided it was time to get married. Impulsively, he headed for Delaware and Dorothy Spence. Despite her parents' understandable objections, Dorothy scrubbed him up, collected an additional hundred dollars in wedding checks, and took him for better or worse in a cabbage-smelling parsonage kitchen on March 16, 1940. (On the whole, Dorothy Spence Mitchum didn't make a bad bargain. The Mitchum marriage has survived almost 25 years with only one brief split-up to date—an excellent score by Hollywood standards.)

The newlyweds moved in with the Mitchums in California, and Bob settled down to a graveyard-shift job as a drop-hammer operator for Lockheed. It was a disaster. In a few weeks he was an insomniac; in a couple of months he went stone blind. A doctor examined Mitchum's eyes, listened to his description of his cramped home-life and his job, which he despised, and told him the trouble was psychosomatic. There was little Mitchum could do to improve conditions at home, but he did give up his job. Not long after, Fate stepped in and he began a new career.

In 1942 an agent he knew took him to a Hopalong Cassidy set where Mitchum, gaping, was asked if he could ride.

"Sure," said Mitchum, who hadn't been on a horse since he left his grandmother's farm at the age of ten. "I used to break ponies in Wyoming."

"Okay, break this one," he was told, and led to a horse that any tenderfoot could tell had a nasty mind.

Mitchum climbed aboard—from the wrong side. The horse gave him a baleful glance and threw him forty feet. Mitchum got up, dusted himself off, and mounted again. This time he flew a mere fifteen feet through the air. "What's with this nag?" he demanded as he was helped painfully onto his feet.

"Nothin' much. He killed an extra last week. Guy that rides him gets the job."

"That's me," said Mitchum grimly. He limped up to the horse for the third time and slammed him hard with the flat of his hand. The horse snarled. Mitchum snarled back, louder. Then he climbed on again, and stuck.

He got the job, and thanks to Bill "Hopalong Cassidy" Boyd, who took a liking to him, was allowed to spend most of his time in front of the cameras leaning against trees with his faithful mount cropping the grass serenely beside him.

After eight Hopalongs, Mitchum could ride well enough to stay in westerns, and act well enough to move on to better things. Sensing that he was beginning to pick up a fan following, RKO rewarded him with roles in *Thirty Seconds over Tokyo* and *The Story of G.I. Joe,* for which he later won an Oscar nomination and star billing.

Mitchum now moved his family—which by this time included two small sons—to an ancient, rambling house off Sunset Boulevard. Things were looking up, but he felt restless. Now that he was among the elite, the studio expected him to show up at the proper parties and hobnob with the proper people. But then as now, Mitchum couldn't make small talk with the fabled aristocracy of filmdom.

He felt at home only with an assortment of low-lifes, mostly drifters who, hearing he was a soft touch, borrowed his money, used his car and drink his liquor. That was okay with Mitchum, who was beginning to develop a sense of guilt about being an actor (it has never left him; he recently remarked that acting was a humiliating way for a grown man to earn a living) and an obsession that he was doomed to failure. "I don't know why I do it (act), except I like the loot."

Just as "the loot" was starting to roll in and Mitchum was beginning to get out from under his old debts, two things happened. He got his draft notice, and served his second documented "stretch" behind bars.

According to Mitchum, just five days before his induction, his wife and one of his sons took sick. While out to fill a prescription, he happened to phone home. To his surprise, a member of his family who had been on bad terms with Dorothy answered the phone. She refused to let Mitchum speak to his wife. Outraged, Mitchum bellowed his intention to come right home. He sounded so menacing that the woman promptly called the cops.

"Upon arrival," Mitchum alleged, "I was met by two sheriff's deputies and arrested." When the woman refused to press charges, Mitchum insisted that justice be done, that *his* side of the complaint be heard. Mitchum further claimed, "I was arrested, roundly beaten and booked at the Fairfax Avenue sheriff's substation." There, he was booked and advised that if he pleaded guilty to being "in an intoxicated condition on private property," he could pay a $10 fine and forget the whole business. Still boiling, Mitchum finally agreed—and then found himself sentenced to two days in jail.

Forty-eight hours after his release, Mitchum reported for infantry basic at Camp Roberts. He found the Army no better than jail ("It's geared to the constitutionally psychopathically inferior. You're in a box—hup-two-three-four. You never get beyond four.") and after a stint as drill instructor at Fort MacArthur, he was awarded a hardship discharge when the Red Cross found his family broke and facing eviction.

Out of uniform, Mitchum, needing money more than ever, plunged into a series of trashy films. His "friends," noting his edginess, urged him to try marijuana. Mitchum had smoked his first reefer as a kid of nineteen and found it uninteresting, but now he discovered that "tea" relaxed him and calmed him down. However, it was marijuana that landed him in the worst trouble of his life.

By 1948, Mitchum's six-one frame housed a network of jangled nerves and painful tensions. On-screen, he invariably got the girl—off, his marriage was cracking under the strain. A psychiatrist he consulted told him that he'd been trying too hard to please too many people, and that he'd better start learning to say no. Mitchum took the advice so much to heart that his wife and kids left him and went home to Delaware. Depressed and frightened, Mitchum began to drink heavily.

On the night of August 31, 1948, with his wife still absent, Mitchum was out boozing with a real estate agent named Perry Ward (a pseudonym). Around 11 P.M., the two men decided to pay a call on Lila Leeds, a blonde starlet they both knew. With Mitchum at the wheel, the car veered off Sunset Boulevard into Laurel Canyon. It was 11:30 when they arrived at 8443 Ridpath Drive, the starlet's hilltop pad. As they climbed the long flight of stairs to her front door, Mitchum looked around uneasily. His old drifter's instinct told him something was wrong.

When the twenty-five-year-old Lila let them in, Mitchum couldn't relax. He extracted himself from the embrace of a pair of rambunctious boxer puppies, nodded to another blonde, dancer Mary Gould (a pseudonym), who sashayed into the living room, and then moved cat-footed to the window.

"What's the matter?" Ward asked.

"Thought I saw someone out there," Mitchum said, peering out into the darkness. There was no movement, so he turned away and sat down on the sofa.

Lila Leeds struck a match. She put what later proved to be a marijuana cigarette between her lips, lit it, and handed it to Mitchum. Mitchum took the cigarette, looked up, then leaped to his feet.

"That's a face at the window!" he shouted.

"It's those damn dogs," Mary Gould squealed. While the other three stared at her, she turned and bolted for the kitchen. Instantly, there was a loud crash from the back of the house. Two men broke into the room, holding Mary in front of them as a shield.

Mitchum reacted with trigger-quick reflexes. Figuring it for a hold-up, he dropped to one knee behind a small table and grabbed it to hurl at the intruders.

"Police officers!" one of the men shouted. Mitchum's eyes for once lost their heavy-lidded, sleepy look. For a moment he crouched, paralyzed. Then the lit cigarette scorched his fingers, and he dropped it on the floor. Instantly one of the cops released Mary and snatched the butt. The other cop snapped handcuffs on Perry Ward, then turned to Mitchum, who silently held out his wrists for the bracelets.

"How long you been on the stuff?" the cop asked Mitchum as he locked the cuffs.

Mitchum shrugged. "Two, three years."

"When was the last time?"

Mitchum looked down at his wrists. "I was blasting weed last week," he said.

Across the room, Mary Gould let loose a nervous giggle. "This is just like the movies," she tittered.

Mitchum turned and stared at her. "Not for me," he said slowly. "This'll ruin me. I'm through."

BOBBY-SOX HERO NABBED IN DOPE RAID, screamed tabloid headlines across the nation. RKO top brass, with some $5,000,000 tied up in three unreleased Mitchum films, contemplated mass suicide. Bookies took bets on whether Dorothy Mitchum would file for divorce at once or wait until Mitchum was tried and sentenced (actually, she promptly rejoined him in Hollywood and has never left him since).

But the public—the never-to-be-taken-for-granted public —responded not with catcalls, but with a burst of wild enthusiasm for Bad Bob's latest escapade. His fan mail increased. His last-released film became the number one box-office smash all over the country. Fan magazine editors, quick to sense the way the wind was blowing, cabled RKO to stand by Mitchum and play up the story along the lines of sin-suffer-and-repent.

Mitchum himself, once he'd been booked and released on bail, took the whole thing calmly. He hired Jerry Giesler, the best legal brain in Hollywood, and sat in court, nonchalantly twiddling a rubber band, while Giesler waived Mitchum's right to a jury trial and threw him on the court's mercy. When the verdict—guilty of "conspiracy to possess" marijuana—was handed down and he was sentenced to two years—sixty days to be served in jail, the rest suspended— Mitchum didn't even twitch. In the Los Angeles County Jail, and at the prison honor farm, he turned in one of his best performances—the model con—and was released one day short of the full sixty on probation.

Nobly offering their valuable property a second chance, RKO put Mitchum back to work, and loaned him money to help pay Giesler's $50,000 fee. For his part, Mitchum made noises like a black sheep returning to the fold, promising the world that from now on he was going to live quietly, shun bad company and keep his nose impeccably clean. He kept that promise for two years.

It took that long for the truth to come out. For months the Los Angeles DA had been bombarded with rumors that Mitchum had been, if not framed, at least deliberately set up as a patsy on the night in question. Newsmen admitted that they had been tipped off *in advance* that a big-name star would be arrested that night. Mitchum, who previously had been as tight-lipped as a corpse about the whole affair, revealed that a friend had been after him all day to visit Lila that night.

Half a dozen film stars had told Mitchum privately that they too had been urged to come to "a party" at Lila's that night, and had high-tailed it away when they'd seen police cars parked out front. Most fascinating of all, Mitchum pointed out that the arresting officers had testified to watching the "tea party" going on in the house for hours but waited for Mitchum's arrival before moving in for the kill.

After months of investigation, the Mitchum case was reviewed by the courts, the guilty verdict was ordered set aside, and the complaint against him dismissed. Neither the DA nor Mitchum chose to make the court's findings public, and to this day few of the millions who vaguely remember the scandal know that Mitchum was railroaded.

That's the way Mitchum wanted it. Having paid society a debt he didn't owe seemed to give him freedom to raise some genuine hell whenever he was in the mood.

In the fifties he was frequently in the mood. He didn't like telephones, and on several occasions ripped them out of the walls when he couldn't get a dial tone, or an operator, fast enough. He didn't like actors (he called them "freaks" and "narcissistic bastards") and brawled publicly with a number of them. Working on *Not as a Stranger*, Mitchum, Frank Sinatra and Brod Crawford had a backstage wing-ding that ended with the entire dressing-room in a shambles and the massive Crawford belted over a railing into the street—an encounter that impressed the three men so favorably that they became fast friends.

Other fist-fights ended less satisfactorily, with Mitchum garnering headlines and the enmity of MP's and Shore Police as a result of his barroom battles with servicemen who wisecracked about the virility of male movie stars. In one such incident, in the bar of a Colorado Springs hotel, he knocked down an ex-heavyweight boxer turned GI. He was also accused of kicking the fallen man in the head.

When servicemen and civilians were unavailable, Mitchum took on his old enemies, the "fuzz." In 1953 a Los Angeles officer flagged him down for doing 74 mph on busy Wilshire Boulevard. Mitchum, who could easily have afforded to pay his fine, gunned his motor and disappeared while the cop was writing out the ticket. An hour later he phoned the police station to complain that an officer had stolen his driver's license. The cop who had tagged him got on the phone and asked Mitchum just what he thought he was doing.

"I didn't know who you were, Dad," Mitchum sassed. "I thought you were a bandit or something, so I went home." He ended up paying a $200 fine to rid himself of charges of evading arrest and resisting an officer.

By now Mitchum's reputation as a champion hell-raiser generated trouble all by itself. From time to time he sounded off angrily when his name was linked to incidents at which he was a relatively innocent bystander ("Hell, I could get ninety days just for shouting in an alley!" he complained), but generally he welcomed trouble with open arms. In the case of French starlet Simone Silva, this was literally the truth.

One day, on a beach in Cannes, Simone decided to make a name for herself by stripping off the top of her two-piece bathing suit on a beach jammed with photographers and celebrities. Everyone else reached for a camera; Mitchum reached for Simone. When the photos hit the front pages the next day, interest was divided between Simone's bare-bosomed torso and Mitchum's bare-faced smirk.

He had done it again.

Today, Mitchum lives in what is for him comparative quiet. While other stars make one or, at the most, two big-budget films a year, Mitchum makes twice that many in the same length of time, many of them second-rate. Although touted as one of the best actors in the business by such as Peter O'Toole, Deborah Kerr, and the late Charles Laughton, and urged repeatedly to have a go at Shakespeare, he laughingly refuses. "I don't want responsibility; I want the money."

Between pictures, Mitchum works like a hired hand on his Maryland farm, which is virtually inaccessible without a compass. The tract borders on Chesapeake Bay, and Mitchum is secure in the knowledge that "If they come at me by land, I can get away by water!"

In spare moments he indulges interests that would flabbergast his public—reading, music, gastronomy—and makes like a proud father over the accomplishments of daughter Petrina, a pre-teen in a Maryland public school, second son Chris, a college boy, and his first-born Jim, now an actor.

Nonetheless, Mitchum can still be counted on to do the unpredictable. Some time ago he bestowed a lengthy interview and a half-dozen home-mixed stingers on a girl reporter, then dismissed her taxi and told her he'd see her home himself.

Instead, he drove the lady on a wide detour up into the Hollywood Hills, deposited her in a houseful of people she'd never met—and disappeared out the back door, leaving her stranded and seething. The news-hen waited weeks, then months, then years for an apology or at least a phone call. None came. Not long ago in Hollywood, she finally bumped into Mitchum again, gritted her teeth, and strode up to him.

"Remember me?" she demanded.

"Why, sure, honey," said Mitchum.

"Then I have one question to ask you," she said. "Precisely *why* did you leave me in that house?"

"Sweetie," said Mitchum enigmatically, "what better place could I have left you?" And giving her a tender pat on the fanny, he ambled off, just like in the movies, over the hills into the setting sun.

HOLLYWOOD'S TOUGH LONER

• TEDD THOMEY

When he was fourteen years old, Lee Marvin was already six feet tall, brawny, and as full of meanness as a tomcat with turpentine on its tail. At Oakwood, a private school in Poughkeepsie, New York, he was known as a touchy, two-fisted kid who would fight at the drop of a pencil or a four-letter word.

One April morning he awoke in a sour mood. Both he and his roomie, a kid named O'Hanlon, had overslept nearly an hour and missed breakfast. Jumping into their clothes, they began racing around their room, trying to clean it up for inspection before leaving for their 8 o'clock class.

In the corridor a buzzer sounded an ominous warning.

"Cree-ap!" groaned Marvin. "Five more minutes! Where the hell's the dustpan?"

O'Hanlon yanked open the closet door. Fumbling through a clutter of shoes and dirty laundry, he wasted a valuable half-minute trying to find the dustpan.

"Get a move on!" urged Marvin, sweeping the floor with quick, furious strokes of the broom.

Finally O'Hanlon located it. He held the pan against the floor while Marvin swept a pile of torn math papers and other debris into it. Then, ignoring a nearby wastebasket, O'Hanlon rushed to an open window and dumped the dustpan's contents outside.

"F'crise sake!" bellowed Marvin. "What'd you do that for?"

"Save time!"

"Dumb ass!" Marvin glared at him with utter disgust. "Now we gotta go outside and clean it up!"

"Don't call me that," shouted O'Hanlon.

"Okay," said Marvin sarcastically, "so you're a smart ass!"

"And you're a son of a bitch!" yelled the other youth.

"Say that again," roared Marvin, "and I'll throw *you* out the window!"

To emphasize his words, Marvin slammed the broom down on the floor.

"You're a son of a bitch!" shrieked O'Hanlon, hurling the dustpan down beside the broom.

They jumped at each other, locked arms and began grappling. It should have been an even match, because redhead O'Hanlon was as tall as Marvin and equally brawny. But he lacked Marvin's imagination and orneriness. Before O'Hanlon quite knew how it happened, Marvin seized him around the middle, jerked him off his feet and dumped him out the window.

It was a second-story window, with a plush sloping lawn below. O'Hanlon landed with a thump that could be heard across the schoolyard. He rolled downhill over the soft grass. Then, unhurt, he leaped to his feet, shook his fist at Marvin, who was grinning down from the window—and began shouting obscenities at the top of his voice.

Marvin roared back, matching obscenity for obscenity. Then he leaped from the window. He tried to drop on top of the other boy the way his burly idol, Victor McLaughlin, did in battle scenes in the movies. But O'Hanlon sidestepped. Marvin landed on his feet, sprang at O'Hanlon and bowled him over like a sack of feathers. Locking arms again, they rolled over and over down the slope, finally halting against the broad trunk of an elm.

Marvin got astride the other youth and slugged him on the cheekbone. Then he slammed his fist against O'Hanlon's jaw. In rapid succession, Marvin landed three more rights and three lefts. They were short crops, but so damaging that O'Hanlon stopped cursing and tried to cover his face with his arms.

Suddenly Marvin heard other voices, coming from behind him.

"Stop it!" they commanded. "Stop it at once!"

Two teachers, both men, ran down the slope. As Marvin turned to look at them, O'Hanlon gave him a vicious kick in the groin. Marvin slugged him a final time, making blood spurt from his nose, before being dragged off by the teachers.

"March!" they ordered, pointing toward the principal's office.

As Marvin trudged up the slope, he heard the laughter of scores of boys. Glancing across the schoolyard, he saw them standing in groups at the windows of classrooms located directly across from the dormitory. From their gestures and rude comments, he realized that the entire episode—starting with O'Hanlon's flying exit from the window—had been performed before the eyes of at least 200 witnesses.

Some of the boys hooted and jeered through the open windows, shouting, "So long, slob! Gonna miss you around here!"

Marvin thumbed his nose at them until one of the teachers slapped his hand away from his face.

His visit with the principal was brief and concise. It was the second time within two weeks that Marvin had been involved in a brawl and he knew what the next step would be, because he'd been through it many times before at other schools.

"I'll phone your father at once," the principal said. "I want him to pick you up tonight, or sooner. As of this moment, you're expelled."

Marvin shrugged. Then he coolly and defiantly drew a pack of cigarettes from his pocket and lit one.

The principal was so startled he dropped the phone. Rising, he strode around his desk and took the cigarette from Marvin's fingers. Then he asked for the pack and the boy handed it over.

The principal returned to the phone. He made no further comment to the boy. But Lee Marvin had finally made his mark in school, an achievement no other student had ever matched. It was the first time in the long and distinguished history of Oakwood School that a boy had shown guts enough to light a cigarette in the principal's office.

That incident occurred almost three decades ago, but the details were still sharp in Marvin's mind as we discussed it while lunching on steak sandwiches in the Beverly Hills Brown Derby. The face of the 41-year-old man who sat opposite me was hard, defiant and a bit proud as he recalled his contempt for the principal and the school. With long, slow drags, he smoked a king-sized, unfiltered cigarette, his dark blue eyes gazing at me coldly through the drifting smoke.

Like that principal some three decades previously, I felt uncomfortable in Lee Marvin's presence. Most people do. He is definitely not a cheerful, outgoing "Chamber of Commerce" type. He does not exude friendliness. He is a big man—6 feet 2 inches tall and 180 pounds—with the large, rough hands of an outdoorsman. As he talks to you, he seems to be restraining himself and there is an undercurrent of tension in everything he says. You have the feeling that if you say the wrong thing—make a comment that's too personal, perhaps—one of those oversized hands may snake across the table and belt you right between the eyes.

It's no act. Although Marvin's trade is acting—and he's gotten so good at it that he earns over half a million dollars a year—at no time during our lengthy conversation did I have the feeling that he was acting. Like Bogart and one or two others, Marvin is genuinely tough behind the facade of brutality and sadism he often reflects on the screen. Perhaps those elements of brutality and sadism explain why Marvin has no close friends. He is one of filmdom's most thoroughly disliked personalities, a notorious loner, a tough, crude man who says what he thinks, does what he wants and to hell with the consequences.

By the time he was 17, Lee Marvin—rebellious and reckless—had been kicked out of 11 private prep schools, mostly for smoking and fighting. By the time he was 20, he'd been through many months of combat hell as a frontline Marine PFC who fought with the 22nd Marines at Kwajalein and Eniwetok and with the 24th Marines at Saipan. He not only shot Japs, but he bayoneted them in hand-to-hand combat. It is written in his Marine Corps records, and also in the deep lines of his face and the silver gray—almost white—hue of his straight, coarse hair.

"I didn't like those schools," Marvin said, referring to the near-dozen from which he was expelled. "And they didn't like me. I guess part of my trouble came from being oversized for my age. I looked big and tough, so it was natural for me to act tough."

During his teen-age years, Marvin lived partially in a dream world, as most boys do. He visualized himself as excessively rugged and courageous, like his movie heroes.

One of the movies he saw several times was *All Quiet on the Western Front*.

"I guess that was when I first fixed the tough guy image on myself," he said. "I identified with the tough sarge in that picture. Shells didn't bother him. Nothing scared him. But maybe what also attracted me was his kindness to the troops. He'd chew them out, but then he'd go out and get them some food."

The word "kindness" seemed out of place in Marvin's vocabulary, which is liberally peppered with four-letter words. He grinned—it was really more of a grimace, showing tobacco-yellow, slightly uneven lower teeth—and began reminiscing about his early life in New York City, where he was born. At times he spoke in a herky-jerky, hesitant way, as though embarrassed by his personal recollections. Occasionally he was vague about certain details (deliberately, I thought) and his voice trailed off into mumbling which defied interpretation. When he wished, however, his enunciation could be crisp, clear and forceful, revealing excellent grammar and a strong, professional understanding of people, places and things.

Descended from Matthew Marvin, who arrived in New England in 1633 and became the first chief justice of Connecticut, Lee Marvin grew up in a wealthy, well-educated family. His father was a top executive in an advertising agency and his mother was a magazine fashion editor. Perhaps his parents were too busy with their careers to give their young son all the love and attention he needed. At any rate, at the age of seven he ran away from home and wasn't found for nearly three days.

"My old man walloped me good," he recalled, "but it didn't bother me. I did what I wanted and to hell with the family. But my father *was* tough. So it's that quality of his —that toughness or whatever it is—that runs through me."

Marvin grew up as a headstrong, bitter boy who resented discipline in whatever form he found it. He finally escaped his father's discipline, only to run into a more despised variety at his first prep school and those which followed. At first, in order to impress the other kids, he only pretended to be tough. But then he had to prove it—again, again and again, usually with his fists. He broke all the rules, paid the penalties, broke more rules, and suffered more punishments. But the cost was greater than he ever anticipated because the expected reward—respect from the kids—did not materialize.

"A lot of them were spoiled brats," Marvin said. "They had too much dough, too much of everything. They didn't like me; I didn't like them. The only thing I liked in school was athletics. I wanted to play football, because I was plenty big enough. But I hated the coach's rules. Rules, rules, rules—nothing but goddam rules and team talk. I couldn't be a team man. So I went out for track, where a guy could be a loner and still do some good."

When he was 16 years old, Marvin starred on the track squad at St. Leo's Benedictine School in Dade City, Florida. It was the only prep school he wasn't kicked out of, and he remained there 10 months, a record for him, discovering for the first time in his life the thrill of accomplishment that wasn't connected with rule-breaking. His specialties were the javelin and low and high hurdles.

"I won all three events consistently," said Marvin with grim pride. "Most of the time I was high-point man. Because of my size, the javelin was a breeze. But my big goddam feet were a problem in the hurdles. I wore the same size shoes then that I do now—twelves—and I looked sloppy as hell going over those jumps. But I kept picking them up and slapping them down, and I kept ahead of those other bastards."

When the track season ended, Marvin talked his father into letting him quit school and join the Marines. The year was 1941 and America was only a few months away from being drawn into World War II. When I asked Marvin why he had chosen the Marines, he did not reply at once. Thoughtfully he rubbed his hand across his oversized mouth. Then he pinched the scarred bridge of his nose before noisily sniffing a large draught of air.

"At school," he said, "I had proved I was the toughest kid on two legs. I'd knocked the crap out of any kid who wanted to tangle with me. But it really didn't prove anything because we were just kids. Inside here"—Marvin thumped his chest with his fist—"inside here I knew I was still chicken. I had this fear that I really wasn't tough at all, that I had a yellow streak running through me as big as a four-lane highway. When you're afraid like that, you want to face it, so you pick the most exciting form to test yourself. So I picked the Marines."

"And what did you find out?" I asked.

Marvin shrugged. "What can I tell you? I was just as chicken as any Marine. In the Marines, everyone wears a mask. If there is one guy in front of you when you're moving into some heavy fire, you feel a little easier and you go a little faster. But if *you're* the guy in front, then you want to lay back, because it's the front guy who always gets it first . . ."

In the battles for Kwajalein and Eniwetok, Pfc. Marvin was a scout often called upon to be the front guy. He paddled ashore on Eniwetok atoll the night before D-Day, landing quietly on the beach aboard a rubber boat containing a squad of twelve men. Their mission: Probe inland as stealthily as possible and find out where the Japs were dug in.

Marvin moved through the darkness in a crouch, unable to see exactly where he was going, trying not to stumble on the beach, which consisted of soft, fine-grained sand and occasional outcroppings of sharp coral. His weapons included a heavy BAR which he cradled in his arms, finger on the trigger; a .45 automatic pistol tucked inside his dungaree blouse, and a razor-sharp Bowie knife in a sheath on one of his three cartridge belts. During the first half-hour after leaving the boat, he kept contact with the other squad men, hearing whispered commands, seeing their shadows nearby.

Then, because of the darkness and unfamiliar terrain, he lost touch with the others. He began walking faster, trying to find them.

"It was a hell of a weird feeling," Marvin said. "I couldn't see anything and I couldn't hear anything. I was wandering around palm stumps and in and out of bushes. Suddenly I walked right into a guy. I didn't know where he came from. We hit head-on, so damn hard we both fell down. He said something in Japanese, picked himself up and got going again. He thought I was a Jap out to take a crap or something. I just lay there on the ground, scared crapless, with my hand on the slide of the BAR. I kept hoping he would not turn around and come back. If he did, I knew I might have to start firing. And that was the last thing I wanted, because if I fired we'd all be dead . . ."

The Jap didn't return. Marvin hurried back toward the sound of the surf, finally located his sergeant and told him what had happened.

"Yeah," whispered the sergeant, "there must be hundreds of 'em. I nearly walked right into their command post."

The sergeant made contact with the rest of his men and they returned to the beach. They sent a radio message in code to a destroyer lying a mile offshore, giving an estimate of the Japanese troop strength and their approximate position. Then the twelve Marines quietly dug shallow trenches in the sand. They spent the rest of the night sprawled on their bellies, waiting for the main elements of the 22nd Marines to come ashore.

Shortly after dawn, Navy cruisers and destroyers opened up with their biggest guns, dropping shells inland, where the Japanese were concentrated. Then the Marine companies slammed onto the beach in amphibious tractors and Higgins boats. Marvin rejoined his company and spent the rest of the day and the next night involved in a series of hot firefights with the Japanese troops, who were dug in on numerous coral islands surrounding a lagoon.

"Eniwetok was a hell of a lot tougher than people remember," Marvin said. "It wasn't a real big one, like Iwo or Saipan. But we lost a lot of guys. At one time, the Second Battalion was down to 125 guys."

Marvin's worst moment came when he and five other men went after a Jap heavy machine gun that had taken a heavy toll in Marines. The gun was dug in near a thick palm stump and roofed over with palm logs and sandbags which were invulnerable to Marine grenades. Wriggling on their stomachs, Marvin and two buddies approached the emplacement from the east side, while the other three Marines came in from the west. Finally someone got a grenade through the emplacement's gun aperture.

The explosion shattered the machine gun and killed half its crew. Marvin leaped up and started to run toward the smoking wreckage. Suddenly he snagged a foot on something and tumbled headlong to the ground, the BAR flying out of his hands. As he rolled over he discovered he'd tripped on a sand-covered trap door which one of the Japs had shoved open while trying to flee from the gun emplacement through a tunnel side entrance.

"He popped out of that hole like a little animal," said Marvin. "For a second I just lay there on my ass, surprised as hell while he blinked at me. Then he lunged. He tried to stick his bayonet in my eye. So I took it away from him. It wasn't hard to do, because he was just a little bastard, maybe 5 feet 2 or so. I shoved that goddam thing into his chest all the way to the gun barrel . . ."

Marvin's heavy brows drew down over his small eyes, which gleamed coldly across the restaurant table. He twisted his big body around in the booth, picked up his cigarettes and accidentally tipped over his water glass.

"Water!" he said with disgust. "Who the hell drinks water?" With a quick hand gesture, he summoned a waitress and ordered a boilermaker—specifying that it had to contain exactly three ounces of gin in eight ounces of beer.

While he waited for the waitress, Marvin lit another cigarette. When I asked him another question about Eniwetok, he shook his head and mumbled something to himself that I couldn't understand. The waitress returned with two drinks, a martini for me and a king-sized, foam-topped glass for him. He looked scornfully at my drink, raised his high and drained half of it in two long, thirsty pulls. With his forefinger, he wiped the foam off his long upper lip. Then he glared at me and demanded:

"Why do you have to keep bugging me about the Marines? All that's been over and done with for years. I wasn't no hero. Sure, I did a few things, like sticking that Jap in the chest, but I wasn't no Sergeant York, you understand? Hell, I was just a scared kid doing what he had to do and getting the crap scared out of him. You ever hear about the khaki Marines?"

I nodded.

"Khaki-colored scivvy shorts and all that," he said. "I was a khaki Marine like the rest of 'em. If they gave awards for combat diarrhea, I'd have medals all over my ass."

Marvin laughed, drained the rest of his boilermaker and ordered another. I'd been told he was wounded in the battle for Saipan, but when I asked him to tell me about it he shook his head.

"To hell with it," he said.

He refused to say anything more. He scowled impatiently at the walls of the restaurant, drumming his long, thick fingers heavily on the table top. When his drink arrived, he grinned at the tall, cold glass and licked his broad lips.

"You know about self-knowledge?" he said. "It's a very destructive thing. An actor looks into himself a lot and you don't like everything you see. So you go out and get a belt, and that's what I think booze is all about. It helps a man study himself. After a belt or two, you don't get quite so disgusted when you start looking into yourself."

For a few minutes we discussed the plans for his next picture, *The Dirty Dozen,* a war film he was to start in London. When I tried to steer the conversation back to

Saipan, he shook his head reluctantly. Then, abruptly, he changed his mind.

"Okay, okay," he said. "It was an ambush and they slaughtered the hell out of us. I was going across a little clearing when I got mine. It hit somewhere below my spine and knocked me flying over sideways. I rolled over and all I could think was: *Shot in the ass, I been shot in the ass.* Guys were running past all around me. I knew I'd never be able to get up by myself, so I talked fast and flagged down a couple of guys. They lifted me up onto my knees. That way I got to my feet and sort of half-ran and half-walked away from that goddam clearing."

Reaching the base of a tree, Marvin fell into some brush. While he was sprawled there, feeling blood soaking the seat of his trousers, some more Marines ran past. They didn't see him. One of them stepped on Marvin's rump, raising so much hell with his wound that he nearly passed out. He lay there 20 minutes. Then, fearing he would bleed to death, he began crawling, dragging himself along on his elbows, his legs feeling heavy and numb. Finally he was picked up by two Navy corpsmen who carried him down to the beach on a stretcher.

"That same night I was on the *Solace*," said Marvin. "It was a hospital ship with clean sheets, music, ice cream and all that crap. I could still hear the sounds from the island, and I really felt cheap, because I knew all the assholes were fighting it out. It's all part of the Marine Corps psychology. You catch one and you're pulled out. They say you're lucky, but you really feel like a coward."

Marvin spent the next thirteen months flat on his back in Navy hospitals in Honolulu, San Francisco and Chelsea, Massachusetts. At first, the doctors weren't exactly certain what caused his injuries, which consisted of a severed sciatic nerve in his buttock, slashed muscles and some bone damage. It was later theorized that a Japanese bullet struck his cartridge belt, detonating one of his cartridges, sending brass and lead fragments into his rump and against the base of his spine. He was in and out of surgery many times, the surgeons' probing instruments removing a score of tiny metal chunks.

"Eventually the nerve grew back," said Marvin. "But I had to learn to walk all over again."

Following his discharge, Marvin—drawing $40-a-month government compensation—enrolled in a stenographic course, despised it and quit. He returned to the family home in Woodstock, New York, and lay around restlessly for a while, trying to decide what to do with his life. Then he got a job as a plumber's helper, digging holes for septic tanks, and hating every minute of it.

One night in 1947 he was summoned to Woodstock's Maverick Playhouse to repair a stuffed toilet. Afterward, dropping his metal toolbox on the floor, he hung around and listened to a rehearsal. He was fascinated.

"It hit me quick," Marvin said. "It was like getting whacked on the skull with a Stillson wrench. I watched the actors move around, heard the lines and knew it was for me. I guess acting was what I always wanted, but I didn't know it until then. They gave me seven bucks a week, room and board—and after a few weeks I got to kiss the leading lady."

When the season ended, playhouse director E. J. Ballentine sent Marvin to New York City where he enrolled in the dramatic school at The American Theater Wing. He acquired technique rapidly. In 1949, when he was 25, he toured with the road companies of *The Hasty Heart* and *A Streetcar Named Desire*. Occasionally he picked up a few extra dollars working as an extra or doing bit parts in movies filmed on location in New York. It was one of these roles—the very minor part of a vicious, tough-talking sailor in *You're In the Navy Now*—which gave his career its first significant leap upward.

The director, Henry Hathaway, was impressed by Marvin's rugged height, his low, smooth voice and grim self-confidence. He built up Marvin's part and took him to Hollywood for more shooting on the picture. Marvin signed up with agent Meyer Miskin, who still handles him, and began grabbing off small but solid movie and TV parts as a brutal S.O.B. An assignment on the *Dragnet* series turned out to be his first important television role.

"I came on strong and mean," Marvin said. "I was a cool punk who killed fourteen hitchhikers. I enjoyed every violent minute of it."

Miskin coaxed producer-director Stanley Kramer into looking at the *Dragnet* rushes and Kramer signed Marvin for his first co-star billing in *Eight Iron Men*. It was a World War II story, with Marvin portraying a hardnosed, savage soldier whose squad was trapped for most of the picture by murderous machine gun fire. During the first day on the set, the cameras were stalled repeatedly by a mechanical problem with the machine gun.

"What the hell's the matter with it?" roared Kramer, bugged by the long delays.

"Damn if we know," replied the chief prop man. "It keeps jamming."

"Get another one," commanded Kramer.

"Okay," said the prop man, "but it may take a day or so to get another authentic model."

While Kramer was tearing his hair, Marvin strolled over to the machine gun. He squatted down beside it and discovered it was a surplus World War II weapon, .30 caliber and water-cooled.

"F'crise sake," he said, "I lugged one of these bastards all over the boonies at Pendleton."

In a twinkling he stripped the gun apart and saw that the cartridge belt was slipping because of a worn groove. He cleaned the parts, reassembled them and showed the other actors how to hold the belt so it would feed smoothly. Then he triggered off a blast of a dozen blanks that scared the hell out of everybody on the set.

"Yaaaaaaaaaaaaaaaah!" he bellowed, shaking his fist at the actors, grips and prop men and showing his teeth in a snarl. "Sons of bitches! Now you're all dead!"

His antics relieved the tension on the set. Kramer was so pleased he named Marvin technical director on the picture as well as co-star. After that Marvin got all the acting jobs he wanted, his weekly salary rising from $250 to $750 and then to $1,000. Typed as a lean, mean heavy, he committed assorted mayhem on all of Hollywood's popular leading men, including stabbing, slugging, shooting and strangling. He enjoyed his work thoroughly, especially when the directors let him invent his own bits of acting business, ranging from sadistic grimaces to flicking his eyes around with the coolness of a born killer.

In one live TV drama, Marvin had a gun-fight scene with actor Rip Torn. Marvin stalked in, put a long, icy eye on him, then abruptly barked a one-word ad lib: "NOW!" Torn was so shaken he committed an unpardonable *faux pas* for a gunman. He dropped his pistol. Marvin, still playing it cool, kicked it back to him, and the scene, which could have been a disaster, came off well.

Recalling the incident, Marvin leaned back in the restaurant booth, stretched his arms and remarked somewhat smugly: "No matter how fast they are, when you've got a white eye for a guy, it really gets them. And when the script calls for me to lean on somebody, I really lean. I try to make a scene as rough as I can. Knock a guy down with one round, then walk up to him and put three or four more in his face. Roll him over and put one in his back. Make it ugly."

He clamped his teeth hard together, drew his lips back and delivered a fierce little sermon: "Today on TV, violence looks so goddam easy that every punk kid wants to go out and try it. I say make it so brutal, make it so cruel, that a man thinks twice before he goes out and does anything like that . . ."

He put that theory to full use in *The Wild One*, the Marlon Brando picture in which Marvin played Chino, leader of a gang of motorcycle ruffians patterned after the Hell's Angels. Marvin's loathsome characterization of a beer-guzzling son of a bitch was almost as powerful as Brando's. He got such a bang out of the role that he let it overflow into his private life. He bought an English motorcycle and proceeded to tear up the California countryside with it. When he wasn't outside racing with other nuts, he could be found battling all comers in saloon drinking bouts, with the main entree massive boilermakers.

One memorable Sunday afternoon at Big Bear, a mountain resort, Marvin downed four boilermakers before entering a cross-country race that was mostly uphill around boulders and scrubby pines. He was flung over the handlebars half a dozen times, but didn't give up until the bike—unable to take more abuse—conked out.

"What about that scar on your rump?" I asked. "Didn't that kind of riding raise hell with it?"

"Sure," he said, "but it quit aching after a few days—and then I could sit down again."

Marvin's motorcycle and booze shenanigans didn't set well with his wife, the former Betty Edeling, a pretty ex-model and UCLA graduate whom he wed in 1951. They had some rousing battles, but the marriage somehow held together for fourteen years, producing four children before becoming unglued in the divorce courts last year.

Commenting on the divorce and women in general, Marvin said: "I can't take crap from a woman. I think dames should keep their traps shut and not speak until they're spoken to. But I've got to admit that women are attractive to me. There's that element of danger when you mess around with them. They are a constant sexual threat. But I can't stand a domineering broad . . ."

Marvin revealed, however, that Betty was right in some

things. "Like having no close friends," he said. "It used to bother her that we didn't know any couples who we could invite in for a few drinks and small talk. When she'd really get sore at me, she'd let fly with this one: 'Why are you so *mean* to people? Why can't you be *nice?* Do you realize you haven't got *one* good friend!' "

He shrugged and then his mouth grew hard. "So I'd tell her to shut up. I'd say, 'That's right, baby. I know about that. Lay off.' "

Through the Fifties, Marvin specialized in killers, but he became best known as a cop, Lieutenant Ballinger of TV's *M Squad.* Even then he was tough, making his cop all-man, like an old-fashioned American folk hero. "I really liked Ballinger," Marvin said. "He was the kind of guy we'd all like to be. His own guy. No broads, no mother, no sleep, no eat—just an honest, fair cop, a little dumb sometimes, the way we all are."

His television image also prospered with *Lee Marvin Presents Lawbreaker.* Meanwhile he continued working in movies (he has appeared in a total of seventy-five), his salary rising into six figures annually, making him a higher-paid actor than many of the stars who were billed above him. Producers competed for his services because of his all-round ability, including a willingness to do his own movie stunts occasionally.

While Marvin was working in *Raintree County,* a stunt man was hired to perform a hazardous scene for him, involving a leap from a balcony. The stunt man went through it several times, but didn't satisfy director Edward Dmytryk. Marvin went up to him and said, "Hell, Eddie, let me try it."

The role called for Marvin to climb drunkenly to the second-story balcony and leap to a huge crystal chandelier. On his first jump, Marvin lost his grip on the light fixture and crashed to the floor. Bounding to his feet, he shouted: "I'm OK, dammit, and I know I can do it!" Ignoring Dmytryk's protests, he went back on the balcony, leaped to the chandelier like a great ape, swung across the room to an oaken banister and slid down to the floor, recklessly waving his arms overhead.

The cameras caught all of it and Dmytryk, although delighted, cried out with mock pain: "Lee, why do you make me suffer like this? One more like that and I'll drop dead with a heart attack!"

During shooting on another scene, a University of Southern California track star was hired to impersonate Montgomery Clift winning a footrace against Marvin. On the first take, Marvin—running the way he did as a high school teen-ager—won the race by a chin length.

"My God, Lee," complained Dmytryk, "you ruined it! You're supposed to *lose* the race!"

Marvin, still jogging around the set, yelled: "F'crise sake, Eddie, you gotta be more specific. All you said was that he would beat me. You didn't tell me to lose!"

Discussing his favorite roles during our conversation, Marvin said he especially enjoyed his work in 1964 in *The Killers,* because it involved pure violence with no attempt to preach or rationalize.

"Like the opening," he recalled, his voice lapsing into a muttered jargon that was part-gangland and part-Marvinese. "It's cold-blooded but jazzy. Me and my partner sidle into this home for blind people looking for a rat double-crosser. I get behind the head blind dame, grab her by the throat and push her almost to the floor. 'Where's Johnny North?' I breathe in her ear. So she tells us. I barge into the room like a bull buffalo, knocking the blindees over—we used real ones—and I say: 'You Johnny North?' He says yeah. So we take out our guns and we put 10 bullets in him straight up and down his middle. It's great. And everybody out front is getting their vicaries."

"Their what?" I said. "What kind of hip talk is that?"

"Hell," he snorted, "you call yourself a writer and you don't know that? A goddam good English word! Vicaries, pronounced vie-*care*-ease. Short for vicarious thrills, which is what the audience gets."

I nodded, impressed by his sudden emergence as a grammar expert.

"What about *Ship of Fools* and *Cat Ballou?*" I asked. "Where do you rank them in the vicarie department?"

"Plenty high," he grinned, "because a guy named Lee Marvin got *his* vicaries out of both of 'em."

In those pictures, made in 1965, a unique new breed of Marvin went on display, revealing his flare for broad, hilarious comedy. In *Ship of Fools,* an overlong, occasionally dull story, Marvin transformed a minor role—that of a whoring, has-been baseball player—into by far the best part in the picture. He accomplished this in one stunning, tragicomic scene, requiring less than three minutes. In it he drunkenly and pathetically explained the torture of being unable to hit a curve ball "on the outside corner."

In *Cat Ballou*, for which he received an Oscar and numerous other honors, Marvin came through with a double parody, revealing unsuspected reservoirs of talent. He played a dual role: Tim Strawn, a black-clad, chilling hired killer, wearing a sinister silver nose because his real one was bitten off in a fight; and Tim's stinking rumpot of a brother, Kid Shelleen, an ex-gunfighter who constantly needed a pint of booze to steady his trigger hand.

The story was a preposterous Western satire, with Marvin performing three episodes in the classic modes of Chaplin, Laurel and Hardy. While practicing target shooting in one scene, he made a drunken grab for his gun and his pants fell down. In another, he stumbled boozily up to a coffin, blew out the candles around it and sang "Happy birthday" to the corpse. In the third scene, the drunkest gun in the West—finally sober—prepared himself carefully for his final battle with Silvernose. While the sound track blared bullfight music, Marvin slowly and bravely adorned himself in natty gunfighter duds, including a tightly laced corset. Then he rode into town, tracked down his brother in a whorehouse and shot him through the heart.

As a result of those performances, the demand for Marvin's services has reached incredible heights and his price per picture has ballooned to $250,000—and up. Commenting on this phenomenon, Marvin said: "Yeah, I've turned the corner. I've busted out. Bogart did it the same way. He started out pretty much as I did, a heel, all rotten. Then, as audiences warmed to him, he became good-bad. Finally he was all good, no matter what the crap he did. I'm gonna make it that way, but with a difference. With me it's going to be comedy and violence, mixed, whenever I get the chance. That's the stuff I really want to do, because that's what life really is. Life is funny, but it's tragic—and violent!"

He emphasized his words by slamming his fist down on the table so hard that cups and glasses bounced up and fell over.

"I say screw 'em!" he roared. "If the producers won't give me parts like that, screw 'em!" He picked up a cup and replaced it on a saucer. "I made that decision a long time ago, back when I was laying around in those Navy hospitals with a shot-up ass. Screw it, man, I told myself. Life is a f—— mess and it's every man for himself! Take what you can get, screw the others—and never let your f—— guard down for a second!"

Again he slammed his fist down. "You know where I'd be now if I'd let my guard down? Buried out in the stinking Pacific with all those other poor bastards!"

To illustrate his point, Marvin related another incident which happened on Saipan, his voice low and deliberately expressionless: "It happened while it was getting dark. Me and another BAR guy were down in a shell hole, trying to improve our position for the night. Nearby was a palm stump and a burning oil drum. We were nervous because we knew there were Japs around, and I kept my BAR about an inch from my trigger finger.

"Suddenly my pal whispered, 'Hey, look at 'em! Over there by the fire!' "

Marvin swiveled his head back and forth. "I looked, but couldn't see 'em, because it was dusk and there was no visibility. 'Where?' I says. 'There!' he says. Suddenly I saw a pair of wrappies in front of my face. Jap wrappies, the bindings they wore on their legs. The Jap had a pistol and he shot my buddy in the head with it. All I remember is seeing him fire and my hand flying back. I carried a .45 pistol in my blouse. I shot him. Point blank in the tit. He slid down in the hole with us, dead as a goddam skunk . . ."

Marvin gave me a long look. "See what I mean? See why you have to keep your guard up? See why I say screw 'em if they get in my way?"

I thought about that for a while. Then I said: "Could you do it again?"

"Do what?"

"Kill somebody, if you had to."

He hardly paused. "I think so. Depending on the circumstances."

He said it very easily. As easily as Lee Marvin, actor, might utter the same boast on the screen.

He might have been kidding. But perhaps he wasn't.

Because the man who spoke so easily was also Lee Marvin, ex-Marine.

"I AM NOT ASHAMED" *

• BARBARA PAYTON

PROLOGUE

In 1950, I was sitting on top of the world. My peculiar acting talents were worth $10,000 a week, and I was in constant demand. Boy, everyone wanted me. I know it sounds unbelievable, but it's true that Gregory Peck, Guy Madison, Howard Hughes and other big names were dating me. Almost everything I did made headlines.

One escapade resulted in a headline: "BARBARA TAKES NEAR-NUDE SUN BATH—JUDGE COMPLAINS."

I was in love with one man, Tom Neal, and was engaged to (and later married) the actor with the most class in Hollywood—Franchot Tone.

In other words I was the queen bee. I'd grow old with 20 servants, three swimming pools and a personal masseuse plus an adoring husband.

Today, I live in a rat-roach infested apartment with not a bean to my name and I drink too much Rosé wine. I don't like what my scale tells me. The little money I do accumulate to pay the rent comes from old residuals, poetry and favors to men. I love the Negro race and I will accept money only from Negroes.

Does it all sound depressing to you? Queasy? Well, I'm not ashamed. I have hope. I don't live in rosy-hazed memory. I look to the future.

I guess I've got to fill you in on the roller coaster ride from happy-town rich to happy-town poor. I always have a

* From *I Am Not Ashamed*, by Barbara Payton, copyright © 1963 by Halloway House Publishing Co.

little too much wine in me but you can bet that every word is true. I'm too old to bull---- the public.

My picture appeared on the front page of every paper in the country in 1949. I was one of the six "Baby Stars" most likely to succeed—Piper Laurie, Mona Freeman, Debbie Reynolds, Mala Powers, Barbara Bates and yours truly. The other five are still fulfilling their promises. Me, I goofed.

It was an exciting year. I was the only blonde among the six. That was something special. It was my first big break. Teen-agers with gaping mouths stuck autograph books in my hand and begged for autographs. Producers asked me to share their beds with them. Big stars told me I was hop-skip-jumping up the rose-colored path to marquee heaven. It was my first brush with fame and I loved the smell of it.

I try to think of what was my biggest moment—my biggest thrill. I think it was in 1950 on St. Valentine's Day. I was going to start a big movie with Jimmy Cagney the next day and I went with Franchot Tone to the opera. I wore a mink stole he had given me and I was dripping ice (diamonds). We marched into the Opera House and it was like everyone had suddenly been struck silent. People stopped whatever they were doing and just stared at us. We were the most glamorous thing since Lily St. Cyr's pasties. And we took advantage of it. Franchot and me, we just stood there and let them gape for a moment. It was heaven.

After that it was up, up, up. Jobs, money, power, romance, and a great future. You may think I was spoiled. I wasn't. I had servants but I cooked, and good, too. I collected antiques and my home was something to see. Not like this dump. Look at it—empty bottles, holes in the ceiling, broken down furniture.

I went out with every big male star in town. They wanted my body and I needed their names for success. There wasn't a column in town written without my name in it. I was hot news. Every morning columnists would call to find out where I was the night before. Sometimes I could tell them—other times it wouldn't have been wise. Then came Tom Neal. He was a beautiful hunk of man. He had a chemical buzz for me that sent red peppers down my thighs. I didn't want to get involved with him on a permanent basis because he was just another bit player with a gorgeous physique.

But he lusted for me and I lusted for him. When I dated someone else he waited at my house for me to come home.

And I wanted him to. You tell me what love is. I don't know. But I think we had a lot going in that department. Trouble is my mind said: "Leave him alone. He can't help your career. He's just another little guy in trouble." But my heart paid no attention.

Tom Neal was a strong, healthy, happy-go-lucky ex-football player, ex-boxer, who had a physique that cried for female attention and got it. I was hung on him. When we made love, buds sprouted flowers and cupid got a medal. Those were toe-tingling days and nights. But it was the train to nowhere. It was the midnight express to dirty diapers and kisses on the cheek for hello's and goodbye's. I had my taste of that and kitchen smell. I didn't want any more of it. So what to do?

Franchot Tone, suave, likeable, quiet, unexciting Franchot, asked me to do a play with him in New York. He was hooked on me. He believed in me, too. That was the route I had to travel. He spelled it out for me and I read him. So I went East with Tone.

I was good to Franchot. He was good to me, too. You'd think that combo would strike oil—but it was a dry well.

We were a hit on Broadway. Light a Roman candle and there's red flashes in the sky tonight. The critics said I was a beautiful girl and could act, too. I got adulation in New York. It was all happy time. But I missed Tom. It had always bugged me that he had never asked to marry me. Here a socially acceptable Mr. Tone was begging to pay my bills legally and Mr. Have-Nothing was living in my house while I was in New York. Tom didn't think he could afford a wife—like me.

Like all feminine romantics, I thought if I stayed away long enough from Tom, he'd beg me to marry him. That's why I held off Franchot until we got back to Hollywood.

But no bells rang when I saw Tom. He just wanted me back in the hay. So I took the joker out of the deck and agreed to marry Franchot. Wanting to make sure that Tom was out of my system, Franchot insisted we all meet like civilized folk and talk it over.

Franchot just couldn't understand what I could see in Tom when he (Tone) was offering me marriage immediately. Simple-minded Neal thought we were great in bed so why complicate the mess with marriage? So we sipped a light wine on a hotter-than-Hades summer night and thought we could talk out our problems.

Tom kept zinging Franchot, "What the hell, you're

twenty years older than Barbara. She's a passionate broad. What happens ten years from now? Are you going to be able to satisfy her?"

Franchot kept debating the subject politely, but I knew he was getting madder and madder. Tone's opinion of Neal was that he was just an out-of-work weight-lifter, and he was pretty definite about it, especially as the wine went down.

I didn't have much to say. I was just like the gold door prize they were battling for. I loved Tom. I liked and respected Franchot. Well, the argument got drunker and we strolled out on the patio. Franchot tripped on one of Tom's barbells and that did it. Not that it hurt his foot, but it was a steel reminder that Tom had been around my house.

Then—atomic bombs! Franchot had to be crazy drunk to throw a punch at Neal. It was like throwing a pebble at an elephant. The elephant roared and speared Franchot to the wall with his tusks. Tom threw about ten fast punches that crushed Tone's nose and stretched him out cold on the pavement.

Both Tom and Franchot told the police and press they loved me and wanted to marry me. Ha, ha—coming from Tom that was a laugh! He had to propose to me via the district attorney's office. His proposal was as legitimate as counterfeit money.

The press descended on me and I gave my decision. The minute Franchot left the hospital, I said, I'd marry him. I kept my word. In May of 1951, I married Franchot Tone, a millionaire success who loved me more than any girl in the world. Sounds like a happy ending to a fairy tale, doesn't it? Sorry—it was just the beginning.

kept my word. In May of 1951, I married Franchot Tone,

Franchot couldn't accept me as Barbara Payton from the beginning. If he could have we might have been happy. But I was the Barbara Payton of Tom Neal's—of my lover's—of my past—all of it. He hated me for what I had been and loved me for what I was.

He tortured himself. I was only somebody for his doubts, fears, recriminations to bounce off. I resolved to let him spend himself of the torture. It was endless. It built. Every part of my body reminded him of another man.

I cried for him night and day. My life was one of re-crimination, doubt, hate and apology. "Just love me," I pleaded. He couldn't do it. His memory was too sharp.

We'd split up and go back together. It was kind of an

unhealthy rhythm. Up, down, sideways, flat and back up again. I learned to love Franchot for his intensity. I was his mania, his phobia—one half of his own split personality. He concentrated on me as if I were a script that he must learn overnight. It couldn't work. I agreed to give him a divorce by default. After days of wrangling and reconciliations our attorneys agreed on a settlement.

Franchot was through with me. It was a relief even though I still loved him. He got off my back and I floated back to Tom again. It was inevitable. His muscles rippled under my hands and we settled back to days of continuous love. I told myself it had to end but hoped it wouldn't.

I got a sweet-smelling wire that I was wanted to do two pictures in London. It paid loads of money so I couldn't turn it down. It wasn't easy to leave Tom but I did.

I was a smash hit in England. The pictures were sensational and I got all kinds of film offers. Counts and Lords begged me be their little pussy-wussy. I gave a couple of them a thrill or two but when Tom came to London, they all looked like male shadows instead of men.

All over England I got offers to stay but Tom was itchy and I caught it. We were offered a road tour of *The Postman Always Rings Twice* and I thought it would be fun to do a play together. I was deliberately foregoing the big time for the small time—to be with Tom.

We did very well in the sticks but not so good in the big cities. After a while we got back to Hollywood and there was nothing to do. We began to fight. One day I told Tom he was a bastard and gave him the air. He said about the same to me and that was the end.

I had an awful lot of money one time. I made it in pictures and I got a big settlement from Tone. But it went fast. One day I was rich and the next I was poor.

So what does a gorgeous young girl do when she's broke? Well, I got married four more times. It didn't work. Husbands wanted my body and not me. Anyway, that's the way it seemed. I don't know why they married me.

I was traveling around without money and it had to end in trouble because I still spent as if I had it.

In 1955, back in Hollywood, I cashed a check for $100 at a supermarket. It was a store I had spent thousands of dollars in. Well, the check was no good. I don't remember if I thought I had money in the bank. I guess I didn't. But the cops pulled me in. I was really going to get the rap because I bought mostly liquor with the money.

My lawyer worked without a fee—because I didn't have a bean—and told the market owner I'd make restitution. Then he asked me for a list of my friends who might give me a hundred dollars to make the check good.

With all my friends I couldn't think of one who would risk a hundred dollars on me. But abracadabra, Milt Golden, my attorney, came up with one. It was Herman Hover, owner of what was then Ciro's nightclub. Herman said I and my friends had spent so much money in his place he felt he owed it to me.

So my lawyer almost got the DA to drop the charges. But I insulted some witch of a newspaperwoman about the same time and she, in the name of her paper, wouldn't let the case be settled out of court. So I got a "Guilty" verdict and had to pay a hundred-dollar fine.

It was the start of a thousand annoyances caused by money troubles. It seemed impossible that I couldn't put my hands on chunks of money every time I wanted to, but face up to it, I couldn't.

CHAPTER I

I don't remember what age I was, but I remember a dream—my first recollection. I could do without it.

I dreamed I was looking at the man in the moon and suddenly it started falling toward me, faster and faster. The huge man's face hit me and crushed me against a rock that I had been leaning on. It was cold and clammy and the moon-face was like gelatin. I was stuck to the rock with this terrible substance. I couldn't get away and I screamed. The scream woke me and the rest of the household, too.

I had that dream all the time. Sometimes, in the summer, the round-eyed man's face was on the sun, too.

When I got rich and could afford it, I went to a psychiatrist to see what my dream meant. He gave me the obvious explanation—I was inwardly afraid of men and their power over me. I didn't argue. It could be. Men have dragged me through all the emotions, top to bottom, and in between. That's what I want to talk about first.

Even in my pre-teen years I wasn't unaware of Hollywood, the glamour, the adoration, the handsome men, the fame, the money. I borrowed fan magazines, cut out the actors I admired and pinned them to my wall. Ten years later I was dating them or sleeping with them.

It was in the movies, where a boy first tried to touch

me. At first I was so entranced with the movie I didn't realize his hands were creeping down the front of my dress—and me about 10 years old with bee stings for breasts! I hauled off and socked him even though he had paid for the movie. He sulked all the way through the picture.

"Know what we call girls like you?" he accused when the lights went on, "Teasers. I'll never take you to the movies again."

This shocked me because I had only a handful of boys with enough money to take me to the movies.

When the lights went out I grabbed his hand and put it down the front of my dress—just for a second, then yanked it out. "You satisfied?" I said.

He grinned. "Boy, you're stacked!"

Wherever did he get that idea? "Shut up," I said, "and let's see the movie."

One night my brother told me James Cagney was coming to town for a fund drive. I always liked him because he was tough and ruthless on screen and it fitted my theory of what a man should be. I found out that admission to the auditorium was $1.25. Not only couldn't I afford that but none of my boyfriends could either. Yet I had to see Jimmy Cagney in person. I got so distraught I was sick to my stomach and couldn't eat.

Then the miracle happened. I was standing in a big crowd by the artist's entrance and a boy of at least sixteen motioned to me. "You're cute," he said. I gave him the razzberry—that's how sophisticated I was. "Want to see the show, kid?" he asked. "Cagney gave my father two tickets —see?"

It was unbelievable but he had two yellow tickets in his hand and they looked professional. But I was cautious. I was learning.

"What do I have to do?"

He bent toward me. "A feel or two. So what? You go inside free. Best seats in the house."

"No thanks," I said coldly, but I was tempted. He shrugged and I watched him proposition another girl a little older. She walked away from him. He tried it on another girl and she walked away.

I realized my position was getting stronger. Sure enough he came back to me. "Okay, kid," he offered. "No feels. Come with me." I didn't really believe him but I had to get inside. I went along with him.

They weren't the best seats in the house but good enough. Jimmy Cagney came out, and I felt my escort's fingers fooling around with my legs, but I didn't care.

Many years later Jimmy Cagney signed me to do a picture with him. I wouldn't have believed it could happen then.

When we got outside the boy, whose name I never learned, said, "You know, you're a strange one—and pretty. You could be an actress."

I thought he was making fun of me. "And you could be a sex maniac," I jeered, then ran home.

That's the way it started. People kept telling me, even when I was a little kid, that I could be an actress. They saw a lot more in me than I saw in myself. I once took it seriously enough to ask my dad if I could ever be an actress.

"I'd rather you'd rely on your mind than your face," he advised. Then he went back to his reading.

CHAPTER 2

At one time, when I was a star, I went twice a week—at twenty-five dollars a visit—to a psychiatrist to see if he could cure my insomnia. I think, in the beginning, I was too much for Dr. Sessan (that's not his real name).

I was very rich but I would beg men to give me their dirty shirts so I could wash them. I just dug it. I had been doing that since high school. At first, he thought it was some kind of sex thing, but then he thought I was just wild —that I liked to wash men's shirts like he liked to play golf.

We tried to remember the first time I washed a man's shirt . . .

I was on a roller coaster with a boy. He stood up daringly as we zoomed down the track and I was afraid he'd be hurt. I tried to pull him back in the seat, and when I grabbed his shirt there was a large rust-colored stain—it almost looked like blood that was washed and didn't come out.

Later in the day I asked if I could wash his shirt. I had to see if I could get that spot out. I felt a little like Lady Macbeth. It didn't come out. The boy thought that was a very intimate thing I had done and tried to get me to lay down in the fields with him. I didn't like him that much so

I never saw him again. But I looked for other shirts to wash.

I think the doctor's summing up was:

"You see, Barbara, the way we cure a transvestite (a man who likes to wear women's clothes) is to give him a girl's handkerchief or panties he can keep in his pocket and hold and feel all day. This, after a while, will satisfy his divergent urge. We hope eventually we can even take the handkerchief or panties away entirely.

"The way I see it is you want many men but there is a moralistic streak somewhere deep inside you that won't let you sleep around promiscuously. So to get a man's shirt, and symbolically cleanse him and you by washing it, gives you some subconscious satisfaction."

That was the summing up of a Beverly Hills psychologist. While it sounded logical, it wasn't true. Today I'm still queer about washing men's shirts—but it's usually *after* I've slept with them.

Well, at twenty-five dollars a visit I stuck it out for six months but I still wasn't sleeping. I had my own theory. I told him, "They give me parts that require talent I don't have. I panic."

He didn't think much of my analysis.

One day he said to me, "Barbara, you are the strangest patient I ever treated. You are so many people and yet nobody. Who is the real Barbara? I haven't found her yet. I don't know if I ever will, or for that matter, if you ever will. I want you to try another psychiatrist for awhile."

I was pretty smart in those days—shrewd—especially where men were concerned. You know how they say girls always fall in love with their psychiatrists. Well, I had the feeling he was falling in love with me—a real switch! He was a fine man and a good psychiatrist and he morally couldn't ask me out as the start of a romance—unless I ceased to be his patient.

My theory turned out to be correct. His name was Jonathan. We spent most of our dates talking about me. It was like getting free treatment. He never made a pass at me. Maybe he had problems.

I asked him once, point-blank, why he didn't try to kiss me or take me away for a week-end. "I'm a married man," he told me.

I had known he was married. I had long ago erased that as a reason for not going to bed with a man I liked, but I didn't say anything. I enjoyed our dates.

I'll never forget some of the things he told me about myself. They were very complimentary. I never trust men's words when they are on the make for me. But the doctor was sincere.

"You have what every woman in the world wants," he explained once. "Adoration, success, achievement, men, fame, everything. Yet it doesn't satisfy you. Very deep inside you there are confused values. You want different kinds of values . . . satisfactions. You want just one man who doesn't exist. A strong man, yet one you can handle. A handsome one, yet one who is of no interest to other women. A rich one, yet one who will live as a beachcomber with you. A talented one but one who won't steal any of your glory. A cheerful one but one who will fit into your many-faceted moods. In that area alone you're in trouble.

"You're a big star, but I don't believe it was ever meant for you. You have great chunks of emptiness inside. Strangely enough, it's your good points—conscience, generosity, love of fun, loyalty—that might mitigate against a continued success. A star and her worship by others must never be parted. Yet somewhere in your heart you realize the hollowness of your rewards. That is dangerous. Once you laugh at the value of what you've been striving and searching for, it's all over. Stardom requires faith in what it is, regardless of its faults."

He was right.

I gave him a kiss on the cheek for that speech. He only smiled—that enigmatic smile.

But I did get under his skin. He switched me to Dr. Irving Bunt.

Then I got a note from Jonathan asking me if I'd have dinner with him at Jack's-at-the-Beach, a romantic eatery on the ocean near Malibu. I was delighted. He was terribly sober all during dinner. With coffee he opened up.

"I'm coming to you with my problems," he said slowly. "I'm in love with you." He held my hand on the table, which was daring for him. "I'm married—contentedly. I have two children. I'm not the kind of man who cheats. I can either get a divorce and ask you to marry me—or try to fight it." He sighed heavily. "I don't know if I'm strong enough."

I was used to men being in love with me, I don't say that with conceit, just stating the facts. I even knew the antidotes which I used when deemed necessary.

"Remember," I warned him lightly, "I'm many Barbaras. Which one do you love?"

"All of them!" He looked miserable.

I was very sophisticated and my solutions for problems were often way out but they worked. "Do you want to go to bed with me?" I asked him point-blank.

He seemed shocked. "Yes, I do, but I love you—" and he explained. "I'm the kind of man who doesn't cheat."

"You deal in theories. I deal in facts. I've been through the whole bit. You love me. I believe you—but you are bursting with wanting me physically. I like you and I'll help you. Once will—might—do it. It often does. Isn't that better than wrecking your home and maybe your life?"

I could see he was tortured. He didn't answer.

"Pay the check. We'll drive up the coast and take separate rooms at the Holiday House, adjoining, for say, three hours. I'll be in the room next to you. If you want me—I'll be there waiting."

He acted like an automaton until we were in separate rooms. I lay down on the bed, fully clothed, and could hear him pacing, even hitting his fist against his open palm. He had to work it out by himself.

In about an hour, he knocked on my door. "Will you kiss me?" he asked. I returned his passionate kiss.

"I'm going home," he said. "I couldn't do it. I'm a mathematical kind of man. It wouldn't work for me. I'd always want you—always!"

I could see he was suffering, but he wouldn't, or couldn't, take my advice.

He only said one thing on the long way home. "I guess I'm the only man alive who would reject such a tempting offer."

It was my turn to smile. I liked him very much and respected him.

I guess he worked it out inside of him because the only contact I've had with him over the years is a Christmas card every year. The word "thanks" is always on it. I just got one last Christmas. I wonder if he knows what I do for a living today and what he'd say?

Dr. Bunt also traveled through my girlhood with me. For example, we moved through my relationship with my father. I think the day my father realized I was a girl—a real feminine girl—I was about twelve or thirteen—he became afraid of me. Not that I didn't love my father. I did. He was a kind, dignified kind of man. I still love him. But that's the way I saw it.

Once when I was thirteen or so, my father came upon me necking, and I mean really necking, in a boy's car parked in our driveway. He apologized and walked away.

My father didn't want to believe that his daughter could or would have anything to do with that mysterious thing called sex.

Dr. Bunt said this kind of father was not uncommon. He was unsure of what was right or wrong, protective or interfering, and therefore stumbled through the relationship haphazardly.

Dr. Bunt explained that the danger in such cases is that the daughter substitutes, without awareness, another father who is also a lover. She looks for the combination lover-father instead of just lover.

It was true and it opened up windows to myself that I had never looked in before.

I remembered some of the ridiculous things I had done. I fell in love with my best girl friend's father. He was very handsome, gray hair, and was a successful architect. I'd see him when I was at my girl friend's house and never showed any outward sign that I was mad about him. I was 15 at the time.

But I told my girl friend about my wild crush and she told her father. After that his manner changed. He was more formal with me and stopped teasing me about things. I was awfully unhappy.

His wife threw him a surprise party—he was forty-five years old—and we kids just happened to be there. They had punch and it was spiked. Everyone was drinking freely. I went upstairs to the john and someone was in it so I just waited by the door. Then the door opened and it was *him* —Johnny. He didn't even walk outside. He was very high. He just grabbed my arm and pulled me inside, locked the door again and kissed me. I was scared stiff someone would see us coming out of the john together.

I'm not going to tell you what happened but what did happen was in the dry bathtub. Someone knocked loudly on the door then and Johnny told me to hide behind the shower curtain until they left. I heard a man enter the room and say laughingly (to Johnny), "That punch is murder on the kidneys." Johnny laughed.

I waited until after the flush of the toilet and then got out.

Downstairs the party was going on as if nothing had happened. That could have been the end of it. A few moments of delirium, delicious delirium, and then back to normal.

But that wasn't the way it happened. I had a lot of electricity in me and men just didn't hit and run with me. They usually came back for seconds and with their tongue dragging.

Johnny waited outside of school for me and asked me to go for a ride with him. I was crazy about him but knew how dangerous it was. Furthermore, I didn't want to get involved. I turned him down. He was like hypnotized. He'd wait for me almost every day after school, leaving his office at three o'clock. He'd walk along with me for a little. I told him the kids were beginning to talk, or whisper is a better word. I asked him to stop seeing me. He begged but I stuck to it.

Then came the explosion. My girl friend was on the phone and said, "All jumpin' hell has broken loose at my house! My father has asked my mother for a divorce. He's in love with someone else. She won't give him his freedom unless she knows who it is. It must be someone at the office."

My heart was skipping beats. My girl friend hadn't the slightest idea I was the third party. And I'll tell you I hadn't the faintest idea of breaking up a home and marrying Johnny!

I decided to do something about it. Next day after school I went to Johnny's office. He hugged and kissed me. I tried to be cool to him. It wasn't easy. I still went for him in a big way.

He told me about all the plans he had for us. But I cut him short. "Johnny, I don't love you. There's a boy at school I love." That wasn't true. "Forget me. I'll stay away from the house. I'll even move away if it will help."

He was stricken but he made me promise I wouldn't move away. I promised, and he and his wife made up again.

That's the way it was. I was always falling for older men —it seemed like gray in a man's hair touched it off.

CHAPTER 3

Dr. Bunt dug out all kinds of painful memories: I was twelve years old and went with the same gang all the time.

One of the boys, nicknamed "Bouncy," was very fat. He had the hots for me, but I always turned him down.

One Sunday we were playing post office. He was in a closet and called me in to receive a special delivery stamp, which meant one soul kiss—tongue, lips, everything. I went into the closet but I kind of brushed him off. He yanked me back and forced his tongue between my teeth. I slapped him hard and started to yell, "Lousy fat bastard—ugly pig!"

He cursed back at me. I broke out of the closet with him still cursing me and chasing me. We both refused to play anymore. The kids were laughing.

I went home for Sunday night dinner. About an hour later Sidney, one of the kids, phoned me. He said, "Did you hear what happened? Bouncy is dead. He was hitching a ride on a tailgate and slipped. It was pulling a tractor on wheels and it ran over him. He was crushed. He just died in the hospital."

I sobbed uncontrollably for several hours until a doctor had to give me a sedative.

Bouncy and his unfortunate death stayed with me through the years.

At this time in my analysis, I got the lead opposite Gregory Peck in *Only the Valiant*. The papers were full of it. I was riding high. You can still see the motion picture on television today. There I am, as I was, beautiful, dashing, a big star playing opposite big stars. And there I am watching what I was. I often ask myself how it could happen. Not that I'm ashamed. I did what I had to do. But how did I fall so low? How? How? How?

How did I go from $100,000 a picture to five dollars for cohabitating with men I have never seen before? I remember once going to bed with a star for a new Cadillac. Cost: $6,000. The second time he came back I asked him what he was going to give me this time. He got mad and I never spoke to him again.

My husband got mad also when he took me to Hollywood at seventeen. I had just recently been married to Captain Payton. It was my first look at Hollywood and our honeymoon. The captain was crazy about me and at seventeen it was enough to be loved. I didn't have to love. Though I was grateful and proud to have such a handsome husband.

Hollywood hit me with a bewildering impact. It was like being let into an exclusive jewelers and told I could have my pick of the jewels. I knew this rich paradise would somehow fulfill my destiny.

My husband was becoming restless. He had to return to his post. I told him to go ahead—I would follow soon.

The town hypnotized me. I was completely in its power. I told myself if I could just get into one picture I would be satisfied to die right after it.

But how did a girl get into a movie?

There was no way any passing stranger could discover me because I had been warned about Hollywood men and was afraid to talk to anyone. Every time a man talked to me I walked away very fast without answering.

I was staying at the Knickerbocker Hotel in Hollywood and Bobby, the elevator boy, told me a casting director, Mr. Griffith, from the New York offices of RKO, had checked into the hotel for a week.

One noon hour on my way out to lunch—the hotel dining room was too expensive for me—a man stopped me and said, "Aren't you the young lady the elevator boy told me about?"

I stammered.

"Tell you what," he said, handing me a card, "give me a ring when you have a moment." Then he left me standing there with my lower lip dragging.

On a Monday morning I went to Mr. Griffith's office at the studio. It was all very business-like.

"Would you like to read for us?" he asked. A tiny man with a tiny mustache, who I later found out was his boss, sat with him.

They handed me a page from *Philadelphia Story* and I read—cold turkey!

"Let's try it again," suggested Mr. Griffith. His boss nodded.

I read it again with more confidence and Griffith said, "That's better."

Griffith came to a conclusion. They'd give me a screen test in a few weeks. In the meantime I'd go to school on the lot. I was cautioned about being too optimistic. They said only one in ten got a part or a contract after a test.

I floated out of the room on cloud twenty-nine. A screen test! It was too impossible to imagine.

I got up very early the next morning to report to the RKO school, which wasn't very far from the hotel. For one hour before leaving I threw up. I attributed it to nerves.

At the studio they gave me scenes from plays to study

and I listened to a lecture on drama. I also played a short scene.

Every morning when I walked inside those gates and said hello to the watchman, it was like coming home. I even loved the smell of the place.

I was sick every morning—but it was nerves. Obviously, it was nerves!

Then the day came when I would do the run-through before the camera. The day after I would do the test. I could feel the pressure building up. I had hot and cold flashes. I knew my part. But I couldn't convince myself I wasn't scared pea green.

They set up the cameras—no film—and the director made the chalk marks for me. I wasn't halfway through the scene when I began to feel sick and faint. I fought it, but I had to stop and get a drink of water.

"It happens all the time," the director said. "Don't think anything about it. It's just nerves."

I had a drink and we tried it again. This time the whole set spinned and I fell down in a faint. A nurse from First Aid used smelling salts on me.

We had a little talk and one word—pregnancy! I cried. I sobbed. I wouldn't accept the verdict. But I agreed to go to a doctor.

"Congratulations—you're pregnant," said the doctor brightly. I cried. I just couldn't stop crying. I went to see Mr. Griffith. He already had the nurse's report. He could see the tears in my eyes. He was very nice about it. I had wasted their time, effort, and money but he never mentioned that.

"Have your baby," he said, "and in a year, if everything works out well for you, and you'd like to, come back. You're a very promising actress."

One year! Maybe longer! It sounded like a death sentence. I was so miserable I wanted to die. I blamed it all on my husband.

CHAPTER 4

You know, I just realized that this is a kind of detective story. I—or we—want to find out what happened that started me on the skids. Could it have been avoided? How? Is it too late to come back—just a little bit?

But first, how did I get up there? To the top. How did I

do what few girls have done? How do you become a famous actress? Well, the magic wand can hit you anytime.

Most of the time a chain of circumstances leads you to a goal and every link has to be in place. For instance:

I had a small part in a movie with Dennis Morgan and Jack Carson. There was a dumpy, grotesque little fellow always hanging around the water fountain where we were shooting. No one ever talked to him and I felt sorry for him.

So one day I had a drink of water and said to him, "Hot, isn't it?"

He stuttered badly but managed to agree with me. We became friendly. He was the director's son and gave me the scoop on what was happening behind the scenes. Like, the young leading woman had ulcers and the medicine she was taking sent her sky high so she had trouble learning her lines and didn't much care.

One day August's (a phony name) car had two flats at the same time and I drove him home. He asked me in—it was a stone mansion in Beverly Hills.

We sat sipping drinks when his father came in. He didn't even know me, I had such a small part. He was cursing his girl star. He had a drink, then he got on an art kick. "You see, Sissie," he said to me, "we wouldn't hire Charlie Chaplin to play Chaplin because the big eye of the audience requires exaggeration, sublimation, distortion to bring out the impression of the real thing. That's how it is with a character in a picture. The writer is never able to draw his portrait as he wants him played. He is exact, and we must distort to make it live. Maybe I don't make my point. I tell you, you walk across the room, Sissie . . . Go ahead—walk."

I got up and walked across the room thinking—"these nutty directors."

"Fine," he said. "Now walk across the room as—what's your name?" I told him. "As Barbara Payton would do it."

I walked across the room, I thought, exactly as I had done it before.

He was delighted. "See—see, there's the slightest bit of exaggeration! You made my point exactly. You have a talent . . . a driving talent. Now you'll go to bed with me."

His son just kept sipping his drink.

I smiled and said, "I only bed down with men I want to bed down with. I don't even know you yet."

He was even happier with that. "Ah, you don't close the door. You leave the calling card of hope. Smart girl!"

After a while I left—after he had passed out. I was fascinated with the man.

Next day on the set he didn't recognize me. But he gave his son a note for me. It read: "Will you have late dinner with me tonight?"

August picked me up at midnight and took me to his father at a small restaurant in downtown Los Angeles. Then August left.

The director, already several drinks ahead of me, talked to me in several foreign languages, none of which I understood. Everyone seemed to know him and we always had someone hanging over our table. He introduced me to everyone as "Sissie."

"Sissie," he finally said to me in English. "You're going to make a big star out of yourself. And you're going to be miserable."

His prediction came true, but it was inconceivable then. "How?" I asked.

"How?" he laughed. "You go home tonight, take a hot shower and go to bed. That's all there is to it."

"And . . . ?" I asked suspiciously.

He roared with laughter again. "In the morning, you take a cold shower, get dressed and come to the set—my set. There I will give you a script of my next picture. In it there is a part for you. And that is how you will achieve the first faltering step to stardom."

I came to the set and he did give me a script. That night I opened the script, which was stamped "Second Draft," and read it through. There was no part in it for me. There were only two middle-aged women and a girl of twelve. I was indignant, hurt and disillusioned.

Next day I had a chance to talk to him. "Why did you lie to me?" I asked, almost in tears.

"What did you think of the story?" he smiled.

"Terrible," I snapped.

"That's what I thought, but no one could give me an honest decision. I knew if you thought there was a part in it for you, you'd read it through—every word."

"You're sadistic," I said loudly.

He laughed and went back to direct a scene.

August saw me in tears and clumsily tried to calm me. "He's strange and uses people for puppets but he always keeps his promise. Just wait him out."

I took heart and did.

A messenger boy brought a new script to my house the

next morning. It had a note attached from the director. "Try the part of Freda."

It was a fine part and he gave it to me without my taking a test. It helped me get my contract with Jimmy Cagney productions.

CHAPTER 5

I guess I was always bugged with that psychiatry kick. On the way up and on the way down. And there must be some substance to it, because the head shrinkers always told me I had the compulsive urge to see myself destroyed ... that in the end it would be my final pleasure. They told me what was wrong but not what to do about it.

Finally I believe them. What makes me believe them is what happens lately. I try to light a cigarette and the flame is three inches to the left or right of the end of my cigarette. It's hard for me to focus. Someone said it's from drinking too much wine.

I like the Negro race because lately they're the only ones who appreciate my blonde beauty—or what I have left of it. White men don't seem to go for me anymore.

I've pawned or sold most of my clothes. I needed the money for Rosé wine.

Mentioning clothes takes me back to my first fur coat. It's the start of something big for an actress—symbol of success to come.

I got my full-length mink on a hot day in July when it was even too hot for a bikini. It was at a 1947 premiere, I was eighteen and beautiful. It feels like a thousand years ago.

As a result of the flurry I caused at the premiere, I was asked to attend a dinner party at the house of an internationally known public figure in Washington, D. C. I won't mention his name because it might cause him embarrassment.

I had no escort of my own so one was assigned to me. He was a taciturn, dignified gentleman forty years my senior, in the steel business. The dinner and entertainment afterwards passed uneventfully. Everyone was charming and on his best behavior.

Mr. Steel, Inc., took me home in his chauffeured limousine. I don't think he was particularly fascinated with me.

Next morning, early, his secretary called to ask me how

well I knew the host of the evening before. Mr. Steel wanted to send the host a small gift of appreciation for the splendid evening and for supplying him such a charming escort. Mr. Steel wanted to know what gift the host might be partial to.

"Napoleon brandy," I suggested.

A week later in Hollywood, Mr. Steel's secretary called me again, merely saying that the famous public figure was delighted with the case of Napoleon brandy Mr. Steel had sent over and Mr. Steel was sending me a gift as a token of appreciation.

The "gift" knocked me right on my ass—it was a full-length white mink coat!

Several weeks later I found out that Mr. Steel, because of legislation that had been okayed by our host, had made several hundred thousand dollars.

It's like I said—the lady with the wand has to touch you.

I can even remember how I got my first diamonds—long ago sent out to the pawn shops.

I was only eighteen but I had a lot of theories about life and people. Nor was I bashful about expounding them. There was a beatnik party in Nicholas Canyon, a narrow, dark place in the hills of Hollywood. Everyone looked as if he didn't have five dollars to his name.

"Men are always telling me how much they love me—how they can't live without me. But when I say the government is after me for taxes and I must have a thousand dollars immediately, I don't hear any voices. I believe if a man really loves me there's no end to what he will do, money or what, to make me happy. Or at least ease any troubles," I said.

Everyone laughed, probably at the way I expressed it, except for one intense, handsome, young boy.

"What do you want?" he asked in a serious monotone. "How much?"

I knew he meant it. But I answered almost mockingly, "I go to premieres and fine parties and I have no good jewelry —like a diamond bracelet for instance."

"How much?" he asked.

"Oh, about three thousand dollars, I'd say."

He repeated, "Three thousand dollars."

"Are you a rich-man's son?"

He shook his head negatively. "I'm a gas pump jockey."

He was so solemn. I felt sorry for him.

"I'll tell you, sonny," I said. "We'll go to the 881 Club and you'll buy me a drink and I'll call it square."

"My name is George Gardner. The drink I can buy you —the diamond bracelet I'm *going* to buy you."

I didn't want this thing to get out of hand. "You remember I was talking about someone who really loves me. I don't even know you."

"But I'm in love with you." He never smiled.

I shrugged, decided he was some kind of nut and moved around the room.

About a week later I got a formal notice from him and an insurance company that I had been named as his beneficiary on a life policy. This was getting serious and I was a little scared. I called him and we had coffee near the gas station where he worked.

He said, "I have no intention of dying yet. It is just a gesture. I'm working on that diamond bracelet. You might say the policy is—insurance."

After a while he convinced me and I was able to eat a sugar donut. I suggested that, being so handsome, he should try and become an actor.

"No," he said. "I know where I belong. I'm hot around cars. They come to life when I touch them."

When I left him I felt better.

A week later there was a picture in the papers of him in a Culver City drag race. He had won second prize.

About a month later, after only talking on the telephone a few times, he asked me if I'd be his guest at a jalopy race he had entered.

It became a kind of publicity stunt and I presented the trophy to the winner, who was none other than George. We had pictures taken together and he treated me to a pizza dinner.

At the table he told me, "I'm in love with you. I know I'm just a kid and in a crazy business compared with a movie star, but I'll make the headlines yet. And I haven't forgotten your diamond bracelet. That was a $500 purse I won today."

I told him to save his money, that I could do without diamonds at present. In fact, I was wearing riding breeches, as I was doing a western movie.

I invited him to a cocktail party at my home but he felt he'd be out of place.

He'd send me clippings from time to time, telling of his wins and near-wins in stock car races.

When he was in a minor accident I called him to say he should give up his racing and take the safer job of movie actor. He laughed at that and said the red eye of the camera would terrify him.

You may know what happened. He was in time trials at a small track near Riverside. His car turned over and caught fire. A small boy sitting on a fence was crushed to death and George was critically injured. A mutual friend notified me and I talked to him in the hospital. Doctors said he had a fifty-fifty chance.

He couldn't talk but his eyes said he understood. I made small talk about movies and racing. I showed him a pair of black panties with red arrows I had just bought. His eyes smiled. He had no family, but racing friends called and came to visit. He seemed to improve, but three days later I was notified that he had died.

It was one of the sadder moments of my life. The insurance company sent me a check for three thousand dollars. I cried. It was a lot of money, but I used every cent to buy a diamond bracelet. Many a tear fell on those diamonds. I know he would have wanted me to buy it.

So I had furs and diamonds at eighteen.

CHAPTER 6

There have been all sorts of rumors as to how I got my contract with Jimmy Cagney Productions. Who should know better than I? Sure, I might lie, but what would I have to gain?

Here's the true story. I had some parts and then I heard Cagney Productions was looking for a blonde. Some madam told me this. I never questioned how in hell a madam plying her trade in Glendale would get such information, but that's the way news gets around in Hollywood.

So I went over to Cagney Productions. It was a scorching hot day. I was a little late and I hurried up the two flights that led to the casting office. I burst into the outer reception room and there were about a dozen girls waiting there. I took one look and knew I didn't stand a chance. They were all cool-looking and at ease. I was hot, disheveled and puffing. What I needed was a trick.

I took advantage of the first one that came to mind. I went through the door into the casting director's office, sat down on the couch, kicked off my shoes and fanned my legs with my dress and said, "S---! It's a hot f------ day!"

Well, the girl the casting director was interviewing just about collapsed in her leather chair and he gulped and admitted with alacrity it was indeed warm.

Then the girl left the office and the casting man wanted to know what kind of a lunatic I was. I was frank. I told him if I hadn't done something spectacular, I would have been brushed off.

Anyway, my entrance became a conversation piece around the studio. Eventually I got a test and was signed.

I could buzz your beanery with the golden gimmicks actresses and actors have used to get breaks. Lawyers tell me I can't use names but you'll recognize some of them or at least think you do.

What about the female singer on-the-way-up who sent the major studio head her younger sister—still in college—to do with what he wanted? And he did. In fact, he did so much she became pregnant and the studio head talked a young leading star into marrying her. Actually it didn't turn out too bad because they're still married and have three children.

I'm sure Fay Spain won't mind if I point out she tested for the lead in *God's Little Acre* and didn't make much of an impression. She then had some nude bust photos taken of herself against a poverty background. She sent them and got the part.

A late-night show hero got his start by buying twenty weekends-for-two in Las Vegas at a small but plush motel and sending them anonymously as gifts to producers who were planning motion pictures in the near future. Twelve producers showed up alone and there were lonely girls sharing the bungalows. Our hero then made it a point to let each producer know he knew they were married and shouldn't indulge in such didoes.

He started getting jobs that led to TV breaks. He was on his way. Twelve producers still hate him but he can get a movie job whenever he wishes even though he doesn't need it anymore.

I think I showed the most imagination in getting a picture job when I was in England. I don't remember the title anymore but there was the role of a nun I wanted to play. Some English actress had firsties on the role but I figured a way. It would cost me a thousand dollars, but it was worth it.

The producer, a very religious man, went to early mass every Saturday and Sunday. This particular Sunday I talked to the priest before mass and introduced myself. I told him I wanted to make a big donation to the church, handed him a thousand-dollar bill—U.S. money—and walked off.

The priest made a big to-do about it at services and I played my part well—mostly down. This producer, who was also a trustee at the church, came over to thank me effusively. From our friendship I got the part I wanted.

CHAPTER 7

There's a saying among the hip set in Hollywood that if the pressures don't get you the habits will.

I guess alcohol in different forms takes the biggest toll. Narcotics create problems. Pills of all kinds enter into it. Sex is a compulsive thing that drags some down and out. Compulsive smoking takes its toll, too. Eating habits send others to an early grave. And some can't sleep, so they keep going night and day. Speed kills others—they are compelled to drive at breakneck speed. Compulsive spending ruins some and gambling hurts others. They are all habits, habits, habits. I know. I've suffered from them all down the line. And I have a record of 100 per cent failure, never having cured one habit in a lifetime.

There are other habits that hang on like an octopus, scaring the hell out of you and never letting go. A girl falls in love with a girl and the whole world turns upside down. You start unlearning everything you ever learned.

At first it's for kicks—something you've never done before.

One evening I had too many drinks. I was at Ciro's with a young actor. He was a Western star and a bruiser when drunk. I said something to him about the state of his sobriety and he kicked me in the shins—a painful, powerful kick that drew blood.

I ran off to the ladies room crying and was bawling away there when a pretty young starlet, whose name you would know, asked me if she could help. I couldn't stop the flow of tears to answer her.

I think it started by her feeling sorry for me. She wasn't a dyke—a butch girl. Actually she wasn't a femme either. But she had some lez experiences before. I hadn't.

She was sympathetic, noticed my bruised leg and put a band aid on it. Her cool fingers felt good on my legs. She told me she just had a fight with her boyfriend.

When I still was sobbing in great big gulps, she cradled

me in her arms. "Men are poisonous," she said. "It always ends up the same way. They're cruel and possessive. I wish to hell we could do without them." Then as an afterthought, she added, "I could, except I need their favors—not love."

I sobbed, "I need love."

"We all do," Jean said. "There are different kinds." Then, in the powder room of Ciro's, she gently turned her face to mine and kissed me on the lips. It was a passionate kiss with her arms around me and I returned it with passion.

I look back now, many years later, at a long series of disappointments with men—phonies, liars, cheats, sadists, even thieves. Not that all men were that way. No, some were honorable and considerate; but in the main, the dating men in Hollywood are opportunists. Just guys looking for a fast - - - and then on to the next cutie.

I looked at Jean and saw excitement. I stopped crying.

"Tell you what," she said, "why don't you come up to my place later for a drink. It's just up the hill behind the club here. I'll brush off Bill. We'll have some girl talk—just the two of us."

I agreed, even though I wasn't sure where I was headed. It sounded mysterious, as if something would unfold for me. Something like from under a rock—unmentionable.

About an hour later I drove up to her pad. She was in a negligée that didn't hide much.

We talked for a long time while we sipped martinis. It was three in the morning but her phone kept ringing—guys. She'd grimace while she talked to them as if saying they were pests. Later she took the phone off the hook. Casually, she said, "It's late. Why don't you stay here? You can use one of my baby doll nighties."

I began wondering if I were all wrong and we were just two girls who had something in common—a mistrust of men. I showered and donned a baby doll nightie that couldn't serve any purpose other than obscuring a freckle. Then I got into bed actually prepared just to have a good night's sleep.

Then Jean got into bed. The light was out but I realized she wasn't wearing anything.

Like an idiot I said goodnight. With that Jean said, "Good night, baby." But she didn't say it like I had. There was a laugh in it. As she said good night, she kissed me and her hands moved quickly, surely, exploratively.

It was the start of my first lesbian affair. They always

happened after men shattered the few ideals or illusions I had left.

Jean and I didn't become lovers like many a dyke and femme. We continued to date men and act normally with them—I mean sex-wise. But we were always there for each other. It was a comfort and a good relationship.

One time in Mexico I used my attractiveness to women to even a score. An ex-boyfriend of mine who had left me rather cruelly, and as a matter of fact had stolen money out of my purse, was spending dough as if he were manufacturing it in Mexico City. It was obvious that his well-groomed girl friend, attractive but a little older than he, was furnishing the loot.

I took one look at her and knew she'd be vulnerable. She gave him the air and he left, cursing me. It was sweet revenge.

Once I even used my magnetism for females to get a part I was after. One of the town's most beautiful actresses, happily married with children, had the lead in a big epic. The role of her young friend was open. The producer told me I wasn't right for it. So I tried another way to get it. I knew this femme star was very powerful, and if she wanted me, I was in.

I was sensitive enough to these things to know the peculiar look she often gave girls was a sign of something. Either she had indulged in lez activities or wanted to . . . or I was wrong all the way.

I decided to gamble. She was doing some wardrobe tests for the picture and I stopped by the stage to look. I told her how beautiful she looked in the gowns. Later she invited me into her dressing room to see some other clothes.

"You just must see the party gown I wear in the picture," she said.

She stepped out of the dress she had on. She apologetically took off her bra, saying the gown had a special built-in bra. Well, she was standing there with the greatest pair of boobies you ever saw sticking straight out. And she just seemed to be riveted to the spot. She just looked at me.

I took the cue. I cupped both her breasts and she swooned onto the couch, writhing in ecstasy. We had a wild affair and I found out it was the first one she had ever had with a girl. She had always wanted to, but never quite had the courage.

She was wise to me. She knew I wanted the part and she knew the price. I got the part and almost every lunch hour we made it in her dressing room. We were very discreet and I doubt if anyone had the slightest suspicion. They just thought we liked having lunch together. They should have known what we had for lunch!

CHAPTER 8

Reading back over what I have written so far, I have the feeling sex was everything in my life. It was important, but not everything.

I had long friendships with men and women that were devoid of passion or sexual feelings—yes, I enjoyed them.

The odd part of it is, I once loved a man who was impotent and I was faithful to him. He left me after a while, thinking it was unfair to me. But it wasn't and I would have loved him and stayed with him the rest of his life.

His name was Johnny Slocum. He was thirty or so and never had a job in his life. He had sidewalk exhibitions of his paintings. He always asked fifty but would take five if he had to. Somehow, out of this he got enough to live on and he didn't want or need anything else.

He painted me maybe ten times in different poses and I expected the obvious request anytime: that I pose nude. Well, he never did, so I suggested it late one night.

I liked Johnny and knew he liked me. But in a month he had never tried to kiss me. I began to think I was losing my chemistry.

Small talk got around to figure models and what they charged—too much for Johnny to afford. I assured him I had a very good figure, and since I was feeling no pain, I did a classical strip tease down to just panties, and then figured the hell with it and struck a pose, completely nude, with flickering shadows from the fireplace flames dancing around my ass.

If I may say so myself, there weren't many men in the world who would, or could, have resisted my curved body. Johnny, who was always smiling, turned sober. "Babette,"—he called me that—"I don't think you should . . ."

Just that. I was annoyed. "No? Well, why not?" He was sitting on a huge pillow on the floor. I squatted beside him on the floor with my head on his shoulder. I knew my perfume was powerful.

He looked like he was in pain as he leaned away from me and huskily said, "Don't!"

As I said, I had a few drinks and this was insulting as

hell. My first instinct was to be indignant. But I was too feminine for that. Coquettishly I said, "Don't you like me a little?" And with that I kind of rolled over on him.

I could feel him shivering—that was a strange reaction. He seemed to be using great will-power to keep his hands behind him so that he didn't touch me.

I kissed him passionately on the lips, crushing him, but there was no response. It was a unique experience for me.

He was saying something when I stopped but it was hard to understand. I strained to hear because he was repeating it. "Eight years old in Switzerland—an automobile accident —my genitals were crushed—impotency . . . no feeling." The last three words I heard over and over.

I cradled him in my arms, his head pressed against my bare belly as he sobbed.

"Never mind . . . I understand. It makes no difference. I love you, Johnny."

His sobbing subsided and he sat up. "Penicillin," he said, "I have no feeling . . . just here." He pointed to his spine. "Like a tingling. Now you know my secret."

I realized my body meant nothing to him. It was a strange feeling. Something else occurred to me. "But an artist . . . I always felt in order to be creative it required response and sensitivity to everything."

"No. Life holds great happiness for me. I don't miss what I don't know. It's only moments like this that I . . ."

I kissed him gently. Then I put my clothes back on.

We lay in each other's arms by the dying flames and I wondered what he was thinking. I knew what I was thinking. I knew I loved him. A new kind of love for me—pity, sympathy, my mother instinct and love for a handsome man, even without balls, all added up.

He stroked my hair and told me I was a princess about to inherit a kingdom—Hollywood; he wasn't far off.

I began to date Johnny steadily. Me, Barbara Payton, who had been called the biggest sexpot in town, was going without it. None of my friends who saw us together ever suspected.

It was a beautiful relationship. I was secure for once in my life that a man loved me for what I was and not just for my body. And he did love me.

Once he begged me to have whatever men I wanted or needed as long as he didn't know about it. I told him I meant it when I said I loved him and that my life was complete with him. I needed no other men.

We went on a long trip together and he used the backgrounds of far-off places for his canvasses. It was a wonderfully inspiring year for me.

An idyll like that had to end, and it ended badly.

He insisted we visit his parents in Bakersfield, California. They were delighted to see him. His mother planned a large family dinner. His brother Richard and his wife arrived for the celebration. The minute I saw Richard I sensed trouble. He was Johnny, but with cruelty.

We had a lot of wine with dinner and everyone was very happy. Johnny's father insisted he show me the gardens. Someone called Johnny's father and I roamed around for a moment among the flower beds. Then I came upon Richard.

"We've been hearing about you," he said. Then he leered, "Don't get much from him, huh?"

At first I thought he meant money, then I realized what he meant.

I tried to be polite and disregard it. My small talk came out: "You people know how to live here."

"I do," he said with hidden meaning. He put one hand on my shoulder and one on my neck. I tried to retreat but his hands were strong. I admit he had a harsh, electric quality.

He pulled my face to him with the grip he had on the back of my neck. He kissed me very hard and roughly. Though I tried not to, I returned the kiss with all the emotions I had dammed up these many months.

"Come with me, baby," he said hoarsely. I slapped him hard because I hated him.

Then he slapped me back and dragged me into the greenhouse. It was part rape—part passion on the floor of the greenhouse. But I won't lie—it was exciting and thrilling. Like animals we were. When it was over I slapped him hard again. A futile gesture. This time he laughed.

The whole thing probably took ten minutes, from the time Johnny's father had been called away. I returned to the house first and Johnny said, "Hope Pop didn't bore you with his Dahlias."

I assured him I liked the flowers very much. The family was still sipping coffee.

In about five minutes Richard came in—no expression on his face. He started talking to his wife and I began to breathe easily. For a horrible couple of minutes I thought he might say something.

Johnny was munching grapes, that boyish grin on his face. I took one look at him and was so ashamed. I wanted to die—or at least get out of there fast.

I used the age-old headache excuse and started getting ready to go. Richard was drinking, not looking up. He was a bitter, sullen man. Then I made the big mistake. I wished everyone goodby and I couldn't ignore Richard. I extended my hand and politely said, "Nice meeting you."

The whole family, all smiling, were wishing goodbys. There was only happiness in the room. Johnny had his arm linked in mine.

Then Richard said it—loud and clear. "Thanks very much for the lay—it was great!" He was looking at me. There was no doubt as to who he was talking to.

To make it worse, his wife either didn't believe what she heard, or couldn't understand, and she said, "What, Richard?"

That's all he needed. "I was being polite. I thanked Miss Payton. We knocked off a piece while you jerks were fooling around in here."

I still thought I could get away with it. Maybe they'd think he was drunk. I tried to pull Johnny along and said, "Good night."

Johnny shook my arm off and stood over Richard. Richard didn't even get up—just smirked as he sipped his drink.

Johnny said something very low through his teeth. I couldn't hear it. But Richard spoke up. "Look, you gotta face it. You couldn't do it so I did it for you. You ought to be thankful."

That's when Johnny went for his throat. He was a strong man and Richard was very drunk. They knocked over the table in their hate and fury. Johnny was on top of Richard and choking him in a frenzy to kill.

The boy's father saved both his sons by clobbering Johnny on the head with a chair. He fell off Richard as if dead. Richard just lay there gasping for breath.

I applied a wet cloth to Johnny's head and slowly he came out of it. There wasn't anger in his eyes as he looked at me—just hurt, terrible hurt. "We'd better go," he told me.

In the car he was silent all the way to Hollywood. I begged his forgiveness. He just stared ahead. I dropped him at his apartment.

Next day I drove over to see how he felt. He had moved, leaving no forwarding address. I never saw him again.

CHAPTER 9

You know what's wrong about getting to the top? You never know what the top is. You think you're going to go higher and higher but there's only disillusionment.

It's the old story—you soon tire of material things and look around for other rewards. I wanted better parts. But I wasn't equipped for them yet. My love life was a mess, seeing both Franchot Tone and Tom Neal. I was torn between what was supposed to be good for me and what I wanted. They never seem to be the same thing.

Some actresses, especially those on top, can handle two or three romances at a time. I never could. When there are two men, no matter how much I care for both, I must choose one.

Take Tom Neal. There were all kinds of rumors about him but the fact is he was a gentle, even though physical man. They talked about our wild sex life. It was no wilder than anyone else's. It's just that he had a circus strongman's physique and I had a great shape, too.

Both Tom and I loved cats and occasionally we'd make-up as cats and play games and eventually they'd end up in lovemaking.

I think Tom loved me for more than my body. We were alike in many respects. He was stubborn like I was and he forgave easily. With Tom nothing was very important except possibly a perfect physique. And both of us lived for pleasure.

Everybody always had Tom marked as an oddball. He really wasn't. He didn't want to get marked—that's true—but otherwise he just liked to sit around and drink beer and make love.

What a contrast to Franchot Tone! Franchot is a lovable, honest, irrascible, masochistic man who loves beauty for beauty's sake. Some core of insecurity makes him insanely jealous. Yet his background, charm, talent and fame should allow him to sit back and allow all the good things of life to come to him.

When I was queen of the May, Tom and Franchot and I were the beloved triangle. When I married Franchot I thought it would be forever. Later, when I divorced

Franchot to live with Tom, I thought that would be forever. But forever is just a weekend—more or less.

Bathing in fame during the halcyon days in Hollywood was delicious. The whole beautiful scene seemed like it was for always. I couldn't begin to tell you some of the world's celebrities I dated during this era. If I did, they or their wives would sue me. But I got around.

I could tell you stories of those wonderful years when the public address system at a premiere announced: "Miss Barbara Payton's car . . . Miss Barbara Payton's car . . ." And there I stood with crowds cheering me, autograph hounds dogging me and the world's most handsome men on my arm.

Why, I remember when four studios wanted me at the same time. Tom and I put their names in a hat and I drew one.

It wasn't all joy. There were heartaches and I tried to be a good human being. Many a time I took food packages to needy families and visited hospitals on my days off.

This was the time when, not only was I making big money, ten thousand a week, but I was Miss this and Miss that and Queen of everything. Make me a Queen, they figured, and people would flash to the event.

Being on top is some kind of miracle. Why, a refrigerator convention would pay five thousand dollars just to have me talk to the boys for a while—in a low-cut dress, of course.

When you go through something like this when everything goes right, when the magic wand taps you, no matter what you do, you know you're leading a charmed life.

This may seem conceited, but I was first to use what now is called "The Method." I felt my power before I even went before the cameras. Jimmy Cagney was the star. I played a girl named Holiday in the movie *Kiss Tomorrow Goodby*.

I just talked and stumbled around and wasn't formal— just had fun. The critics loved it. The word "natural" was used in all the reviews. Sure, I was scared before I went before the cameras, but it all worked out perfectly.

There were stories that I was an idiot with money. I guess I was because I must have gone through a million dollars during my good years. But I had so many friends and there was always someone in trouble. The young starlets were always about to go to the party or the premiere that would change their life. They needed clothes or they couldn't go. And money! It seems the hundred dollar bill was the only medium of exchange. Everyone needed a "C" note. Then when they came to repay me, I didn't have the heart to take the money.

I suppose the wildest spending for a star, though, takes place in the gift department. The boys who work on the pictures—the crew—do such a great job, I always had to give them something—gold watches, traveling bags, suits, cameras.

I guess the wackiest thing I ever did was buy a cameraman a house. He had made me so beautiful in the movie I just had to repay him.

Oh, I know you're going to say, "Why didn't she put the money in the bank?" Because I felt I'd be earning big money all my life—it was so easy to earn it . . .

Maybe I didn't have much sense when it came to money but I sure had a lot of fun. I must confess I could work a man for expensive gifts and did it just for the hell of it. Often I would be given a watch or a ring, then give it to someone who needed it more than I did.

When it came to dresses and furs, I'd often wear them a couple of times and give them away.

You know, getting beautiful gifts from men is a game, or at least it was with me. I could look at a man and know how far I could go. And I also knew how far I'd have to go . . . to get the gifts. It was a delightful chess exercise.

CHAPTER 10

When you start going in the wrong direction you hardly notice it at first. There are a few less autograph hounds outside the theater. The studio boss rushes past you on the lot, but you are sure he didn't see you. The market manager politely reminds you your account is running a little high. You don't get quite the "A" treatment at the beauty parlor. Your agent sends you just a few less scripts. And most important, you look in the mirror and you don't look quite as good. You don't know why but that's the way it is.

Then all of a sudden you find yourself doing a Western with "Jesse James" in the title. I did one. *The Great Jesse James Raid* with Willard Parker. It was no disgrace but it didn't mark a step up. When people at parties ask you what you're doing, you find yourself excusing your role.

And all the while you're getting nervous and bitter and you can't quite understand why. It's a vicious circle with the scene of self-destruction set into being by career problems.

You drink a little bit more. You get on that sorry-for-yourself kick. If you're like me you need more affection and sex because you have to prove there's one area of living you can still score in. You go to pills—push'em up pills, sleeping pills, slow'em down pills, bennies, passion pills and pills of all colors, shapes, sizes and power. After a while you aren't as careful. You take pills for anything in any quantity. It doesn't make much difference. They all seem to work. It's psychological.

Eventually you give up. I have a theory about beauty too. You start losing your looks—the natural process of growing older—and they stop buying. I started putting on weight. I was still a glamour girl, still attractive, but not quite as many men were interested. Or let's say not the same high caliber of men.

Yet as a person I was more mature, more intelligent, and had a better sense of humor. See, I was more valuable, but the advertising wasn't as good.

Many women are aware of this and hate to be loved for their looks alone. They know it's a temporary façade at best.

One time Tom Neal took me to a Photographer's Dress Ball. I had the greatest make-up job—putty nose, cotton in the cheeks, painted on pimples. Well, the men stayed away from me as if I were a witch—which I looked like. Then I went to the john and got back to normal. The wolves flocked to me. I told them to go screw.

Really it's all ridiculous. I had a roommate once named Sybil who had a big pair of boobies. When she went to a party in a tight bra and no cleavage showing, she was given the icy shoulder. Let her show a little of what she had and she was candy at a kiddie party.

Even a name, like I was Barbara Payton, an actress, a star, served as a magnet. When I started slipping, men weren't as attracted to me—but as soon as someone told them who I was, they were fawning all over me. Wouldn't you say we live in a superficial society? And don't tell me this only happens in Hollywood.

I'm not just blaming the men. There are plenty of girls who look up a man's credits and bankbook before they'll date him. If a man has money, they like him. Otherwise, no.

On the way down the real kick in the pants you get is

from the Studios. It would be wonderful if a producer, for instance, had said to me: "Your pictures aren't making any money, you're getting heavy and you're getting hard to handle, so when option time comes up, you're through."

But that kind of honesty you don't get in Hollywood.

It's when you're starting to slip that one night you might say to yourself, "What's a whore?" Because when the big money stops coming in, but you're still living the same way, money becomes something real instead of figures on a business manager's pad. Now money means paying the rent, food, clothes and drink. And that last item is the most important. If not for that, you'd be thinking twenty-four hours a day about paying the first three.

Then there's always the man you genuinely like who feels sorry for you. Somehow he can tell that you need money. And after you've gone to bed with him a few times, you find an envelope on your dressing table with a few hundred dollars in it.

You might be appreciative but indignant and your first instinct will be to give it back. But you realize that your bills are enormous and you must pay them. So you rationalize and tell yourself it's a loan until you get your next big break. But the next big break never comes along and you never pay back the "loan." In fact, you borrow more money—and never pay that back.

Sooner or later you must face it. You never will pay it back. You are taking money for giving a man your body for a night. Yes, but you rationalize—"I'm no different than the thousands of women every year who marry rich men for their money . . ." Yet society considers it differently. You have another escape. You tell yourself a whore sells herself to anybody for up to a hundred dollars. But you will only sleep with men who you would sleep with without money—and the amount of money is much more than a hundred dollars.

But the awakening has to come. With me it happened like this: I had been dating a young actor-singer who was really starting to get into the chips. He had asked me to marry him but he was just a kid. So I wouldn't marry him but he was good company and we went away a few times for weekends.

He was very generous and always gave me a few hundred. He was very diplomatic about the money and would stick it in my purse when I wasn't looking.

It was a delightful romance and I was very fond of him.

Well, one weekend we went to Las Vegas, had a fun time and then flew home. Well, as I always did, I looked around for my envelope. I really did think I had lost it. So I called my young friend and innocently enough said, "You know something terrible has happened. I think I lost the money you gave me."

He must have been in a bad mood because he snapped at me, "You didn't lose any money, baby. I just didn't give you any. I wanted to find out if I was making love to a girl friend or a whore. Well, I guess I found out!"

I was shocked . . . and furious. "Why you little ingrate," I screamed. "I slept with you because I liked you and because I felt like it—and because I felt sorry for you because you're a boy trying to act like a man. I wouldn't sleep with you again for a million bucks!"

His answer was, "I'd hate to try you on a million . . ."

I slammed the phone down. But it gave me cause for thought. Was I a hustler, a whore, a call girl? Of course not! But the question rankled. I took stock of myself. It was almost true. My prime source of income was from men—just a handful—but men who gave me money when I spent the night with them.

The conclusion hit me with such impact—even though I was still getting small parts—that I knew I had to get away from all this. I had to think and to act on it. It led me to my favorite spot on earth—Mexico.

CHAPTER 11

They say when you hate yourself it does no good to change the people or the places. That's not true. Because under the right indoctrination you can learn to love yourself again. I did.

It was time to re-evaluate and I did. A blonde movie actress in Mexico is always cause for celebration. At first I liked the adulation. But then I realized it was empty. I was admired for face, body, reputation, but not for *me*.

I wanted to get back to earth again. I took to hanging around the bay. I love boats. No one was rich—everyone was poor, and happy. Everyone was also always in love. Sex was a robust thing that held no shame. It was expected that every night everybody would make love.

I got tanned, and took off weight swimming. I had offers to star in Mexican movies but turned them down. I was finding myself through a wonderful fisherman who fell in love with me. He didn't have a dime, but he did have a skiff and he had me for better or worse. Because we were married!

My husband fished and I just relaxed on the boat in the hot sun and gentle breezes. I tried to think good thoughts. I washed out all the bad memories—and there were many.

I planned never to go back to Hollywood again. And I honestly believed I'd never return.

I found myself. I knew who I was. It wasn't too bad and I felt I was repairable. Writing poetry seemed to satisfy my creative urge. No one would have recognized me walking the streets of Fusian, the little fishing village, in jeans and a bikini top. I wore old sandals or went barefoot. I never felt better in my life.

There was something about the sea air that dampened the skin and made it come to life. I was full of pep and a new kind of vitality. I felt I could never go back to the life of a glamour girl. In fact, I wondered how it had ever come about . . . and how I had lived that way.

I read American newspapers in complete wonderment. Could it be that I once donned furs to go to a premiere? Had I been mixed up in nightclub brawls? Had I dated the big stars and become engaged to them? I looked at my firm tanned body, unemcumbered by jewelry and fine clothes, and marveled.

I think if I had remained in Mexico the rest of my life I would have been happy. But the career virus is virulent. Like TB you can arrest it but can never cure it. And worse, it becomes more active each time it infects.

I thought of the people I loved in my village. My husband—it was enough for him to fish and make love. He read my poetry and scratched his head. Then he told me how great it was. I knew he didn't understand it but he wouldn't for the world hurt me by saying anything else than it was wonderful. And so it was with these people. They lived only to be happy. And who's to say they weren't right . . .

The more I mulled it, though, the more I knew I needed a second chance. I felt I now knew what mistakes I had made. Success came too fast. I couldn't grasp all its facets. But now I knew. The years in Mexico helped me to understand what life is—something between living just for daily happiness and throwing everything you have toward one goal.

For two years I had been trying to be someone else. It

can't be done. I am Barbara Payton, an actress. Not Barbara Payton, a vegetable.

So I left Mexico. I was awake after a two-year-dream. Destination: Hollywood.

CHAPTER 12

I came down the runway at Los Angeles International Airport, fit and raring to go. It was good to be home.

I hadn't notified anyone of my arrival. Los Angeles is like New York in that no one pays any attention to you unless you call attention to yourself. Most of the time people don't even listen to you. For years it was a gag of mine to say to store clerks, gas station attendants, waitresses or messengers: "F--- you very much . . ." Never was I challenged or even got a smile. People just don't listen or observe. They live in their own little world and don't want to be bothered.

I took a hotel-apartment and read the front page news that I had started divorce proceedings to end the marriage to my Mexican husband.

Most papers used old photos of me taken when I was under studio contract. I looked much better now. I was tanned and thinner and, whether true or not, felt better equipped to take on the world.

When the stories broke about the divorce, lots of my old friends called and one asked me to a cocktail party.

I dressed simply with a high-necked dress, no jewelry and a new hair style. I was no more the sexpot. The new image had dignity and style.

It was a typical Hollywood party held at the Crystal Room of the Beverly Hills Hotel. I got nothing but raves on my looks. The two years in Mexico had paid off. There was just one thing. I had to get a job—a picture job—and fast.

So I moved from circle to circle hoping by conversation to be directed to the right man who could help me. Luckily it was all shop talk and most of the guests were in the picture industry. But time was slipping by and people were starting to leave and I had made no contact.

Then, I met a man who helped me through the next few months in a unique way. He owned a dramatic school. We chatted a little about young kids on their way up and, out of nowhere, he asked if I'd like to teach at his school.

I didn't realize how much I would appreciate such a chance. I showed the kids how to dress, get a job, walk, speak and act. It was fascinating work. I tried to show them how to avoid all the trouble I had.

They seemed to respect me and could name all the pictures I had made, which was more than I could do. They could even quote the reviews.

So I was happy. But I had earned close to a million dollars as an actress and now I was broke. Even my jewels were pawned. I had made it once as an actress and this was where I must make it again.

I called some of my friends. They all would lend me money but that wasn't what I wanted. I wanted respect and adoration again—the very qualities I thought were superficial when I was bouncing around a boat in Mexico.

Strangely enough I got a break because I liked a horse called Breakaway. I liked to see him run, so I conned someone into taking me to Santa Anita. At the bar between races a director asked me what I was doing.

I was frank and told him I was looking.

He was planning to do a picture. He had a script but needed financing. I was used to these stories. Nothing ever happened. But I told him where he could reach me.

A week later he called, said he had arranged financing and would I meet with him. Would I!

He was an old man in his seventies but he had all the enthusiasm and drive.

And I had a part—not the lead—but a part.

It was wonderful to be working again, even though it was a small-budget picture. I felt it was the beginning of a new and brighter career.

Then the roof fell in. In the middle of the picture the director's partner, the moneyman, bowed out of the picture. There was panic. The director couldn't raise another penny. He needed $75,000 to complete the picture. I promised him I would get it for him.

How do you raise $75,000—just like that? I put in calls to oil, steel, stocks and banking friends. I knew so little about business that they just laughed, but one man with an investment in a brokerage company made a lunch date with me.

He put it right on the line: "Sweetie, $75,000 is a lot of money, but I probably could spread it around among friends—especially if we got the negative as collateral. But that's tough and I'm going to have to ask for favors. What's in it for me?"

"Well," I said. "Maybe you'll make money on the deal."

"I'm not interested in money," he said. "What else?"

"What else is there?" I asked—but I knew.

"I've always been attracted to you. You're kind of out of my circle—but I'd like to go away for a week with a star like you. Far away—like Lake Arrowhead. What do you say?"

Never play easy to get. "Let me think it over—I'll call you tomorrow."

Three days later the picture was pumping again with $75,000. A week after that I went away with Mr. Shellout.

Incidentally, the picture was released quietly and never made a dime. But I had one more credit. The public never knows quite how pictures are put together.

CHAPTER 13

When Fate is on your side, you can do nothing wrong. But when she's being coy, nothing is right.

I could do all sorts of things, and do them right, and it might look like they would lead to fame and fortune but . . . down, down I skidded with nothing to hold onto.

So I did a "B" picture. Nothing. I began to have doubts. Should I have left Mexico?

At a bar in Hollywood called The Coach and Horses, I met a prop man who had been on one of my pictures. It was fun talking over old times when I was riding high. We had a few drinks and went to a movie—*Trapped*. I was the star in it.

We ran into a friend of his and the three of us went to a bar. They got into a fight and I found myself with the friend, who was a bit player. He tried to get me to go home with him. I refused and when he got nasty I went to the prop man's house.

The prop man was married but I convinced his wife someone was trying to harm me. They let me sleep on the couch.

During the night the prop man tried to ease his way into bed with me. He lost the silent struggle and I sobered up and went home, where I should have been long before.

I resolved to stop drinking. I noticed I was getting a little puffy. Also, I decided to bury my pride. I called producers I had starred for and told them I'd do walk-ons, bits, anything in their pictures—that I needed work.

Many of them came through, but it was hardly a living.

I was worried. And my pride was pulverized. I began drinking again.

But I was destined to have one big fling before the light dimmed again.

I went with my roommate Iffy, to Santa Monica Beach on a hot Saturday. The beach was obscured by tons of people. After some searching we staked out our four foot square piece of beach by the water. We stripped off our clothes, leaving bikinis to cover the vital places, and lay down on our backs so that the full rays of the sun hit our faces.

I was in that land just between sleep and wakefulness when I felt an annoying sticking in my right side. A grinning young fellow was digging his toenail into my side, trying to get my attention.

"Get lost," I said.

He dug again.

Now I sat up indignantly. "Kid," I said, "I'll give you to three to scram or I'll call the fuzz."

"You're going to be my star so why should I scram?"

He looked to be about twenty-one, handsome, dressed immaculately even though he was at the beach.

I gave him another "get lost" look and lay back again.

"It's like this," he said. "I'm going to make a picture. And you're going to be the star. I knew it the minute I saw you stretched out like that. My uncle's in the real estate business and he gave me the money to make a picture. We'll win an Academy Award." He continued to babble on. "It's a short called *Empty House*. It's the story of a girl who's been dead thirty years, coming back to see the man she was going to marry, and what he's up to. Of course, he can't see her."

"Of course," I said sarcastically.

"I'll pay you a thousand dollars a week," he said. "I figure a four-week schedule. We're really going to take our time with this one. I want to start tomorrow. The only thing holding me up was I couldn't find a star. You're it."

I admit he had my curiosity. Iffy continued to sleep. "Sit down," I said.

"Meet Timothy Ryan, Irish," he grinned.

"Barbara Payton, American."

"Barbara Payton, Barbara Payton—that's a familiar name. Are you an actress?"

That used to burn me up when people didn't recognize my name. My ego, I guess. "Yes . . . an actress."

"Great," he said. "That's my Irish luck! I'm giving you a ten per cent cut of the pictures, too, because I can see it's all going to depend on you."

I had to put him down. "I've been getting fifty thousand dollars a picture. What do you do about that?"

It didn't bother him. "This is art. Maybe you'll be enchanted with the script—I know you will! I wrote it. It'll make them realize what a great actress you are. And we'll have fun doing it."

Iffy, now awake, sat up. She was a bit actress and a dancer. "What have we here?" she asked. "A little boy lost? Let's turn him into the Lost and Found."

"Meet Timothy Ryan, writer, producer, man about town," I introduced.

They shook hands. "And you," he said, "would be perfect for Margaret. Just a day's work but I'll pay you $250 for the day."

"He's crocked," Iffy said to me.

"I don't think you girls understand. I know the word is used loosely but I'm a genius. Everything I do is brilliant. That's why I want you to be in my picture—to make it perfect. What do you say?"

"I just don't feel I'm the caliber actress to fit into such an artistic picture," I kidded.

But he wasn't taking any kidding. "Tell you what," he said. "Why don't you girls have dinner with my uncle and me tonight. We'll have a fine sea food dinner and sign the contracts. You'll be fond of my uncle—and he's stinking rich."

"I don't like sea food," Iffy said.

"Then beef stroganoff. My uncle cooks it. He has a house with forty rooms."

After some conversational exchange we agreed to meet his uncle and left the beach. Timothy made a phone call and we went to his beautiful Brentwood home in our beach clothes.

Soon the conversation got around to the picture. His uncle put it on the line. "I invest here and there in pictures and plays. Timothy is my favorite nephew, but I don't think he's ready to make good pictures."

Timothy started to protest.

"Oh, I'm not going to renege," his uncle went on, "but I think he should do his little short with unknowns."

"No one can be more unknown than me."

His uncle went on, "There's a picture I'm interested in

titled *Bride of the Gorilla,* starring Raymond Burr. I believe I could set you, Barbara, as the co-star. Would you be interested? And your friend I could get a small part, too. What do you say?"

We were both delighted. Timmy was unhappy but his uncle assured him he could find some other girls on the beach.

Next day I got the lead in *Bride of the Gorilla,* and that's how you sometimes get a part in Hollywood—getting sun at Santa Monica Beach.

But that was my last big picture break. I worked several weeks, made some money and had my confidence restored.

My friends felt sure I was started on the way up again. I had many conferences with producers and scripts poured in for me to read.

But I wasn't clicking. I didn't have the brass, the confidence, the luck to get the big ones. The men made passes faster than they used to and more frequently . . . without pretense that it was love.

When jobs are scarce I'll tell you what it does to you. A fat slob asks you to go to dinner with him. You despise him but you know he'll take you to a class restaurant where you might meet someone who will lead to a job. Ordinarily, when things were good, not only wouldn't you have gone out with him, you would have hung up on him.

So you go out for the evening after spending money at the hairdresser's, ward off both his physical and conversational passes, and hope something good happens.

During the evening several big shots come to your table and are pleasant. But it all adds up to the big zero. At the end of the evening, as you hold your breath while this ape kisses you good night, you realize it was a wasted evening.

Repeat evenings like this and you get pretty discouraged. I've heard people say, "Well, she can't get acting jobs but there are other kinds of jobs—secretary, receptionist, typist, waitress . . ." Sounds simple. But when you're an actress you're an actress. It's a disease. You just rebel against doing anything else.

I don't just mean me. I mean thousands of actors and actresses in the same spot. Sure, we're wrong. So is a dope addict or a drunk, but it's hard to do anything about it.

I had been married three times. It was a way out. But it was no answer for me. Maybe if a great guy came along I'd do it again. . . .

That's how life is. You keep changing goals and its gets

complicated. In the back of my mind was: get an acting job or even get a nice, considerate man with a good job. That's how my values had changed.

Now I saw qualities in a man because I wanted to see them, and often they weren't even there. I was put off my guard and put out when I shouldn't have.

Take Donald, for example. I met him at one of those cocktail parties for an author whose book was being made into a picture. Donald was a lawyer who had written several textbooks dealing with law. Don't ask me how I got involved with him. We were unlikely companions. He was very deliberate and cautious. I was just the opposite. He wasn't particularly good-looking but he was a gentleman. Put quotes around that word if you wish.

When we met, he knew who I was and that helped.

That first night he took me home and we just sat around while he told me how he got through law school. No pass. No compliments. No complicated relationship. He just talked and I just listened. It was different.

Then Donald called me and asked me to go to a concert. We had a nice evening ending with ice cream sundaes at Browns on Hollywood Boulevard. I had never been there before. We took a long walk later, and that I had never done before, either. I felt a nice compatibility with him. He was easy to be with. I began getting ideas. How would it be married to a lawyer—to him. I liked the dream . . . me reading all about his brilliant defense of accused murderers. Even though he now was a corporation lawyer.

When he kissed me good night, it was with lips barely touching.

This was all new to me—and I liked it. I looked forward to Donald's calls and less to the calls of my agent.

Knowing men, I was sure the Big Pass would be made anytime. And frankly, I couldn't wait!

Donald was very thoughtful with little gifts, and proud that he was going with a real, live movie star. I never told him I wasn't getting the roles I used to. But he got his kicks from people asking me for my autograph. And when he saw my name, or sometimes our names, in the columns, he'd clip them out and save them.

Still the pass didn't come. Hello and goodby kisses were the order of the day and that's it. He once explained I was no ordinary girl and he wanted me to respect him and his work. I could have done with a little less morals and some warm loving.

Actually, our evenings were uneventful. We'd go for walks, or the movies or just sit around talking. I was a zombie waiting for just one thing—a proposal of marriage. Oh, I used tricks, but none worked.

Well, something had to happen and it did. About six weeks after we started going together, we came home from a long walk and I made tea for us. He liked some almond cookies and I always had them at hand.

We were sipping tea when he began by clearing his throat. I thought, before he started to speak, that this was the proposal.

"Barbara," he said, "there's something I've wanted to talk to you about. I've wanted to bring it up sooner but I was never as sure as I am now."

Finally!

He got up and paced, then stopped and faced me. "Do you believe in me? In my future?" he asked.

"I certainly do!"

"You know," he went on, "we're from two different worlds. In your world money flows easily and is rather unimportant. In my world money comes hard and sometimes a man has to use every weapon at hand to make good."

"It's unimportant—money," I said, "as long as people love and respect each other."

"A man's got to put up a front," Donald said. "A professional man has to have a front."

I was getting uneasy. It was a strange way of proposing, and without any physical contact. "I don't understand," I said.

Donald paced again. "I could buy all new furniture, a law library and new offices and hire a couple of good assistants and a receptionist for fifteen thousand dollars. That's all I need. And I'd pay you back in three years."

I couldn't believe my ears. He was asking me for fifteen thousand dollars as a loan! But did he mean it would be a kind of dowry—me with the $15,000?

I was through with subtlety. "Tell me, Donald. You want fifteen thousand dollars. Do you want me, too? Do you want to marry me?"

"Well," he said, "if you lend me the fifteen thousand dollars, in three years perhaps we could marry."

Three years! I felt disillusioned, humiliated. I started to laugh. I was almost hysterical. Me, a con girl in specialized areas of living, being used! All because I was an idiot with my guard down.

He still didn't understand my reaction. "Maybe I could get along with $12,500. But not a cent less. And I'm honest. You'll get your money back."

Just $12,500. I had only recently borrowed $150 to live. It was crazy. How could I get him out of there—immediately?

"Well, what do you think? I would never forget you if I could get a $15,000 loan."

I decided to handle it with dignity. My God, had he been seeing me for six weeks just to borrow money? "At the moment, Donald, I couldn't swing a $15,000 loan. My business manager has all my money tied up in real estate. I'm terribly sorry. I would if I could."

He was stunned. I guess he was sure I would give him the money. "Could you work out something like $5,000 now and more as we go? I really need it. You won't be sorry."

My head was spinning. I hated him. I hated his whining. I hated myself for being a fool. "Please, Donald," I said. "I have an awful headache. I'd like to go to bed. Will you excuse me?"

But no. He had to wring it dry. He still had a little hope left. "Do you think when you get your next picture we could work it out?"

Then the dam broke. I gulped one Scotch at the bar and said, "You are a f------ idiot! I am a movie star with not a pot to p--- in! I owe everybody money. I was depending on you to bail me out. I thought we might marry. You earn the daily bread and I take care of the house like other couples do. It sounds so simple. But you are despicable— romancing me for a few bucks. Why, even if I did have the money, I wouldn't give it to you! I pray that I never look at your hypocritical face again. Do you hear? Get the hell out of here and stay out!"

I slammed the door and laughed and cried. And mostly I vowed never again to get out of my element. I'd rather be conned by the con men I was accustomed to.

I did marry again—later—a short marriage that I don't even want to talk about. He was husband number four, age thirty-one and his name was George Provas. It didn't last long. There are good things and bad things I want to forget. That's my privilege. So I prefer not to dig up certain things.

Talking about things I don't want to talk about, I was given a hundred-dollar fine and a year's probation for passing a phony check in a market. You may ask how a girl who made the money I did can reach the depth where she has to write a phony check.

It's easy. When the money is pouring in, you just can't believe it won't always pour in. I'd venture to say—and this is no alibi—I loaned friends and relatives enough money that, if I had it now, it would guarantee me a life of ease. But I don't regret it. That was my pleasure, loaning money, so I did it.

In the market where I passed the bad check I had spent thousands of dollars—a lot foolishly—over the years. And do you know why I wrote the bad check? To get liquor, not food. Not that I'm a drunk. I'm not. I do drink a lot of wine, but when I don't want to drink I can go days without it. But there is something festive about having liquor around and inviting people to have a drink.

I've always acted on impulse and I just had to cheer myself up. So I wrote a bad check—just one—to be happy again even if it were just for a day. I know you won't, or can't, understand this, but believe me if I didn't give in to my little whims, I'd die. That's the kind of cat I am.

After the market catastrophe came the realization, finally, that I didn't have any money and that it wasn't going to be easy to get some. Also, that I wasn't a movie star anymore . . . In fact, I was nothing—a has-been, a nobody.

I found a cheap place to live, but while that sounds sensible, it wasn't. I couldn't raise one hundred dollars a month rent any easier than I could raise four hundred . . . and at least the latter gave me the mysterious "front" that often ends with a job.

I got a job helping in a beauty parlor but I was so impractical that I'd forget to pick up my salary or I'd lend most of it to others. Fifty dollars sounded so unimportant that I couldn't worry about it. I was lost . . . lost in a practical world . . .

CHAPTER 14

My rent was overdue a week and I only had one dollar in my pocket. I had had two warnings from my landlady. In my refrigerator there was some American cheese and soda water. Also a can of peaches that would see me through a day or two.

I took the dollar, my last, and went to see one of my old pictures, *Kiss Tomorrow Goodby* with James Cagney. I enjoyed it very much but it was ironic that I had been paid so many thousands to do it and I only had a dollar left to see it.

All during the picture I kept my mind off my troubles— I couldn't solve them anyway. Then I walked home.

I hadn't eaten all day so I opened the can of peaches. They were delicious and they filled me. Then I looked through all my things to see what I could pawn. There wasn't anything. I was down to bedrock.

But I still had a telephone. I went through my address book. I had borrowed from everybody. Some, more than once. There were still men who would take me out to dinner. But how do you live with no money at all?

I didn't answer the knock on my door because I knew it was the landlady.

I looked in the mirror. To me I looked the same as ever —just as I had in the movie. What had happened? I undressed and looked at myself in the nude—not much change. I could lose five pounds but not more. I put on a dressing gown.

There was a knock on the door. I opened it this time. It was the landlord, a tall, kindly man browbeaten by his wife. "I'm sorry," he said, "but my wife says your rent is overdue."

"Come in," I said, with what charm I could muster.

He stood looking uncomfortable. "Wasn't it a lovely day?" he said finally.

I nodded. I knew landlords had heard every excuse in the book but decided to try one anyway. "Mr. Gordon," I explained. "My husband's alimony check, which is usually here long before this, should definitely be here tomorrow. I will slip the hundred-dollar check under your door before noon."

He looked miserable. "My wife said—I have nothing to do with it—that I should either get the rent money or ask you to move out . . . tonight."

"Don't look so sad," I said. "If that's what she wants, that's what it will have to be. I really don't have any money."

We both just stood there. "Could I . . . lend you five dollars for food?" he said.

I just shook my head no. Then I suddenly burst into tears, great gulping sobs. It seemed as if the whole world was collapsing on me.

Mr. Gordon patted me on the shoulder and tried to give me a handful of crumpled bills. I wouldn't take them, but I put my head on his chest and continued to sob.

"Please," he said, "don't cry. I've collected other rents and I have some money. My wife won't know—if you can pay in a week it will be all right."

A week. It sounded glorious, but what then?

I tried to stop crying. "Don't worry about me. I'll be all right—honest I will."

He patted my head. Then he kissed my forehead gently. "I'd help you if I could. My wife . . ."

I nodded understandingly and went to brush my hair back with my hand. It hit his hand by accident and some of the money fell to the floor. I bent to pick it up for him, and when I handed it to him I noticed he was staring. I looked down and my dressing gown was open, showing almost everything I had.

"I'm sorry," I said.

He swallowed hard. "You . . ." I don't know what he wanted to say, but he moved to me as if a trance and his hand traveled from my neck down past my breasts. I didn't try to stop him.

He kissed me gently again, this time on the lips. "The hundred dollars," he said, "is in my wall safe. I'll pay your rent. It's my fishing vacation money. I need you—to prove I'm a man. To prove to me . . . I mean."

I would have gone to bed with him for nothing. I had a great compassion for him. I locked the door and dropped my dressing gown.

My rent was paid for one more month.

After that I found out from other girls in similar spots that they could exist without working. They had dinners with boy friends, and clothes could always be obtained with the right hint. Lots of girls got cab money to go home, then took a bus instead or overcharged their boy friends.

The one problem was the rent. That's why, in choosing an apartment, a girl will always study the landlord. That judgment might give them the rent.

My conscience didn't bother me—this time. I liked Mr. Gordon.

When my rent came due again I was in no better spot than a month before. In fact, I was in a worse spot. Mrs.

Gordon came this time and asked for her money. In fact, she was raising my rent to $125 dollars a month. She just didn't want me living there. She said she'd give me twenty-four hours to come through with the money—or else.

I was sunk unless Mr. Gordon came up. I wondered if she suspected anything.

Next morning as I was leaving the house, Mr. Gordon was coming in with some packages. He said, "Good morning, Miss Payton." I smiled. "I guess," he said softly, "you heard your rent was raised."

I told him I knew. "Don't worry," he said.

That evening Mr. Gordon came in, nervous and embarrassed. "Would you rather owe me the money?" he said.

I smiled and admitted I didn't have a bean. "Can we do business some other way?"

"You don't think I'm forcing myself on you?"

I assured him I liked him very much, then asked curiously, "What if your wife should come up?"

"She went to the movies," he answered. "We—er I—have a couple of hours . . ."

"Then let's make the best use of them," I smiled.

When we were in bed he said, "Don't worry how much she raises your rent. Stay. It's her money and she's getting it back. It's a bookkeeping trick. I hate her."

So the rent was paid again.

Things were not getting better. I got a part-time job in a modeling studio and made no effort to include the rent in my budget. As for my other expenses, I just juggled, hoping for the best.

And so rent time came around again. In between firsts of the month, I never saw Mr. Gordon. On rent days there was a note in my mail box saying my rent was being raised to $150. Just on intuition Mrs. Gordon hated me and wanted me out. But it was easier not to pay $150 here than to pay $75 somewhere else.

This time things worked out differently. Mr. Gordon sneaked up in the middle of the night—I was sleeping—and handed me $150. He told me to pay Mrs. Gordon and whispered he'd see me some evening soon. I paid her the next morning and she eyed me suspiciously. I merely smiled.

A few nights later Mr. Gordon came up and said he thought I should move because Mrs. Gordon was suspicious. He had no idea why. When I tried to lead him by the hand into the bedroom, he backed away frightened. So I gave Mrs. Gordon notice, which seemed to cheer her.

Two weeks later, late one evening, Mr. Gordon came up. His wife had gone to her mother's overnight. Her mother was ill. He wanted to talk to me. No, he didn't want to make love to me because it made him feel guilty and nervous, but he insisted I take $350 which he had saved.

"You gave me the only real pleasure I've had in twenty years and I want to show my gratitude," he told me. "I probably will never have such enjoyment again. I want you to take the money. It will make me feel better. I would appreciate it."

I did take the money. But I also got him into bed, clouded his conscience with love and made him feel good. When he left he looked for a long time into my eyes and then turned and walked out.

That was it. Goodby, Mr. Gordon. You were a sweet, kind man—crushed by captivity.

CHAPTER 15

Hustling is a creeping thing, a disease that comes from nowhere and you don't know you have it until you study it carefully. And even then you can rationalize it. The "look," though, gets stamped in your face and eyes—it must, or how would men know you have a price?

For instance, a producer I had an affair with three years before called and asked me to dinner. I went, and point blank at dinner asked him to give me a part in his next picture.

"Tell you what, Barbara," he said. "I could give you a small part. Maybe you'd make $250 or $300. Then I'd ask you to have an affair with me. And knowing you, you probably would. But the movie business is different today. The plush times have gone. Bookkeepers are breathing down my neck every minute. If I put you in my picture, there'll be someone who'll know we used to date. There will be questions and innuendos. I'll be under suspicion."

He took my hand in his. "I hope you're not insulted, Barbara, but I'd rather give you $300 from my own pocket. I'm no hypocrite. Sure, I'm not giving it to you for nothing. I dig your body. Stay with me tonight. Then the transaction is between you and me and it's only our business. What do you say?"

"That's kind of cold," I told him.

"I suppose it is. But I'm being honest. We're having dinner. It's a date. I'll buy you flowers and wine. I care for you in a way. You know that."

I nodded. I didn't know if he did. But I wanted to believe it.

We went to his place after. I drank until I was stoned. Next day I found three hundred dollars in my purse.

That kind of thing became the rule rather than the exception. I kept telling myself it was just a temporary thing. Yet I'd wake up sometimes in the middle of the night and call myself all the names I deserved. I was a high-line broad—a high-priced hooker. I was—and I knew it.

One night my producer friend called to ask me to dinner. I accepted, knowing I needed the money. We went to the best places and then back to his house. After some talk and a few drinks, he led me into the bedroom. Soft music played and I was determined to please him because he was a font of ready money.

For several hours we made love until he was exhausted. What am I talking about—I was too! He put some money into my purse and asked if I wouldn't mind taking a taxi home.

When I got home I took the money out of my purse—it was only a hundred dollars, not the usual three hundred. I was furious and called him. He didn't answer the phone. I decided to have it out with him the next time we went out. A few days later, I put it to him right at the table at Chasen's.

"You owe me two hundred," I said.

"Oh?" he smiled.

"Don't be charming, please. Anything but that. When we made love in the past you gave me three hundred dollars. But last time you only gave me a hundred. So you owe me two hundred dollars, right?"

"Wrong. I don't want to hurt you, Barbara, but you've lost a little since I gave you three hundred dollars. To me, mind you to me, you are worth about a hundred dollars, which is considerable. However, I didn't know it was so cut and dried. I thought we were friends and we went to bed for kicks. The money changed hands because you needed it. But Barbara, if you're saying you're a hustler and your price is three hundred dollars I've got to pass. You've priced yourself out of my range."

It was humiliating for me. I had refused to look at

myself as I was. Now I was being forced into it. I was a whore. I excused myself and went to the powder room, where I cried in solitary. My attitude, I decided, should be —all right, I'm a whore and by God the men are going to pay dearly for me! I'd show them.

I went back to the table and my friend asked me if I was okay. I said I was and my price was three hundred dollars.

He smiled and said he'd just take me home. I kissed him several times in the car and teased him but he was adamant. Home I went. I was mad now and determined. Now I knew what I was and wanted to cash in on it. I called a director friend of mine who was mad for my big bosom, and I said to him, "I'm lonely. Would you come over? I'll leave the light on in the hallway. I won't get up. Just come on to bed with me."

"I'd be delighted. I'll be right over."

I'd show him.

He slipped into bed with me—and he stayed all night. In the morning he almost left with just a kiss.

"Didn't you forget something?" I asked. "Like two hundred dollars."

He seemed surprised. "I thought it was for free because you were lonely. But . . ." He dug into his wallet and tossed some bills on the breakfast table. "But darling, next time you're lonely call a millionaire."

I had almost charged him three hundred dollars, but at the last minute lost my nerve. Well, the two hundred dollars would buy a lot of groceries.

It's funny how supply and demand, sex appeal and talent regulate a girl's price. I found out soon enough that my price was a hundred dollars and not a cent more. At a hundred I found enough friends to keep me living well. At times I still fancied myself just a kind of date and not a hustler, because I wouldn't make love to a man unless I liked him and knew him. Also, I wouldn't go for any wild perversions. I was like any girl having a little fun.

I could maintain that illusion as long as I could keep high above the unhappiness level with wine. If the wine content dropped I'd know I was a whore, and I was ashamed and unhappy.

It was seldom now that people made a fuss about me because I was Barbara Payton, the movie star. It wasn't even so much that I had changed in appearance, but the name was beginning to fade.

One night a friend sent over his friend, a kid of twenty-one. He was so awed by me I went to bed with him and then wouldn't take his money. That's how lousy a hooker I was.

CHAPTER 16

It was Christmas Eve, I was drinking more than usual and was full of the sad sentimentality of the season. I was broke and needed a trick or two. I made some teasing phone calls and finally hooked an actor friend, but he only had fifty dollars. I told him to come over anyway. I laughed and said I'd give him half a —. It was a mistake. When you bend a price for one it spreads like a fire and you never can get it up there again.

It made me a fifty-dollar hooker, and I realized I was on the skids fast.

Disaster was hot on my tail. I was panicky. I better get a typing job or something because the handwriting was on the wall. Receptionist, that's what I'd do. No more hustling or I'd end up in the gutter doing it for a bottle of wine. I had heard about those endings.

Next day I was scared enough to make the rounds of the employment agencies. But I knew nothing. Worse, I looked battered. I could tell I was on the trail to nowhere. I better get to the beach for a few days before I tried for a square job.

I checked in at a motel at the beach and lay in the sun, swam, ate and drank vegetable juices and food. I was scared and knew what I had to do.

I had everything beaten but the nights. I couldn't sleep. I didn't want to think. I needed my sleep. Panicsville again. I walked the beach. I met a kid I liked and we sat around a bonfire and talked.

We necked a bit and he tried to take my bikini off but I wrestled with him. I didn't want a lover—I wanted a friend.

Then he said, unkindly, "Are you a pay broad?"

I didn't realize it stuck out on me. I threw some sand in his eyes and ran away. I couldn't stand it, and drank a bottle of wine. I knew I would undo all I had done to help myself but I had no discipline anymore.

I decided to drive back home. So I was a fifty-dollar whore. What the hell, at least I admitted it. I decided I'd better get married again. What I didn't know is that it takes two to make a marriage and apparently I didn't look like a marrying-type girl.

I'd bring up the subject of marriage among my tricks, but it was bad business, and I found myself losing customers.

Life began to drag in a dream. Wine and bare bodies and nightmare sleep and money that was never enough to pay the bills. It seemed that everything was deadened. There were no joys, no sorrows, no thrills, no nothing.

I couldn't snap myself out of it. Then one day I suddenly became aware again. I don't know why or how but I noticed it was fall, my windows were dirty, my clothes had been stolen and a John had just paid me twenty dollars. Twenty dollars! How did that happen? My price was three hundred dollars. I almost called him back and demanded the rest of my money.

But no, I remembered. My price had fallen. What happened when it hit bottom? What would happen to me? I locked myself in for a day and wouldn't let anyone into my apartment. I wrote some poetry, called a writer friend and read it to him. He said it was good and he thought he could sell it. Three months later I got a seven-dollar check. He had sold it to some beatnik journal for me.

But writing poetry gave me a lift. At least I was above the ordinary whore. I was different, more cultured. But I was broke. I couldn't even buy wine. Money just disappeared.

I decided it was all right to be a hustler as long as I wrote poetry—even in bed with a trick I could think of lines.

Now I realized, as I sobered up some, that not only was I being paid twenty dollars by some tricks and ten dollars by others, but some weren't even paying me. It was hilarious, but I couldn't laugh. They just slept with me and left. My bookkeeping, clouded by wine, wasn't very reliable.

One night I realized I was in bed with a Negro. He was gentle and kind to me. "You aren't capable," he said, "of running this kind of operation. You need a protector, a pimp. Someone who watches out for you, pays your rent, collects money for you." He gave me five dollars. Five dollars! Then he gave me a name he suggested I call.

A week later with no wine or food in the apartment and no money either, and after I called all the names in my book and none showed, I called that name, Ray.

He came over that evening. "Girlie," he said, "you're in

the hell category. Might even be too late to pull you out.
You got too much weight and the alcohol is sticking to you.
But I like blondes. If you want to try, I'll see if I can help
you."

"Sure," I said and went back to sleep. He brought me
food and put me in his apartment and I started to take on
a few Johns a day and he saw to it I wasn't cheated. I
never saw any money but he kept me eating and drinking.
I was grateful for that. When I had time I would write
poetry and my pimp, that's what he was, liked it. He was
proud of my writing.

I had crying spells though and once a John knifed me
because I wouldn't do what he wanted. Thirty-eight stitches
from my fleshy belly down.

Sometimes everything became water-clear. I thought of
the days I walked into the Presidential box at the opera
with my mink dragging and on the arm of handsome
Franchot Tone. And how everybody looked at me with
admiration. I thought how at a premiere of my own movie,
during which I was paid $100,000, the press fought to talk
to me. I was really something.

How, or why, had I fallen? What had happened? Yet,
somehow, I wasn't ashamed. It was in the cards. I played
them as best I could.

And then one day recently I went into the hall to take a
phone call. It was Frank Sinatra's office. They asked me if
I'd like to do a walk-on in his new movie *Four for Texas*.

I couldn't believe it! I didn't even question how, or why,
they had found me. I shouted, "Yes!"

I went to the beauty salon for the first time in a year.
I even got a manicure.

I was on a set again and everyone was so nice to me.
Life was good. I asked myself over and over, "Can I make
a comeback? I'm only thirty-five years old. It's not impossible—is it?"

An old friend of mine said to me, "Barbara! Where have
you been?"

"I've been living," I said.

Don't judge me harshly just for living.

TRAGIC DEATH OF ALAN LADD

● *TEDD THOMEY*

He was doomed. As mercilessly as if a loaded pistol were aimed at his temple or a shiv at his throat.

His luck had run out. Even though he was Alan Ladd, a multimillionaire film star with vast holdings in real estate and oil, he was powerless to stop the unseen forces which were about to take his life.

Countless times on the screen, slim, blond Alan Ladd had played the role of a tight-lipped man of action marked for death. Countless times a neat twist ending had spared his life at the last moment. But this was different. This time death was enormously real, a part of him, walking wherever he walked those final two days in his $150,000 mansion in Palm Springs, California.

Death breathed the very desert air he breathed, lurked in the pills he swallowed, concealed itself in the liquor he drank.

Worst of all, there was nothing Alan Ladd could do to prevent what was happening to him. Because he didn't know it was happening. Because, like any man caught in the same trap, he was ignorant of the deadly chemical attack which was taking place within his nerve centers and in the deeper recesses of his brain.

All he knew was that he felt more restless and high-strung than he had ever been in his life. He had come to the desert a few days before for solitude, relaxation and escape from the tension of Hollywood, where he had spent exhausting months doing the role of hard-eyed, rock-fisted Nevada Smith in *The Carpetbaggers*. Always before when he had come wearily to the desert, its clean, warm air had worked miracles on his nerves, easing the tensions of emotion-charged days before the cameras. But this time release failed to come.

On the night of January 28, 1964, Ladd paced through his palatial home like a neurotic puma restrained in a palatial cage. He chain-smoked. He drank whiskey after whiskey. In desperate need of something to do, he emptied ashtrays and wastebaskets throughout the house. Then he walked out to the glistening blue water of his lighted pool. Deciding not to take a dip, he swept the concrete poolside area with a broom, although it was perfectly tidy, and then he went back indoors and turned on the TV. But he couldn't concentrate and snapped the set off angrily.

The phone rang. Ladd's butler, the only other person in the house, answered it. "It's for you, Mr. Ladd," he said respectfully. "Your wife."

Sue Carol Ladd, four years older than her fifty-year-old actor-husband, was calling from their main family residence in Beverly Hills. A former actress who had given up her career to devote herself to managing Ladd's business affairs, she was still attractive at an age when most women begin to dry up and wrinkle around the edges.

"Alan?" she asked. "How are you tonight?"

"OK, I guess."

"Do you still feel all tied up inside?"

"Yeah," he said, "And this time I can't seem to shake it. I feel like a clock wound so tight it's going to blow up."

Sue Carol sighed, then spoke softly. "Alan, you know you shouldn't worry so much. And how many times do I have to tell you that everybody says you're sensational in *The Carpetbaggers*? If you would only—"

"Let's not go through that again," he said grimly. "All I know is what I feel. And in my bones I know I stank. Maybe one scene was OK, the fight scene. But in the rest of it Alan Ladd stank like Alan Ladd never stank before. So let's just not talk about it, OK, honey?"

"Certainly, Alan. And try to get some rest tonight. I'll call again in the morning."

When she hung up the phone, Mrs. Ladd was unaware that she had just had her final conversation with the man to whom she had been married for twenty-two years.

Ladd went into the master bedroom and stripped off his clothes. He swallowed several more of the sleeping pills and tranquilizers he had been taking steadily since his arrival in Palm Springs eight days previously. He put on his pajamas, drank another glass of whiskey and lay down on his king-sized bed.

But once again sleep would not come. His head ached

and throbbed. Nervously he crossed and uncrossed his tense legs. He put his hands behind his neck. He smoked one cigarette and then another. With each puff he had a strange sensation of heat. He felt as if the skin of his body were as hot as the burning cigarette tip. Even worse, his nerves felt as if they were in a giant centrifuge, spinning faster and faster, winding up tighter and tighter.

He sprang suddenly out of bed and put his hand over the air conditioning register. Cool air struck his palm, proof that the unit was working. But he still felt as if he were burning up. He put more ice cubes in a glass, poured in more whiskey, drank it and lay down again.

Now his brain seemed to be spinning, filled with mixed thoughts tumbling against one another. Thoughts of his family. Thoughts of Hollywood and his sagging career. Thoughts of Alan Ladd, the washed-up actor. Alan Ladd, who'd made it big for over twenty years even though he was just a runt, five feet, six inches tall.

Only five feet, six inches tall. He groaned quietly to himself. Because down through the years that had been the hardest thing of all to bear. His lousy freak height. His lousy short legs that made it necessary for him to be "planked" for all his scenes with actors and actresses of average height. Planked. A phony way to build up height and a career. Wherever he walked on the sets at Paramount or Warner Brothers, there were special boards which raised him high enough so he could look his screen foes level in the eye, or bend down to kiss his leading ladies on their luscious rouged lips.

He knew by heart all the wisecracks that were made behind his back by some of his taller and less successful colleagues: *"Yeah, I'm working on the latest Alan Ladd Western. You know who he is, don't you? Mickey Rooney on a horse!"* (Big laugh.) Or: *"Hey, did you hear how Alan Ladd nearly broke his neck over at Paramount today? Naw, he didn't fall off his horse. He fell off his plank!"* (Bigger laugh.)

A film set can be a cruel place where professional jealousies cut and undercut one another in the continual battle for better billing and more flattering camera angles. As a result a lot of those cracks were deliberately made within earshot of Ladd by actors who resented the star privileges he received.

Although he was extremely sensitive about his height, Ladd shrugged off their remarks, refusing to be drawn into the petty sniping which occurs on most sets. He never criticized other actors or actresses for their shortcomings, no matter how many times they loused up his scenes by blowing their lines.

He knew they were aware that he had one magnificent physical achievement working for him whenever he stepped before the cameras. This was the fact that Alan Ladd was 6 feet 4 from the waist up. Whenever he was seated with a group of men, he towered over them, even over those who were 6 feet one or 6 feet 2. He had a large chest, excellent shoulders, long muscular arms and oversized hands formed during the early years of his life when he did hard manual labor as a carpenter.

Those attributes gave him masculine strength in film closeups. But they were of little help off the screen. Because he refused to wear lifts in his shoes like other small actors, he was a constant disappointment to his fans whenever they met him in public. Expecting him to be a six-footer like the heroes he portrayed on the screen, they could not conceal their surprise when they found him to be short in real life.

As a result of this, Ladd developed a dislike for meeting the public early in his career and kept away from night clubs and parties where he might encounter skeptical strangers who would look down their noses at him. Later in his career, his dislike of the public changed into fear and hatred, and he often lived in seclusion, seeing only close friends and members of his family.

Those were a few of the thoughts which chased like phantoms through Alan Ladd's tortured brain during that long night when nothing he tried would induce sleep, or alleviate the searing pain in his head. He took more sleeping pills, but he knew they wouldn't help because he'd taken so many in recent weeks that he'd become immune to them. Whiskey seemed to be a better sedative, so he poured himself another glass and sipped it, hoping that soon he would begin to feel it ease away the tenseness of his breathing and the taut discomfort in his legs and arms.

Again his thoughts began to tumble in a montage effect, with old memories and new mixing like images on a badly edited film. He was certain his role in *The Carpetbaggers* meant the end of his career, because he felt he'd been so lousy in it. He hadn't wanted the part and had fought bitterly with producer Marty Rackin, his long time friend, arguing that the role was wrong for him.

It was the first time in over two decades that Alan Ladd had accepted second billing in a film. It was a lousy comedown for a man who had starred in scores of major films, every one of which had made a potful of money, despite the criticisms of reviewers who called his acting flat, unemotional and uninspired. He knew what such a comedown meant—that he was finally face to face with the age spectre which every leading man dreaded. It meant he was too old to play the clear-eyed, slim-jawed hero any more—too old for anything but secondary character parts.

He lay back against his pillow, rubbing his temples in an effort to make the pain stop. He cursed the pain and cursed the career which had brought him to this state of agony, trembling and wretchedness. Because he knew in his heart that he had never wanted the damn career. He'd never wanted to be a star. All he'd ever sought was peace of mind. He'd gone into film work only because it paid better than carpentry. All he'd wanted was to make enough money to buy a ranch, settle down and enjoy life the way his parents had once hoped to do. No matter how hard they worked, they hadn't found security. It had also been denied to him, but in a different way.

Now the pain was diminishing and he could feel a blessed drowsiness coming over him. It was a heavy, peculiar feeling, but he welcomed it the way an exhausted and defeated boxer welcomes the blow that lets him finally find peace on the canvas. He began to doze. Fitfully at first, his mind still churning, mingling images of the poverty of his childhood with equally stark images of the catastrophes he'd encountered after becoming one of Hollywood's wealthiest citizens . . .

Alan Walbridge Ladd was born on September 3, 1913, in Hot Springs, Arkansas, and the bad luck which always hovered near him struck its first blow when he was four years old. His father, a public accountant, died. This was the grieving boy's first bitter taste of insecurity, because he'd been deprived of his father before he scarcely knew him. His mother took the boy to Denver where she met and married James Beavers, an itinerant house painter.

The marriage was the beginning of years of grinding poverty for young Alan and his mother. Beavers was a willing worker but jobs were scarce during the depression years of 1921 and 1922. Packing their few household articles into an old Model T Ford, the family decided to move further west, taking four months to reach California. En route, Beavers painted houses to keep them in food, and Alan's mother took jobs washing and cooking.

When their final dollars expired, Beavers was forced to sell his precious paintbrushes to buy the last few gallons of gasoline they needed. When they arrived in Pasadena, the Model T was a gasping, worn-out derelict, running noisily on four metal rims because its thin tires had blown out one by one crossing the mountains and Mojave Desert. A battered kerosene lantern hung on the radiator in place of the headlights which Beavers had traded for three quarts of badly needed crankcase oil.

Like the characters in John Steinbeck's *Grapes of Wrath*, Alan, his mother and stepfather set up housekeeping in a rickety tent and shack town on the outskirts of Pasadena. They existed on the cheapest foods they could find, eating mostly potato soup and tough greasy mutton. Ladd became so sick of the taste of mutton that in later years all his cooks had strict orders never to serve it, or even cook it where he might notice its odor.

Alan's stepfather finally found a steady job painting backdrops for Hollywood movie studios. "It was the opportunity my stepdad had been looking for all his life," Ladd once recalled. "He had the brains to be a studio executive but he had no confidence in himself. He was even scared to be the foreman of a paint crew."

When Alan was ten, the family moved to a cottage in North Hollywood. During his first day at his new elementary school, Ladd—an undersized brat with an oversized temper—got into trouble which dogged him for months. When he bent down for a drink, a bigger kid shoved his head deep into the fountain. Ladd stood up, water dripping from his yellow hair, and discovered he was surrounded by jeering boys. He tore into the kid who had ducked him, a bully a head taller, and managed to whale the stuffing out of him.

As he turned away from his fallen tormentor, a shout went up from the throng. Ladd mistakenly thought he was being cheered for his victory. Instead he had the shock of discovering he was under attack by an exact duplicate of the boy he had just clobbered. The bullies were twin brothers and the second one seemed twice as big and tough.

Ladd suffered a bruising defeat, including a slashed left nostril, a blackened eye and a walnut-sized lump on his head where twin No. 2 thumped it upon the concrete base of the drinking fountain. But far worse than his physical beating was the emotional defeat he suffered. As he staggered away, mopping his bloody nose on his arm, someone in the crowd hollered scornfully:

"Better luck next time, Tiny!"

The loathed nickname stuck. From that moment on he was Tiny Ladd, runtiest of the runts in his class. In the weeks which followed he battled every kid who called him Tiny, whipping most of them because his fists were fueled on anger and outrage. Repeatedly he was dragged to the principal's office, ordered to explain his poor grades and warned that he would be expelled if he continued fighting.

Surrendering to the pressures, he kept his fists in his pockets whenever he heard his nickname. But his grades did not improve, wavering near the bottom, until he found out about sports.

In grade school and junior high, Ladd went out for track, and although he was too small to be a record breaker, his successes were sufficient to restore his self-confidence. His grades climbed to a B average. When he entered North Hollywood High, he was still shorter than average in height but his chest was filling out. He became one of the school's star athletes, playing varsity football for three years, even though he weighed only 140 pounds. He held the 1931 San Fernando Valley shot-put record, no small accomplishment for someone his size, and became the 50-yard free-style interscholastic swimming champ.

He was still called Tiny—but now the name was one of the most honored and respected in school. During his senior year, his swimming coach decided he had the timing and muscles for high diving. Tiny Ladd became not only the school's champ diver, but was the finest diver in the San Fernando Valley for the next decade.

He also was captain of the school's swimming, track and football teams, head of the Hi Y and president of the student body. He started to enjoy clothes and girls and became the nattiest dresser for miles around. A clothier gave him free suits in exchange for his exhibiting the newest fads: loud neckties, belts, crazy socks.

An English teacher noticed the confident way he carried himself and coaxed him into trying dramatics. Ladd played the part of Ko-Ko in *The Mikado*, and the following month, qualified for tryouts at a small Hollywood studio which was trying to form a stock company. But when he spoke his lines, he suffered an acute attack of stage fright and sounded as if he had a mouth full of dried apricots. The director looked at him incredulously and said: "Would you repeat that, please?"

Ladd spoke again, words which sounded like "*Glubba glomp glibb, glibb.*"

"Oh, my God," said the director. "I don't believe it."

He excused Ladd from the audition and suggested that he seek a career as far removed from acting as possible.

After graduating from high school, Ladd went to work for eighteen dollars a week on a local paper, the *Sun-Record.* In two years he worked his way from printer's devil and copyboy to columnist-sports editor at thirty-five dollars a week. Then he quit and used his savings to open a hot dog stand called Tiny's. Much to his surprise, the place was a success, thanks to a tangy special relish which his chef put on the dogs.

But abruptly Ladd's luck went tragically sour. His stepfather, working overtime as a studio painter, had a heart attack and died. The following year Alan's mother, still depressed, committed suicide.

For three days, 21-year-old Alan stayed in seclusion at home, finding solace in reading Christian Science. Then, revealing an iron self-discipline, he went back to work, submerging his feelings in long fourteen- and sixteen-hour shifts at his hot dog stand. In three years he paid off the $6,000 mortgage on his parents' cottage.

He then hired a day manager for Tiny's so he could work nights as a $75-a-week radio news reporter for an oil company. In his spare time, such as it was, he picked up $25 checks as a movie dress extra, wearing his own flashy wardrobe, which included a loud, fawn-colored suit and suede shoes. When he showed up in the suit one night at the radio station, its manager—a stuffy Ivy League type— called him into his office.

"Mr. Ladd, do you like the clothes you have on?"

"Why, yes," said Ladd, taken aback.

"Well, I don't," replied the manager. "So make up your mind, Mr. Ladd. Do you want to stay in radio and dress like a gentleman, or would you rather gallivant around the movie studios in that God-awful thing you've got on?"

Ladd flushed with embarrassment which turned to anger. "I still like the suit!" he exploded. "And I quit!"

He went back to work full-time running his hot dog stand. The next month a studio worker who owed him a sizeable tab for dogs, chocolate pie and sodas offered him a job as a grip—trade name for a film handy man. Ladd went to work for Warner Brothers.

The first day he made every possible booboo and was fired. A friend interceded for him with the boss.

"Why the hell should I rehire him?" demanded the boss. "He's got ten thumbs!"

"Well," replied Ladd's pal, weakly, "he used to be one of the best high divers around."

"OK," said the boss, biting off the end of his cigar. "He's hired for the high work."

For the next year Ladd worked as a carpenter on beams sixty-five feet above the stage floor for $42.50 a week. Once he lost his balance, fell on a set rigged below him and wrecked it. Another time he dropped a plank through a piano, creating discordant pandemonium on a stage where a musical was being filmed. Later, being a swimmer, he was sent under water to steer a miniature frigate through a tank while a calm marksman shot bits off the model with a high-powered sniper's rifle. As the cameras turned, several bullets kicked up geysers only inches from Ladd's submerged hands.

"Was I scared?" said Ladd later. "You bet your sweet rump I was!"

One day Ladd looked down from his perch in the scaffolding and saw an actor friend lazing around reading magazines. The friend did nothing else for ten days. "How come?" asked Ladd. His friend replied that he got fifty dollars a day for waiting around to play his role. Ladd promptly decided he was in the wrong end of the movie racket. He sold his hot dog stand for $1500 and entered a school of dramatic training.

On the night of his graduation, he was offered a reporting job with International News Service at three hundred dollars a month, starting immediately. But Ladd turned it down, preferring to gamble on a hit-or-miss actor's career, a decision he regretted for years.

Casting directors repeatedly rejected him, saying he was too small and his blond coloring wouldn't photograph properly. During the next two years his only acting work was bit parts in radio melodramas over Los Angeles radio stations. His salary ranged from as little as twenty dollars a week to a high of forty dollars.

One evening an agent named Sue Carol listened to a radio show and was impressed by the voices of two of its characters, an old man and a brash youth. Miss Carol was a doll-faced, dark-haired Chicago beauty who had starred in Hollywood "B" pictures from 1929 to 1932 when she was in her early twenties. When her career began to slip, she organized her own theatrical agency. Deciding to add the old man and the youth to her list of clients, she invited them to her office for interviews and was surprised when only the youth showed up.

"Where's the old man?" she asked.

"I'm both guys," said Alan Ladd modestly. "Think you can use me?"

Sue Carol nodded eagerly. As far as she was concerned, it was love at first sight. "He was the cutest boy I'd ever seen," she told her friends. "He was very shy, had sun-bleached hair, a wonderful smile—and muscles. He was for me."

She immediately got him a film job playing a sailor at $250 a week. He worked in only two scenes, but they happened to be the first and last filmed, so Ladd was carried for sixteen weeks. On the strength of that, Sue got him work in a bloody war movie, *The Beast of Berlin*, which was shot in five days at a total cost of $20,000. It was filmed amid such chaotic confusion that Ladd clearly could be seen on the screen in two different parts—first as a young anti-Nazi and later, resurrected, digging a grave for someone else.

The small roles which followed were shrewdly judged by Sue who selected only parts that showed Ladd to advantage. She was so convinced he had a big future that she dropped all her other clients to concentrate on him. In 1941, the break they had both been working for came at last. Ladd was offered his first important role as a youthful gunman in Paramount's *This Gun for Hire*. His selection was remarkable in that it broke Hollywood's long taboo against short, blond leading men.

Ladd was a sensation as Raven, a cold-blooded cop killer. The camera was on him throughout the picture and at the end, when three dozen policemen closed in on young Raven for the kill, the crowd at the preview booed.

Paramount swiftly put Ladd into a second picture and again his personal success was phenomenal. But the studio chiefs didn't fully realize what a bonanza they had until they let Ladd carry a picture all by himself. The film was *Lucky Jordan* and it eradicated any lingering doubt about Ladd's mesmerizing power. *Lucky Jordan* was made for

$375,000—rummage-sale money at Paramount—and it returned over $4,000,000.

Studio bosses were astounded by what they had stumbled upon. They were familiar with the problems of certain actors who gave great performances on the set, only to see their scenes flatten out on the screen. Ladd was exactly opposite. The cameras took this slight blond and brought out a powerful personality which was not at all apparent in the flesh and blood Ladd.

Ladd's luck now began its giddy upward spiral. He married Sue Carol (it was her third marriage and his second; he had married a childhood sweetheart in 1936, divorcing her shortly thereafter). He made several more extremely successful gangster films, receiving $750 a week, and then interrupted his career in 1942 to enlist in the Army Air Corps. After he worked up to corporal at a Southern California base, he was offered a commission, but refused because he felt his star status had influenced the offer.

He was not happy in the Army. The other soldiers liked him, but he took a lot of kidding about his height and it rankled him, although he tried not to let it show. When he was taken off the garbage detail, by a fawning officer fan of his, he begged to go back. "I don't mind garbage," Ladd said. "In fact, I like it. It may stink, but it's uncomplicated."

The following year, 1943, he was given a medical discharge for nervousness and chronic stomach ulcers. The latter were cured by a diet of Sue Carol's soft-boiled eggs and cup custards, and he went back before the cameras. Unlike many stars, his fans had not forgotten him during his absence. He made such pictures as *Salty O'Rourke* and *Two Years Before the Mast,* and his salary rocketed to $3500 a week.

During the next decade and a half, Ladd starred in over 50 pictures. In 99 per cent of these, he played a typical Alan Ladd character—steely-eyed, soft-spoken, but a man of rugged action. Most of his pictures were mystery or Western suspense dramas. His performances ranged from that of a wandering gun fighter in *Shane* to the bumbling characterization of a Sir Lancelot-type in *The Black Knight.* In both he rode horses; one in blue jeans and the other in iron pants. The first was a movie milestone which won him the greatest critical acclaim of his career; the second was a medieval mishmash. But, significantly, both made large amounts of money.

Ladd was so consistently potent at the box office that his films eventually returned a total profit of over $100 million. In the mid-1950s he formed his own company, Jaguar Productions. In addition, Warner's paid Ladd a $150,000 salary for each picture and cut him in for 50 per cent of the profits. This unique setup enabled him to earn nearly a million dollars in 1957, his most lucrative year.

Although Ladd made his biggest profits during a time of bitter tax bites (he kept only 15 per cent of what he earned), he hung onto enough to make handsome investments in land and oil. His multi-millionaire status permitted him to have a personal staff of fifteen people; an eleven-room French provincial home in Beverly Hills, and a $450,000, sixty-acre ranch in Hidden Valley, forty-five miles northwest of Hollywood, where he raised chickens, cattle, race horses and turkeys.

In Palm Springs, in addition to his seven-bedroom winter mansion, he owned 110 acres of strategically located real estate, plus a swank downtown hardware store worth $225,000. His oil investments were scattered through California, Oklahoma and Texas.

As he advanced into his late forties, Ladd maintained most of his slim good looks, troubled only by sagging flesh beneath his chin and the deep broad part in his blond hair, which occasionally needed the assistance of a small hairpiece. He gave the outward impression of being a serenely happy film star enjoying life with his wife and children.

In truth, however, all was far from serene. Carefully concealed from the public was the fact that he was one of the most restless and neurotic personalities in Hollywood, constantly worried about his future, plagued with thoughts of bad luck and death. Much of his insecurity stemmed from the poverty of his childhood; he was fearful that another depression might destroy the wealth it had taken him years to accumulate.

Once he confided to his close friend, Marty Rackin, producer of six of his pictures: "I guess I'm the most insecure guy you know in this town, right? But I can't be like those guys who've had it good all their lives. They figure things can't ever get bad. But if you're like me, and once had it real bad, you keep wondering how long the good can last."

More than once, Ladd told Rackin that he had never

expected to be a star and that he would have been a lot happier if he had remained a $42.50-a-week carpenter at Warner Brothers. "The trouble with being a star," he said, "is that you have to stay a star. You have to battle to stay on top and it's a battle that never ends."

Ladd was convinced that the taboo against small blond actors which he had once broken would some day get its revenge, and that Hollywood would toss him on its scrap heap. Each time he starred in a new picture he was convinced it would be his last, either because the public was finally tired of him or because he might not live to complete it.

Although he was nearly always in good health, he brooded about the bad luck he was convinced hovered nearby, ready to swoop down on him with its deadly talons. One of his few fights with Sue Carol occurred when she dropped one of his $100,000 life insurance policies without informing him.

"Get it back!" he commanded. "You never can tell when you might need it!"

In the early 1960s, Ladd's long expected bad luck began to descend upon him. To combat television, Hollywood turned exclusively to large budget extravaganzas or hard-hitting sex movies. These bore no resemblance to the Alan Ladd films of old, which were now regarded as shallow trivialities. Producers continued, however, to recognize the box-office value of Ladd's name and offered him co-starring roles or high-paying secondary parts in their new dramas. Unwilling to take less than top billing, Ladd rejected offer after offer for roles.

For most of three years Ladd was among Hollywood's unemployed. For him this was torture, because his creative energy was still at its peak and he had no outlet for it, no long scripts to memorize, no twelve- and fourteen-hour days on the set which brought the blessings of fatigue and a good night's sleep. The culmination of his frustrations came one night in November 1962, when he was involved in a mysterious gun accident on his Hidden Valley ranch.

Ladd had gone to the ranch in a vain effort to seek solitude and relaxation. Shortly after midnight the phone rang at the Lake Sherwood fire station near the ranch. The caller was Mrs. Ladd, who had remained in their Beverly Hills home. She was agitated and distraught.

"I just had a call from Alan!" she said. "He's been shot!"

Fireman Robert Price raced to the ranch and found Ladd

lying in blood-soaked pajamas on the bed in his bedroom. He had been wounded in the chest by a .38 caliber revolver which lay on the rug. He was semi-conscious and breathing with great difficulty. Price stopped the bleeding with towels and called an ambulance which took the actor to Woodland Park Hospital.

The police were unable to question Ladd because he was under heavy sedation. When they contacted Mrs. Ladd, she said Alan had told her on the phone that he had "shot himself while fooling around with his gun collection."

Three days later, in a bedside interview with detectives at the hospital, Ladd gave a different account, stating that he had shot himself while chasing a prowler. "I was alone in the house," he said. "About midnight I heard a noise so I jumped out of bed, took the gun from a night stand and started for the door. I tripped over something and fell. I hit the floor and felt a concussion as the gun went off."

"What did you trip over?" the officers asked.

"I don't know," said Ladd.

The detectives who had investigated the possibility of suicide (part of the routine of all gunshot wound inquiries) said they were satisfied with Ladd's story and considered the case closed. They revealed that the bullet, after missing his heart by two inches, had ricocheted around inside his chest, breaking three ribs and deflating a lung.

While recuperating, Ladd had many bull sessions with his pal Marty Rackin, chief of production at Paramount, who was then casting *The Carpetbaggers*. Again and again Rackin urged Ladd to play the sympathetic role of cowboy Nevada Smith in the picture, arguing that it was a meaty part which would restore him to the ranks of sought-after actors.

Again and again Ladd refused, saying: "It's no use, Marty. I'm washed up and I know it. I'm too damn nervous and I'm scared. I know I wouldn't be any good in the picture."

Rackin refused to give up. He enlisted the aid of Sue Carol and they started a persuasive campaign to restore Ladd's self-confidence and change his mind. Finally Ladd, exasperated by all the arguments, threw up his hands and exploded: "All right, Marty, I'll do it! But only because you're my friend and you've stuck by me. But I'm warning you that I'm going to stink!"

Now Rackin and Mrs. Ladd began a campaign to get Ladd back in physical shape. He had been hitting the bottle pretty hard since his gun accident and had put on weight. They got him to knock off the booze and start exercising. Rackin hired an ex-boxer who showed up at Ladd's Palm Springs home every morning to do road work with him. They jogged for three miles before breakfast, rested and then jogged three more miles.

When Ladd arrived at Paramount to start work, his waist was trim, but he was the most nervous man on the set. He felt better when he saw the special arrangements Rackin had ordered to make him feel more secure. Rackin gave him the full star treatment, including his former posh dressing room, complete with new furnishings and red carpeting. Rackin also saw to it that the cameramen, grips and other workers were familiar faces, old pals who had worked Ladd's pictures in former years, and who could set up his planking without offending him.

Ladd worked harder on the picture than he'd ever done before, but throughout its long shooting schedule he was wracked with forebodings of misfortune. Despite Rackin's pleadings, he refused to see the rushes of each day's scenes.

"But you're terrific, Alan!" Rackin said. "If you'd only come and look at yourself, you'd know I'm telling the truth!"

"I've heard all that guff before," said Ladd, walking hurriedly past the projection room.

When the picture was finally in the can, Ladd went straight to the desert, remaining in seclusion for ten days and nights. But he was defeated in his long battle to find relaxation for his anxieties and twitching nerves. His struggles reached their climax that night in January when he tossed and turned on his bed, his temples aching, his body burning with feverish heat.

At 10 o'clock the next morning, his butler, Wendell Tyler, ventured into the darkened bedroom to see if Ladd was ready for breakfast. But the actor was in an exhausted sleep, his breathing deep and slow. Knowing how badly Ladd needed rest, Tyler did not return to the bedroom again until 3:30 in the afternoon.

Immediately he saw that something was wrong. Ladd lay twisted across the bed. His mouth was open, but he did not seem to be breathing.

Tyler sprang to a phone and summoned a doctor. When the doctor arrived, he confirmed what Tyler feared. Ladd was dead.

When Sue Carol received the shocking news in Beverly

Hills, she was told that the authorities presumed death had been caused by a heart attack. But an autopsy was ordered.

Over 1200 fans and top film stars attended Ladd's funeral the following Saturday at Forest Lawn, where he was eulogized as a man "who was prouder of having worked as a carpenter on Stage 5 at Warner Brothers than he was of being a movie star."

On Monday, Riverside County Coroner James S. Bird revealed the findings of the autopsy. The report was a second stunning shock to Ladd's family and friends. The medical examiners discovered that death had not been the result of a heart attack. Ladd had been the victim of a freak accident, caused by a rare combination of drugs and alcohol.

Coroner Bird disclosed that each time Ladd swallowed a sleeping pill or tranquilizer he had contributed to the lethal chemical forces building up in his body. Finally the accumulation had become so powerful it resulted in cerebral edema—swelling of the brain caused by excess fluids.

The drugs he'd taken were identified as seconal, a barbiturate; librium, a tranquilizer, and sparine, a medicine which quiets the nervous system. The coroner's report added, however, that the drugs had been the secondary death cause, with the major factor being "the high level of alcohol."

Ironically, Ladd's luck had run out just when he was on the brink of what could have been a brilliant new career. Because of his refusal to see *The Carpetbaggers,* he'd died without realizing Rackin and his wife had told the truth about his performance as Nevada Smith.

When the picture was released a few months later, critics across the nation hailed Ladd's portrayal, calling it the best in the film. Some went so far as to say his work as Nevada Smith even overshadowed his great portrayal in *Shane*.

Had he lived, Alan Ladd might not have agreed with them. But their words would have made him feel better.

THE FRENZIED WORLD OF JACK CARTER

● *NORMAN WILNER*

I was sitting in a Miami nightclub with Jack Carter and his beautiful blonde wife when Jimmy Durante introduced Carter as "Pound fuh pound, America's greatest entertainer . . ."

Then Durante sniggered coyly. "Next tuh me, of course."

A shy, abashed look came over Carter's face. He stood up to acknowledge the applause and knocked the table over, inundating everybody within a three-foot radius with celery, shrimp cocktails and whiskey. "Oh, my God!" he quavered.

The audience howled under the erroneous impression that it was part of the show. Carter smiled weakly and slunk out under cover of the darkness. Paula Carter and I followed him outside where he stood muttering to himself. "As an encore, I should have blown my brains out," he said. He hailed a cab and we all got in. Carter dusted off the seat and sat down, daintily hitching up his pants. "The Fontainebleu," he said.

The cab shot off into the heavy traffic. We heard what sounded like a kitten mewing. Carter started nervously. "What the hell is that?" he grumbled.

The cab driver turned around and grinned at us. "That was me. I'm learning how to be a ventriloquist. Pretty good, huh?"

"Turn around, you idiot, you'll kill us all!" Carter bellowed. "Watch where you're going! . . . That's a red light . . . You're going too fast! . . . Watch the taxi on your right! . . . Where'd *you* learn how to drive? . . . Look at that meter, eighty cents already! The bastard's got one of these trick meters! . . . Ten dollars a day I'm paying for a rented car, and I won't use it because it costs ten cents a mile." Carter struck himself on the forehead. "Oh, how I hate myself!"

As Carter nervously harangued him, the cab driver kept mewing like a kitten. At the red light, he turned around and evidently recognized the comedian. "Hey!" he said delightedly to Carter's wife. "You know who that is?"

"I hope so," she smiled.

The cabby leaned out the window and shouted at the driver of the adjoining cab as Carter fussed and fumed at him. "Hey, guess who I got for a fare, what's his name?"

"Chakrin's the name," Carter snapped.

"Go *wann,* your name ain't Chakrin. I know who you are. You're uh . . . uh . . . ," he kept snapping his fingers. "I got it on the tip of my tongue."

"Tongue," Carter said. "That's my name, Jack Tongue."

The light changed and the cab started again. Carter dabbed gloomily at the shrimp cocktail sauce on his jacket. "Twenty-five years I've been in show business and they still don't know my name."

"They know your name, darling," Paula said, comfortingly. She turned to me. "Sammy Davis, Jr. says Jack is the greatest crowd pleaser in the business—"

"I don't please me. I'm very dissatisfied with me." He took out his immaculate white handkerchief and absently began to wipe the window. "Nobody knows me. For a performer, I'm very untheatrical. Milton Berle steals gags, Joe E. Lewis drinks, Buddy Hackett talks out of duh side of his mout' like dis in that beautiful nasal voice. What have I got going for me? I'm masochistic. I'm depressive. Somebody up there doesn't like me and I think it's me."

To what did he attribute this unhappy frame of mind?

He shrugged. "It's the fashion nowadays to blame your parents. I blame me. I'm the kind of guy, if they crowned me king of England, I'd be *furious* because they didn't make me prime minister, too."

I said he sounded like a stereotype of a neurotic comedian. Had he ever been analyzed? "By three different analysts and I gave them all nervous breakdowns. The last one took off for Europe and is doing my act in Vienna."

The cab pulled up at the Fontainebleu. The cabby turned around. "I got it. Jackie Mason, right?"

Carter looked pained. "The name is really Chakrin. In Russian, that means 'philosopher,' and that's what you've gotta be in this business."

We got out and Carter said, "It's a good thing he didn't know me. When I play New York or Miami or Vegas, the word gets out, 'Jack Carter's in town.' It's like jungle drums. The bastards refuse to take me in their cabs because I drive them crazy. All right, I'm the first to admit it. I'm tough to live with. Thank God, my wife understands me and puts up with me."

As we walked into the Fontainebleu lobby, a middle-aged woman in a mink stole rushed up with an autograph book. "I saw your show last night and I never laughed so much in my whole life. So many jokes. You really work very hard!"

Carter smiled wanly and signed her book. In the elevator, he said, "I resent it when people come up to me and say, 'Jack you work very hard.' What am I, a truckdriver? Sure I work hard," he added incongruously. "I have to *crush* an audience or I'm not happy. I swarm all over them, give them forty jokes instead of four, even though I know it's wrong. I should give them the charm routine like Danny Kaye, not 196 jokes a minute."

"Don't you like Danny Kaye?"

"Certainly I like him!" Carter said indignantly. "I admire the man. He's a cool worker and he lays the language in well."

We got off on the sixteenth floor and went into his luxurious suite. "Jack isn't the average run of comedian," Paula said.

"I speak twelve languages," Carter said proudly. He began ticking them off on his fingers. "English, Spanish, French, Italian, German, Hebrew, Yiddish—" He paused.

"That's only seven languages."

Carter fixed his hooded blue eyes on me with hostility. "What are you, a certified public accountant?" He turned to Paula. "Why is the whole world against me?"

"The whole world is not against you, darling" she said patiently.

"I just got hungry or thirsty, I don't know which. You feel like a drink or a sandwich or something?"

"I'll have a Screwdriver," Paula said.

"Bourbon, hot water and orange juice," I said.

Carter scowled at me. "What kind of a drink is that? I'm *dying* for seltzer."

He talked about his childhood when he, his two sisters and mother and father lived somewhat less than luxuriously in three rooms in back of a candy store his father owned in Coney Island.

"My father had a Jewish still in the basement, a seltzer machine. It always scared me. I never liked to go near it. The damn thing was almost human. It had metal arms and coils and wires like a Rube Goldberg invention and it made a dull, humming noise—*mmmmmm, mmmmmm*. One night, my father sent me down to the basement for a box of Tootsie Rolls. It was dark down there and I stumbled against the seltzer machine and the arms grabbed me!" He let out a hoarse scream. "I've had seltzer trauma ever since."

Paula said, "Sometimes we're watching a horror movie on the Late Show and I'll say 'Boo!' and he jumps."

"I still sleep with one eyeball open," Carter said.

He phoned room service for the drinks and a hamburger for himself. "Make sure you bring sliced tomatoes with the hamburger," he emphasized.

"Jack ad libs a totally different show every night," Paula said.

"I really make a tough job tougher," Carter frowned. "I enjoy torturing myself. I do a bit where my mother keeps hitting me in the head. 'Where's your brains? Where's your brains?' She hits and she hits and finally, I say, 'Keep hitting, Mom, they'll be right out.' "

He excused himself and went into the bedroom to change his clothes. I asked Paula whether her husband was difficult to live with. "Jack drives me crazy but I can't imagine being married to anybody else. He's the most unpredictable person I know, and that's part of his charm."

She told about inveigling him into accompanying her to an auction at the Parke-Bernet galleries in New York. Carter had never been to an art auction before and he viewed the proceedings with a jaundiced eye. He sat there, grimly silent, while she bid on a grotesque cigar store figure of Punch that was well over six feet tall. When the auctioneer knocked it down to her, Carter leaped up, his eyes blazing, leveled his finger at the gargoyle and bellowed, "Not in *my* house!"

"It took Jack weeks to get over it," Paula said. "He would close his eyes and make horrible faces every time he looked at it. Then somebody offered me double what I had paid for it but Jack had a fit. 'What are you, crazy?' he screamed. 'I *love* that Punch!' "

The bedroom door opened suddenly and Carter's head

popped out. "That's the story of my life," he rumbled. "I have to hate something before I love it." He came out, fumbling with the buttons on the jacket of a new tuxedo. "It's warfare when I get dressed. Even my clothes are against me. Buttons pop, zippers snag. Some of my worst battles have been against clothes hangers. I've never won a fight yet."

"When we're home," Paula said, "he hangs around all morning driving me crazy. He finally gets all dressed, kisses me goodby, goes to the door, and as he's on his way out, he changes his mind, comes back and drives me crazy for another hour. Then he'll go downtown and call me twenty times to look in the pocket of his suit for his cigarette lighter. 'Which suit?' I ask. 'The gray suit.' He has maybe fifteen suits in different shades of gray hanging in the closet. I look in the pockets of his gray suits, his brown suits, his blue suits, I look through all his suits and finally he finds the lighter in the suit he's wearing."

Carter stared in the mirror with a curious mixture of admiration and loathing. An impeccable dresser, Carter insists on buying not only his own clothes but his wife's as well. For some mysterious reason, however, he invariably brings home dresses that fit tall, emaciated girls and Paula is not, by the wildest stretch of the imagination, emaciated. I asked her if he had good taste.

"I have excellent taste!" Carter shouted. "I could have been the Jewish version of Christian Dior!"

I asked if he had any physical idiosyncracies. "What the hell kind of an insulting question is that?" Carter roared. "What are you, a goddamn Peeping Tom?"

Paula gave me a funny look. "I didn't mean Krafft-Ebing," I explained. "All I meant was—oh, let's strike the question."

"He's ambidextrous," Paula said.

"That's right," Carter said. "I can talk lefty or righty."

"He punches me lefty."

"But she bleeds righty."

He strode around the room restlessly, hacking and clearing his throat. He sounded very much like a seal barking for herring. "They gave me a — — air-conditioned virus room!" he suddenly shouted. "Did I come down to Miami to freeze or to get a little sunshine? I don't know how I can do the show tonight, but if I lay down, I'm dead. If I keep moving, I'm better off. Maybe I better go in the bathroom and take steam for my throat, huh? What do you think?"

He looked at his watch and turned pale. "It's almost time for me to go down and make a fool of myself. God, I hate this business!"

"Can I watch the show tonight?" Paula asked.

"Paula, for God's sake, you *know* how I feel about that."

Carter does not like his wife to be in the audience while he is performing. During a recent engagement, she sneaked into the nightclub disguised in a brown wig and horn rim glasses and hid behind a pillar. There were 3,000 people in the nightclub, but in the middle of his frenzied gyrations, Carter suddenly halted. "I see you, Paula! Out! *Out!*"

"And he refused to go on with his act until I left," Paula said. "I don't know why he did it. I'm his greatest audience."

"You stink," Carter growled affectionately. "Where's my hamburger? I'm starved and I gotta go on in ten minutes."

Red Buttons came in and Carter fell upon him like a tiger. "Red, you gotta help me! I'm all out of material!"

Buttons laughed. "Last year, Jack was opening at the Copa and he got panicky. He phoned me and said he had nothing to say, nothing new to offer the audience. I come over, thinking I'll help the poor guy out. He's done it for me and other comics countless times. Jack sits me down in a chair and for four solid hours, he rattles off his nothing to say. I give him maybe one joke. He was a bloody riot at the opening—"

"You think so, Red? I thought I was lousy that night."

"He started eight P.M. and got off the floor like three shopping days before Christmas." Buttons chuckled. "And then he tells the audience *I* wrote his entire act."

Carter gazed moodily out the window at the Miami lights glittering in the dusk. "I was a strange child. I had a constant fear of being left out and I had to be the best."

Carter considers himself physically grotesque. "I'm 5 foot 11 or 11 foot 5, depending on my mental state. I weigh 185 stripped . . ." He leered. "I have a very strong, weak chin. My eyebrows are bowlegged. I've got 20-20 vision in one ear . . ."

"We call him 'Brillo-Head,'" said Buttons.

"That's right. I don't comb or brush my hair, I scrub pots with it. I'm so ugly I should be fined and sent to jail."

He was joking and yet he was serious. "You're crazy," I said. "Why, you're handsome!"

He shook his head. "I don't believe it. I would have done me over." He brooded a moment. "Whenever I drive out to the suburbs, all I see are beautiful children. You don't see ugly kids any more. They must throw the ugly ones away."

Buttons turned to me. "Jack is a very bright, nervous kind of guy. He hasn't changed a bit in the seventeen years I've known him. He drives everybody nuts but everybody loves him."

"I've got enemies in this business, Red."

"You're your own worst enemy," Paula said.

"And who has a better right?" Carter bellowed. "I'm Jack of all trades, master of nothing. I'm not me, I'm not Jack Carter. I'm a chamelean. I'm potpourri. In Texas, I say, 'Ah reckon' and I walk like I've got saddle sores. In Miami, I use Jewish routines even a Nazi would laugh at. In Boston, I used to talk like J.F.K. . . . . It's almost like I'm ashamed of my own talent."

"Jack is so talented he could be anything," Buttons said. "When I got back from Japan after making *Sayonara*, I brought a scroll with me. Jack made up a poem on the spur of the moment and hand lettered it on the scroll for me—

CLEAN FLOOR
DIRTY STREET
PLEASE REMOVE
SHOES FROM FEET.

"I have a terrible phobia about cleanliness," Carter said gloomily.

"He waxes and polishes every inch of the apartment the day before the cleaning girl comes," Paula said. "When people come to our house, he makes them take their shoes off before he lets them in." Carter is forty, and for his thirty-ninth birthday party, one discerning friend brought him one thousand pairs of paper slippers. Lucille Ball and Gary Morton presented him with a mop and pail and fourteen large bottles of Mr. Clean. Knowing that Carter entertains a morbid interest in medicine, one physician friend brought him a moldy dissecting kit.

"Jack is the kind of guy who steps out of the shower to take a leak," Buttons whispered to me.

"He loves his carpet more than he loves me," Paula said. "Once I fell down the stairs and he hollered, '*Look* what you did to my beautiful carpet!' It drives him crazy when

I walk on my high heels on that damned carpet. He follows me sniffing like a bloodhound on the trail with a vacuum cleaner picking up every last tiny particle of dirt—"

"But my entire life is disheveled," said Carter running his finger over the windowsill and inspecting it.

"We went for a drive the other night and had to stop for a red light," Paula said. "Don't you think he jumped out with a cloth and began polishing the hood?"

Carter is the fretful owner of a 1956 Thunderbird which is as spotless as the day he bought it and still has the original plastic covers over the seats. He has driven in it perhaps a dozen times. "I curse the dealer who sold it to me, I curse the insurance company for letting me have insurance on it and most of all I curse the State for issuing me a driver's license."

The phone rang and Paula answered it. "It's your press agent."

"I don't want to talk to him," Carter snarled.

"What shall I tell him?"

"Tell him I died and I'm not expected to recover."

Paula murmured her apologies into the phone and hung up.

"That character," Carter rumbled. "One thousand a month I'm paying him and he can't even get me into the *Christian Science Monitor*." A look of intense anguish came over his face. "And he has the *chutzpah* [nerve] to charge me extra every time he uses a five-cent stamp! He'll probably send me a bill for this ten-cent phone call."

The waiter came in wheeling a tea cart. Carter threw his arm around Buttons and asked if he would join us. "You know I only touch organic foods," the diminutive comedian said.

"I forgot! A glass of balsa wood for my friend!" Carter shouted. With elaborate, ceremonious gestures, the waiter took the serving plate and lifted up the large silver cover, disclosing a dried-up little hamburger.

"Where's the tomatoes?" Carter asked, his voice shaking with rage. "I *distinctly* said tomatoes. Did you hear me say tomatoes?" He looked at me.

"You distinctly said tomatoes," I said.

"A dollar-seventy-five for a stinking hamburger plus a dollar extra for room service and I can't get a lousy slice of tomato," Carter said, visibly trying to control himself.

"I bring you tomato, yes?" said the waiter, bowing obsequiously.

"You bring me tomato, no!" Carter roared. "By the time you bring me the goddamn tomato, I'll be on the plane back to New York!"

The waiter cringed. Carter tipped him five dollars and pointed majestically to the door. "My compliments to the chef and tell him to drop dead." The waiter scuttled out, a broad grin on his face. Carter bit into his hamburger savagely. "Either I overtip or I undertip, there's no in-between," he mumbled, his mouth full.

"Jack is the bull and the bear of our business," Buttons said. "He's either way up or way down, there's no happy medium."

"Jack E. Leonard says I'm the only guy he knows who sends back restaurants," Carter said. "I should have had my mother cater this hamburger, only she drives me nuts too. She makes 'watch-out' food. With every dish, you get a warning—'Watch out for the bones; watch out, it's too hot; watch out, it's too spicy; watch out, don't eat too fast.' My father is the umpire. 'Let him alone, let him burn his tongue, who cares?' "

Carter glanced nervously at his watch. "Red, pray for me. I got a feeling in my bones I'm not gonna make it tonight. I got a feeling the audience is gonna rise up and walk out on me tonight."

"That's about par for the course," Buttons said. "All the little Carter enzymes are waving the flag. Don't worry, Jack, you'll knock them dead the way you always do."

"I'm an actor, damn it!" Carter roared. "What am I doing telling jokes for a living?"

"Are you a Method actor?" I asked.

"No, but I've read Stanislavsky and all these inwardly-within guys . . ." Carter's mouth contorted suddenly. He clutched his hands to his stomach as though he were in pain. "You mus' sufferrrr!" he bellowed in a pseudo-Russian accent. "Them, not me. I do enough suffering on my own time."

Carter's closest friend, Mickey Hayes, a Miami haberdasher, shudders when the comedian bestows his patronage upon him. He has, on various occasions, diplomatically suggested that Carter take his trade elsewhere but the latter is adamant in his loyalty. Says Hayes: "Jack can come in for thirty fittings on a suit before he's satisfied. He pulls at the sleeves and the crotch and the lapels until the suit is all out of shape. Then he says, 'See? I told you it didn't fit right.' "

Hayes was best man when Carter married Paula and, since it was impossible for him to come to New York for the wedding, Carter impulsively chartered a plane and flew the entire entourage, bridesmaids, rabbi and all, to Miami.

I met Hayes the next day in the Poodle Room of the Fontainebleu. A four-piece Cuban band was clattering away noisily, waiters scurried around with drinks, amorous couples clutched at each other and everybody seemed to be whispering at the top of his lungs. Sodom and Gomorrah, I couldn't help thinking as I furtively regarded a redhead with a spectacular bosom dancing with a wizened old man.

"To me, he's a fantastic guy," Hayes said. "When I opened my new store, Jack flew from Los Angeles just to cut the tape. It was in Winchell's column. Jack likes to hang around my store and wait on customers. The other day, he fitted somebody for a suit and the guy happened to see Jack perform that very same night. The guy was amazed. 'Hey!' he said, 'This comedian's a *tailor* in the daytime!' "

Hayes fingered the ice in his Scotch reflectively. "Jack has the most immaculate wardrobe hung away in his closet, maybe seventy-five suits like brand new he's too nervous to wear."

Hayes is friendly with all the big-time comedians but feels closest to Carter. Why Carter? "This is the kind of guy Jack is," Hayes explains. "I've seen him turn down an appointment with an important Hollywood producer because he was going over to his parents' house for supper. Jack has no faith in himself. He'll be the last one in the world to find out how great he is. The funny thing is, in spite of the public image of him as a loud, brash comedian, actually he's a very shy person."

Hayes stubbed out his cigarette. "If he were here, this ashtray would be cleaned out already."

Carter came over wearing jazzy pink cotton slacks, a yellow zebra-striped polo shirt and red loafers. He didn't look particularly shy. The Cuban band began to play again, the bongos thumping and the maraccas chattering. Carter looked back over his shoulder. "Did something fall down?" He sat down, took a napkin and meticulously wiped off his side of the table, then emptied the ashtray into a nearby wastebasket. Hayes burst out laughing. "See what I mean?"

Carter grinned self-consciously. He crumpled up the napkin and threw it away. "The Vegas bit came out like pure gold last night," Hayes said. "I can't even remember the *shtick* [bit] I did," Carter said pensively. "If I'm on a venom subject, I get vicious funny."

"You couldn't be vicious if you tried," said Hayes.

"I'm the most vicious sonofabitch that ever lived," said Carter, nudging the crumpled napkin with his toe.

"I was with Jack one night when a total stranger came up and said, 'Here's that hundred dollars I owe you.' Jack looked at him. 'What hundred dollars?' He didn't even remember the guy. He's always doing things like that. Vicious," Hayes snorted affectionately.

The band played an Afro-Cuban jazz number and Carter jumped up suddenly and began jitterbugging. "The first dance I went to, everybody was Lindy Hopping all over the joint. I didn't know how to dance so I went home and for two weeks, I practiced. When I came back, I was a Jewish Fred Astaire. I was born with this crazy gift for mimicry, so I mimic dancing and singing and acting and eating and even living. I'm not me. I'm not Jack Carter. I'm fourteen other people." He sat down just as suddenly, breathing hard.

"How do you relax?" I asked Carter. "Or aren't you able to relax?"

"I was a basket case for four years on the golf course. I got so angry at myself once, I threw a wood and wrapped it around one of the Strafaci brothers' neck. Frank or somebody. That's when I decided to give up golf. I'm too competitive."

"Are you a poor loser?"

"I'm a *born* loser."

"You're forty—have you arrived at a philosophy of life yet?"

Carter looked amazed. "Here? You want the Lin Yutang bit *here?*" He had to raise his voice over the infernal din of the cha-cha band and the cocktail glasses clinking. "Thou shalt not fart!" he snarled.

Carter's leather-lunged voice has been likened to a bullfrog suffering acute dyspepsia. He attributes this to his humble beginnings, one summer, when he was a towel boy at the Washington Baths in Coney Island. He stood around naked and shivering all day, assiduously scrubbing the customers' back and hoping for a nickel tip. The bathhouse employed a regular barker who fell temporarily ill and Carter, eager to get back into dry clothes, volunteered to substitute for him.

In order to attract more customers, Carter prayed toward

Mecca, bellowed crude insults at the gaping yokels and developed the machine-gun attack that characterizes his present work.

He attended Public School 100, where he was walloped regularly because of his imitations of the principal. He didn't do too well scholastically but graduated with more welts than any other student. At Brooklyn's New Utrecht High School, he specialized in art and dramatics. Carter is privately convinced that he might have been another Rembrandt except for his unfortunate proclivity for drawing caricatures of those in authority. Art, however, did not satisfy his lust for theatricals, so he accepted the leading role in a school production of *Cyrano de Bergerac*.

("I make over $300,000 a year in nightclubs and television, but the guy with the nose is buried deep inside me and I can't get him out. Anthony Quinn would give his right eye to be a nightclub performer, and I would give both of mine to be a dramatic actor.")

In 1939, Carter won first prize in a Major Bowes amateur hour. He did a raucous imitation of Jimmy Durante, pigeon-toed around the stage in a glassy-eyed facsimile of Boris Karloff as the monster in *Frankenstein*, and rattled off jokes. Through the peculiar logic of show business, this won him a dramatic scholarship in the summer stock company run by Christopher Morley.

The famed author told him, "My dear boy, you are that rarity—an actor who can clown and a clown who can act." Morley took a fatherly interest in the young comic and even went so far as to write some rather literary jokes for his act which Carter stealthily discarded.

Carter's first professional engagement was a one-night stand at a saloon not too far from the Swift slaughterhouses in Manhattan. "I got seven bucks and all the blood I could drink." The patrons, a singularly uninhibited lot, cheered him to the rafters when they discovered that he had neglected, in his stagefright, to zip up his fly.

Emboldened by his success, Carter demanded a fee of eight dollars for his next engagement. A somewhat spirited argument ensued. The proprietor, a large, burly individual, hoarsely informed Carter, "I don't wanna have to lean on you, kid." Carter hastily agreed to work for seven dollars but was cancelled, nevertheless, when the disenchanted patrons discovered that he was mouthing Henny Youngman's routine, word for word.

Carter played a number of smaller niteries and was then

booked with a Major Bowes unit along with Frank Sinatra, Robert Merrill and other hopeful unknowns on a cross-country tour. "I was just a kid and I had never been away from home before. I cried all the way on the bus to Syracuse because I was so scared." The sight of Carter so unnerved Sinatra that the emaciated crooner sat on the other side of the bus and refused to have anything to do with the blubbering comic.

After a stint emceeing for the Les Brown band, Carter was drafted and served in the Medical Corps. The young comic, who turned queasy at the sight of a hangnail, was soon transferred to a radio quiz show under Air Force sponsorship. Among other phobias, Carter had a fear of height. For the next three years, ashen faced with fright, he flew the Pacific war stations, while starring in a military review, *Flying Varieties*.

It took Carter many years to overcome his aversion to airplanes but he appears to have mastered his fears.

Actually, Carter's most vivid memories of the war center around the town of Needles, California, which enjoys a mean temperature of approximately 130 degrees. "We would come out of a cold shower, drenched with perspiration. I took my O.C.S. test standing at attention, stark naked. Four officers sat at a desk, reviewing my case, stark naked too. I mean it was *hot!*"

When the war ended, Carter returned to nightclubs and vaudeville and began to earn important money. His bright, fresh monologues caught the attention of the TV tycoons and in 1948 he was starred in a variety minstrel show.

"I was only twenty-six and didn't even know how to blow my nose, but I ran the whole show. Berle used to watch me in action and smack his writers—'Why can't you write sketches like that?'" Berle was so enamored of the whirlwind technique that he signed Carter to pinch-hit for him on the famous Texaco hour.

In 1950, Carter was signed by NBC to star in the hour-long segment before Sid Caesar's 90-minute show. Although Carter got a towering 48.7 rating, he immediately ran into difficulties with the NBC brass.

"They would tell me, 'You can't wear a robe because Caesar wears a robe. You can't have an opera bit because Caesar has an opera bit.' You can't do this, you can't do that. I, like a *nebbisch* [nothing], stood at attention and saluted. 'Yes sir. Yes sir.' Finally, my sponsor, Campbell Soup, got mad. Hell, they were spending *millions* and they said, 'Goddamit, if Jack wants to wear a robe or do an opera bit or anything, he'll do it and nobody's going to order him around.' "

Carter shrugged philosophically about the financial aftermath. "Caesar was protected for ten years by his lawyers and agents, Berle was protected for life, Gleason they hadda give the building and I ended up with heartburn."

During the ensuing decade, Carter landed starring roles in Broadway musicals, *Mr. Wonderful, Top Banana,* and *Call Me Mister.* In 1958, with his unerring sense for disaster, Carter turned down the Robert Preston role in *The Music Man* to play Sganarelle in a musical flop based on a play by Moliere.

"I was flattered because the producers auditioned for me, little Jack Carter, the guy with the biggest inferiority complex in the business bar none. Opera singers were in the cast. Wright and Forrest, who wrote *Kismet* and *Song of Norway,* wrote it. It was one of those Alfred Drake-type musicals—"

Carter leaped up and propped one foot on a couch, stroking his imaginary beard lustfully. He began to sing a melody from the show in a rich baritone, leering at the imaginary soubrette as only Alfred Drake can leer. I was surprised at the quality of Carter's voice and asked if he had ever tried opera.

"Robert Merrill once said to me, 'Idiot, let me take you to my voice teacher. You've got a voice big enough for opera. All it needs is training.' But I wouldn't go because I only do the things that are wrong for me. When I was twenty-five—it sounds like the beginning of a Robert Frost poem—'When I was twenty-five and terribly young and alive'—Guy Lombardo said to me, 'You have a terrible, driving ambition to be a star. Wait ten years, you can't hurry up success.' "

Carter squinted one eye up at the ceiling musingly. "Settle for something less than your ambition. I read that somewhere."

"The thing Jack doesn't realize is that he *is* a big star," Paula said.

Carter looked pleased, but he loftily ignored his wife. "Success is a step backward in the right direction. I read that in a book."

"Do you read a lot?" I asked.

A dreamy, poetic look came over his face. "Everything that comes out," he said.

Paula giggled. "Don't let him kid you. He makes me read all the latest books and review them for him. Jack is like a Hollywood producer—he's too busy to read."

Not too long ago, Carter made a movie for MGM entitled *The Horizontal Lieutenant*. Before the screening, there was a party and everybody commented on the delicious hors d'oeuvres. What might be tactfully described as an awkward silence prevailed when the picture ended. It had evidently not been one of the studio's more notable efforts. Carter stood up and shouted, "But wasn't the *food* wild?"

Paula laughed as she told the story. I said, "You enjoy your husband, don't you?"

"I *kvell* [thrill]."

"Don't be a phony," Carter said. "You're only half-Jewish."

"The only reason we stay married is because it's cheaper than getting a divorce," Paula said.

"Many's the time she's threatened to go home to her mother, only her mother is divorced and living with *her* mother," Carter said. "That's no gag, either. Paula's grandmother just got married at the age of eighty-five to a kid of seventy. Can you imagine anything like that happening with *my* parents? They're so old fashioned, to them divorce is something you read about in the papers that happens only to Hollywood actresses. My father, God bless him . . ." Carter shook his head lovingly.

Carter's father owned a small candy store in Coney Island and eked out a precarious living. Many of the freaks who appeared in the Coney Island side shows came into the store. "My big thrill was when Houdini's dog bit my sister. I have two sisters and we get along fine."

Carter recalls that he once timidly sidled up to his father and whispered, "Hey, Pop, it's my birthday." His hard working parent, absorbed in his own private woes, fixed him with a malevolent stare and said, "We should break out the American flag maybe?"

Paula reminisced about the first birthday party she threw for him. "He stood in the corner like a shy little boy. He couldn't believe it. He was positive nobody would show up."

He was wrong. A Carter party is a show business attraction.

"Jack is the funniest present opener in the business," says Ed Sullivan. "People have parties nowadays just so

Jack can open the presents. You can't imagine what belly laughs there are in three silk hankies when Jack opens the box. I literally fell down on the floor laughing and pounding my fists, begging for mercy. Jack is funny on my show but he's ten times as funny at home. Paula and he once did a double on my show and he upstaged her. His own wife. Jack goes on to win," Sullivan chuckled.

"How'd we get on the birthday kick?" Carter said. "We were talking about Pop." Carter smiled. "My father is a peculiar man. He loves Paula, but he's still testing her. If she tells my mother she doesn't feel like gefilte fish, he'll say, "See? *See?* A *shikseh* [gentile girl] wouldn't eat that." Carter chuckled. "Even my mother, good natured as she is, I'm the original 'No One's Good Enough For My Son' momma's boy. Years ago, every girl I would bring home, my mother would say, 'She's not for you. She's not for you.' Finally, one day I got mad and I hollered at her, 'Mom, for God's sake, is there a girl walking around with a sign 'This Girl Is For Jack?'

"My folks *live* to be hurt. They pray that I don't phone, so they can go around and tell all the neighbors, 'See what a rotten son we've got? He never telephones.' "

Carter told about recently kissing Miss America, Mary Ann Mobley, on the lips. The following day, she contracted the mumps and the doctor told him to check with his parents to see whether he had had it as a child. He phoned his mother. "Mom, did I have the mumps?" "Who remembers?" "Mom, you've only got one son. It's important! Try to remember up to age twelve, I'll take it after that." Meanwhile, his father was rumbling in the background, "Who? What? Where? Tell Jack not to give him his right name."

"My pop really believes in the old joke where the doctor says, 'Stick out your wallet and say Ahh.' He never tells anybody he's Jack Carter's father because he's afraid he'll be overcharged. This is the first year I couldn't get my parents to come down to Florida. Their apartment was robbed so all winter long they sat by the door waiting for twelve Puerto Ricans to come in. The place looks like Langley Collier moved out thirty years ago. They leave the plugs out of the sockets because they're afraid to waste electricity. I laugh but I'm the same way."

He lighted a cigarette, took one puff and grimaced. "What am I doing with this," he said, stubbing it out. "I hate cigarettes."

"I bought him that cigarette lighter just to light my cigarettes," Paula said. "Some smoker . . ." She giggled. "He puffs but he doesn't inhale. He can't *stand* cigars, the smell drives him crazy. Jack is very sensitive to odor. He's got a whole closetful of men's cologne but he doesn't even use it—"

"I never sweat unless I'm onstage," Carter said. "Then I *giss*. There's something cockeyed about my sweat glands." A gloomy expression came over his face. "I can't even have B.O. the way any normal, average guy has it. I only shower every other day. I don't know, maybe it's a psychological reaction from my Washington Baths job as a kid in Coney Island."

The following day, I met Carter at his cabana. He was stretched out on a beach lounge. He blearily opened one bloodshot eye and glared at me. "I took one of those sleeping suppositories at five o'clock in the morning," he croaked.

"Were you able to fall asleep?"

"No, but my ass yawned all night."

He closed the eye, his face twitching slightly in the burning sun. "Let's forget about the interview today. Have lunch but not near me. The thought of food makes me nauseous."

"Relax. I promise not to ask any questions."

"You're a liar. You're going to sit there and stare at me with your pen." He lay there, gasping at regular intervals, then mumbled. "Go ahead, ask me some more of your stupid questions."

Just then Paula came over, looking voluptuous in a polka-dot bikini. I asekd her if Carter is a hypochondriac.

"He's the opposite. He doesn't even know if he's sick. He never wears rubbers or a scarf or anything."

Carter suddenly sat bolt upright as a redhead undulated by, and he leered at her. "Get a load of that shape, will you?"

"Uh huh," she said, unenthusiastically.

"How much do you give your wife as a weekly allowance?" I asked Carter.

"One hundred fifty dollars." He paused. "Actually, I give her a hundred dollars but I enjoy lying."

"One hundred dollars isn't much for a big star like you."

"That's just for her bobby pins, you idiot!" Carter

roared. "She spends a thousand dollars a month just for long distance calls."

Jack Tirman, one of Carter's many press agents, later told me. "He's frugal but *crazy* frugal. Once he raised hell with Paula for throwing out three cents worth of soup greens, then in the next breath he went out and bought her a $10,000 mink."

A jeweler-friend sat down on the adjoining lounge and Carter began to haggle with him. He loves to buy gifts for anybody even remotely associated with him. A nightclub dishwasher was astonished when the comedian came charging in one night and presented him with a handsome wristwatch. The dishwasher, a Puerto Rican, was properly grateful but had difficulty making out the numerals. They were inscribed in Hebrew.

Last Christmas, Carter was shopping in Bergdorf-Goodman for lingerie for his wife when a well-dressed stranger approached him. Talking out of the side of his mouth, he informed Carter that he would be willing to part with his $1,200 diamond ring for a mere third of the cost because he was temporarily strapped. Leading the amazed comedian over to a nearby phone booth, he gently pressed him down in the seat and delivered a persuasive sales talk. To prove beyond a shadow of a doubt that it was a perfect diamond, the impeccably dressed charlatan began to rub the ring against the glass door.

"Now he's got the glass of the phone booth door cut to shreds," Carter reminisced. "I'm saying 'Yeah, yeah, yeah' even though I *know* he's conning me and I end up buying the ring for eighty bucks cash. I've even convinced myself it's worth twelve hundred. I quick run over to a jeweler who's a friend. He takes one look at it and says, 'What's with the crackerjack?' I tell him, 'You're *crazy*. That ring is worth thousands.' He brings his partner over and the partner squints at it through his jeweler's loupe and says, 'Nice cheap stone you got there, but somebody ruined it by rubbing it against glass.'

"Not only did I forget to buy Paula the lingerie, but when I got home that night what do you think she bought me for Christmas? A diamond ring!"

Carter shook his fist at a cloud that had covered the sun. "All right, we saw you. Stop showing off. Move. Beat it. One hundred dollars a day I'm paying for sunshine. Paula, why don't you sit in the sun and get some color? Any color. Get blue." It became increasingly cloudy.

"How do you like that," Carter raged, "an anti-Semitic cloud!"

"What is this green ring I see on your pinkie all the time?" I asked.

"It's a green ring you see on my pinkie all the time."

The waiter came with food on a tray. "Excuse me," Carter said, heaving himself to his feet. "It's time for my swimming lesson. I may drown just to get a laugh." He walked down to the pool.

I asked Paula how she met her husband.

"Every time I saw Jack, he was with a different beautiful girl. Not just beautiful but intelligent, so I couldn't help but be impressed. When he asked me for a date, I wouldn't go out with him at first. He kept phoning and phoning, and finally I said to him, 'All right, but you'll have to take my mother, too.' I was a little afraid of him. He had the reputation of being a playboy—"

"You mean a wolf?"

She laughed. "Some wolf. We were going together four months, and finally I told him, 'If you don't kiss me tonight, I'm never going out with you again!' "

After two years of seeing each other constantly, Paula asked whether his intentions were serious. Carter turned pale and changed the subject. She then wrote him a letter saying she thought they ought to get married. Carter's first panicky impulse was to leave the country. He wrote back that he was impossible to live with. Paula countered with another letter stating that she wouldn't dream of letting his little peccadilloes come between them. She received a letter several days later stating that he loved her too much to make her unhappy.

The impassioned correspondence built up to the inevitable climax when Carter reluctantly permitted her to announce their engagement. Paula wanted to get married immediately but Carter blushed modestly and insisted on a long engagement so they could get to know one another better.

"Jack was thinking in terms of fourteen or fifteen years, but I wouldn't let him get away with it."

It was a war of nerves and almost a foregone conclusion that Carter, who has always been a nervous individual, would lose the uneven battle. At the last minute, however, Carter left her waiting at the synagogue. Undaunted, Paula went to work on him again. The end came one morning at four o'clock when she was awakened from a sound sleep by Carter calling from Los Angeles, where he had a night-club engagement. He sounded a trifle hysterical.

"Listen, Paula," he said tensely, "something terrible has happened—"

"Oh my God! Are you all right, darling?" Paula inquired anxiously.

"Me? I'm fine but I forgot to water my plants before I left. Will you run over like a good girl and water them?"

"Now?" Paula inquired in a dangerously restrained voice. "At four o'clock in the morning?"

"Paula, I swear I'll marry you when I get back from the Coast. Only please, *please* water my plants or they'll die!" he blubbered. True to his word, Carter married her when he got back, but he was so angry at himself for giving in, he virtually ignored her for one solid month afterwards.

For a while, they maintained their own apartments because Carter was convinced the marriage wouldn't last. The Broadway columnists called it "Carter East" and "Carter West."

At the time, Paula was playing the ingenue in *Wildcat,* and Lucille Ball refused to give them a wedding present until they moved into one apartment. "Your marriage isn't a real marriage until you live together, you silly kids," she told them. Again, Paula had a tough job convincing him, but they finally gave up their individual apartments and moved into a luxurious eight-room apartment on Central Park West. Carter took one look at the opulent furnishings and snarled, "I hate this crummy joint!"

According to Paula, the reason Carter doesn't like the apartment is because it's on the nineteenth floor and he can't lean out the window and scream at strangers. This is one of the few pleasures he has in life.

One day, he unwillingly accompanied her to the showroom of the company that makes furniture for the White House. Paula selected a blue couch and for once he liked what she had selected. When it was delivered six weeks later, he glared at the inoffensive couch and demanded, "What's this hunk of junk?" Paula reminded him that he had given his okay.

"I don't like it! Send it back!" It reminded him of a couch his family had in the old days when they lived in back of the candy store. After some rather heated words, Paula gave in and sent it back. The following day, Carter went to Bloomingdale's and ordered another blue couch.

"It's almost exactly the same couch, but to this day Jack won't admit it."

Several weeks later in New York I phoned Carter just as he was about to leave for Palm Beach to star in *A Thousand Clowns*. He told me he had fired the public relations firm that represented him and rehired his former press agent, Jack Tirman. I was to get in touch with him for any further biographical material. I phoned Tirman and told him what Carter had said. There was a stunned silence, then Tirman laughed uproariously.

"How do you like that crazy bastard? He never told *me!*"

I met Tirman the following Saturday at the Friars' club. A slender, balding, rapid-talking man, Tirman said Carter had been his most eccentric client. He told me about the time the comic had just concluded a big TV spectacular and scored a personal triumph. "Jack was secure for maybe twenty-five minutes."

Tirman persuaded the TV editor of New York's *Daily News,* the country's biggest newspaper, to interview Carter. They met in Sardi's restaurant. The TV editor told him what a marvelous performance he had given and various show business friends came over to the table to congratulate him. Carter stared at the caricatures of actors on the walls and became increasingly gloomy.

"Jack had just played to something like twenty million people," Tirman explained, "but he was terribly upset because he didn't make the walls at Sardi's."

According to Tirman, Carter is a highly sensitive man who lives in perpetual fear of offending people. "Jack screams at you, and five minutes later, he forgets why. I liked him so much I did publicity for him for nothing even after our contract ran out."

Tirman signaled the waiter for some more coffee. "Worry. That's his middle name. I've seen him on his way to a date in the old days. He'd telephone and make another date for later that same evening, just so he shouldn't be hung up. Once he went out with six different girls in one night. In the middle of a handball game with me, he'd be worrying what he was going to be doing a half-hour after the handball game.

"Jack is a great comedy star," Tirman added, "but that's not enough for him. He wants to be a big dramatic star. But if he ever got to be another Barrymore, say, he wouldn't be happy because he'd want to be another Caruso."

Tirman stopped a plumpish man in his early forties and asked him to sit at our table. "This is Jay Burton, the gag writer. He can tell you a million stories about Jack Carter."

"This is a nut of nuts," Burton said, recalling an occasion ten years ago in Miami when he, Carter and Sid Caesar, another notoriously indecisive personality, felt like having a bite to eat at two A.M.

For fifteen minutes, they couldn't make up their minds whether to take Jack's car or Sid's car or a taxi. Then Burton was seized by inspiration. "Fellas," he said, "I tell you what, let's take Jack's car." Grateful that Burton had made the big decision for them, they all piled into Jack's car and drove off.

"Jack drives around the safety island," Burton recalls, "cursing and screaming like a madman at the other cars. Then he drives right back to the hotel and says, 'I can't take this Miami traffic, let's grab a cab.' They went to six restaurants and never even touched the food. Either they didn't like the looks of the headwaiter or the menu was too fancy or the hatcheck girl was blonde instead of brunette," Burton recalls. "Finally at four o'clock in the morning, they're still arguing about where we should eat and I said the hell with it. I lost my appetite and went to bed."

Tirman told me that Carter enjoyed an exceptionally busy year in 1961. He was booked every week for fifty solid weeks and earned considerable sums of money. During the two free weeks Carter grew increasingly nervous and began to gnaw at his nails. He pestered his agent every day until the latter finally secured him a booking. Carter turned pale at the news.

"My God, I've forgotten how to talk to an audience. I say hello to the people, right? *Then* what do I do?"

When the Carters returned from Palm Beach several weeks later, I met them at the office of Bullets Durgom, the comedian's manager.

I asked Carter how he liked Palm Beach.

"It's a disaster area," he said. "The youngest couple is ninety. Two of them died while the show was on. We didn't tell them because we didn't want to spoil their evening."

At the conclusion of the play, as the audience was filing out, Carter yelled, "Come on back! There's a fourth act!" Carter chuckled. "They couldn't believe their ears. They never heard a play talk back."

He told about introducing actress Penny Fuller to the audience. Miss Fuller, who hails from North Carolina, played the part of Sandy Markowitz from the Bronx. Carter said, "B'nai Brith made her a retroactive Hebrew. She's entitled to twenty-five years of retroactive persecution."

Carter willingly sacrificed a month of lucrative nightclub bookings to work in *A Thousand Clowns* for $2,000 a week. "After taxes and agents and managerial fees, I maybe had a dime left for a cup of coffee, but I was happy."

I asked if he had somebody who watched his money.

"I watch my money," Carter rumbled. "I watch it go."

"I never know what we're going to do any evening until positively the last minute," says Paula. "God forbid I should make plans. Jack *hates* to make plans. Either we have dinner at the corner delicatessen or in Hong Kong, there's no in between."

"We'll be having dinner in Las Vegas next Thursday," Carter said. "I'm booked for six weeks there." He brooded for a moment.

"There's not much dignity in the nightclub world. I have a terrible tendency to put it down myself. I remember we were rehearsing *Mr. Wonderful* and Julie Styne, the producer, said about a certain bit, 'That's no good. That's *nightclub*' like it was a dirty word. Sammy Davis, Jr. who was in the show with me—or rather, I should say I was in the show with him—tore off his jacket and flung it on the floor, he was so mad. For 30 solid minutes, he told poor Julie off about the wonderful heritage of nightclubs, how so many big-time performers have started in nightclubs.

"The trouble is, we all yearn for the legitimate stage because it has prestige. I worked a solid month in *A Thousand Clowns* in Palm Beach for peanuts when I could have made ten times the money in nightclubs . . ."

Carter glowered at me darkly. "That ——— David Merrick knocked me out of a play once just by saying, 'Carter isn't Equity.' You know what he meant, don't you?"

"Let's go somewhere for cocktails," Paula interjected.

"I feel more like seltzer," Carter said.

Carter drinks sparingly and is probably the only performer who wakes up in the morning suffering a hangover without benefit of alcohol. Says Red Buttons, "I've never seen him drunk in my life. He has a mental high going all the time." He enjoys, if that is the proper verb, a simple Spartan breakfast of coffee and self-flagellation. The coffee is almost but not quite as black as his mood and is rarely hot enough to suit him.

One morning, annoyed by his constant carping at the temperature of the coffee, Paula invited him to stick his finger in the cup and test it. Carter's eyes almost popped out of his head as he dipped his finger into the scalding coffee. Manfully restraining a scream of pain, he kept his finger in the coffee and smiled at her nonchalantly.

"See? I told you it wasn't hot enough."

Paula didn't say anything but gazed at his submerged finger, which was slowly but inexorably blistering. Carter held out as long as he could, then pulled his boiled finger out and ran, screaming and cursing, around the house.

I met Carter and Tirman backstage at the Americana Hotel in New York, where he had been booked to play a benefit. Tirman told me that Carter's agent had come up with a $5,000 club date afterwards, but Jack had turned it down. Carter was pacing back and forth backstage, peering out behind the curtain at the waiting audience, muttering and cursing to himself.

"Jack," Tirman said, "it's only a lousy benefit, for God's sake! Not only are you not making a nickel on the deal, you're dropping five gees to boot. Stop aggravating yourself."

Carter ignored him as he peered out from behind the curtain. "Looka that skinny bastard at the front table. He looks like a non-laugher to me . . ."

Tirman was amused. "It's like talking to the wall to tell Jack to stop aggravating himself. That's his only pleasure in life."

We heard the master of ceremonies announce Carter's name. A roar went up from the audience. Carter turned pale, then walked onstage, looking as though he were headed for the electric chair . . .

HOLLYWOOD PUG

● TEDD THOMEY

One punch, a violent left hook to the Adam's apple, changed the life of Jack Palance. Exploding like a bomb, it shattered his throat and his life-long dream of becoming the world's heavyweight boxing champion.

It happened one wild night in March, 1942, at the Ridgewood boxing club in New Jersey, long before Palance thought of trying to bull his way into the acting racket. A crafty veteran of fifty-nine amateur and pro fights, he had been boxing since his early teens in the rough and tumble coal mining towns of eastern Pennsylvania.

As he bounced up and down in his corner, tensely awaiting the first-round bell, Palance heard boos mixed with the cheers the crowd had for him. He knew jeers and boos were a necessary part of the game, but they filled him with quick anger because they were directed at something he couldn't help—his ugly Slavic face.

His nose had been broken so many times it was a flat mass of flesh, one nostril gaping like a gorilla's, the other beaten partly shut. His hazel eyes were small and evil-looking beneath a shelf of scarred, bony brows and his huge jaw looked like a chunk of rock a sculptor should have thrown away.

Because of his ugliness, great menacing size and arrogance in the ring, Palance was regarded as a villian by many of the fans who watched him fight in clubs around Jersey City and New York. They came to his bouts hoping to see him get his head smashed. Palance had frustrated them badly by winning eighteen of his last nineteen fights. He was regarded as a comer by fistic experts who predicted that, with a few good breaks, he could be a leading contender for Joe Louis' crown.

Stung by the boos, 22-year-old Palance rushed out at the

133

bell looking for blood. His opponent was Corky Kelly, a cunning, burly-shouldered bruiser as strong as a Percheron. Both men weighed two hundred pounds, but Palance—six feet four—stood three inches taller than Kelly and had a longer reach. Before the first round was a minute old, Palance had the fair-skinned Irishman bleeding from two deep cuts high on his right cheek.

In the second round Kelly worked in closer, clinching and hammering his big fists into Palance's flat belly. In one of the clinches, Kelly butted Palance. The Irishman's thick, bony skull rammed Palance alongside the jaw, bursting the skin. The crowd yelped with delight as Palance backed up, blood dripping onto his chest.

From that point on the fight was a bloodbath, with both heavyweights covered with gore. Palance, clearly the superior boxer, hacked up the right side of Kelly's face until it resembled a slice of prime rib au jus, rare. Then a crashing right by Palance closed Kelly's left eye. The crowd leaped to its feet and howled as Palance began stalking Kelly from his blind side, preparing to land the finisher.

Desperately Kelly clinched. Once again he butted, his skull catching the tip of Palance's big jaw, tilting his head upward. At the same moment, Kelly brought up his left. It was a scorching hook, aimed at Palance's jaw, but it missed. Instead it struck Palance's momentarily exposed Adam's apple.

It was by no means the best punch of the fight. But it was the luckiest. Palance felt something break in his windpipe. His throat flooded with pain and began to swell shut, affecting his breathing. He got through the rest of the fourth round and then flopped panting onto his stool. He spat out his mouthpiece and began coughing blood.

"Good God!" shouted his corner men. "What's wrong, Jack?"

Palance, unable to talk, gestured at his throat with his glove and kept coughing up blood.

At the start of the fifth, Palance swung with all he had, trying to end the fight quickly. But his best shots missed and he soon ran out of gas, his breath wheezing in his throat. He spat out his bloody mouthpiece, but it didn't help. Unable to get enough air, he was forced to fight defensively, staggering backwards, holding Kelly off with weak thrusts of his arms.

Unaware of what was wrong, the crowd screamed insults at Palance, calling him a quitter and a bum, screaming for

Kelly to kill him. Somehow Palance got through the round, but he was near collapse when he reached his stool. He was bleeding from the nose as well as his mouth. His handlers told him they were going to throw in the towel, but Palance shook his head and wobbled out for the sixth round.

Now the sounds of Palance's torture could be heard clearly above the jeers in the arena. The referee listened to his wheezing for ten more seconds, saw that he was out on his feet and raised Kelly's arm in victory.

The crowd booed Palance as they had never booed him before. They also booed the referee for depriving them of the pleasure of seeing Palance fall, and they booed Kelly for his inability to finish off his opponent.

A ring doctor gave the loser a perfunctory examination and told him his throat would be all right in the morning. After paying off his handlers, Palance had thirty-five dollars left from his seventy-five dollars loser's share of the purse (he would have received four hundred dollars for winning). Dejected and sullen, he hopped a bus and rode from New Jersey to New York, holing up in a decrepit hotel in the Bronx.

Palance stayed alone in his room for a week, going out only for meals, spending the rest of the time pacing nervously or lying tensely on the brokendown bed, trying to decide what to do with the wreckage of his life.

He was scared. Not only because he had lost his voice and his throat pained and burned. He was scared because he realized now what damage a freak punch could cause. One or two more like that one and he would wind up in the condition every fighter dreaded more than death— maimed for life, blind or a punch-drunk idiot shuffling around asking for handouts.

As he sweated it out, the big ugly man didn't realize that his decision would in a roundabout way lead him toward a career as an actor. He never dreamed that some day he would become one of the world's foremost screen villains, projecting an evilness that would make audiences shudder with fear and loathing in theaters throughout the world. There was no way for him to know in 1942 that the punches which had broken and scarred his face would help him earn fame and millions of dollars in such films as *Shane, Sudden Fear* and dozens of others.

Born in 1920 in the small mining town of Lattimer, Pennsylvania, Palance had battled poverty all his life and had gone into prizefighting in a desperate effort to escape the plight of his family. His real name was Walter Jack Palahnuik and he was the son of John and Anna Palahnuik, Slavic immigrants who had come to America from Austria-Hungary in 1908. The Palahnuiks raised five children in the hard coal slums of eastern Pennsylvania, and there were many times during the Depression when the parents went hungry so their offspring would have enough to eat.

Young Jack grew up full of hatred for the coal mining company which kept the Palahnuiks and other townspeople in economic slavery. The Palahnuiks had no property of their own. They lived in a company house, on company land, wore company clothes and ate company food. The symbol of all their troubles was the "snake," the long wavy line on their father's pay slip that meant "no cash." It told them that the family owed more money to the company store than Palahnuik was earning with his backbreaking pick-and-shovel labor in the dark anthracite tunnels underground.

There was no way the family could get ahead. They had to buy at the company store and they kept falling deeper and deeper into debt because the store's prices were higher than elsewhere. When butter was $1.25 in the company store and 87 cents a pound in other groceries, Mrs. Palahnuik didn't dare buy the cheaper butter. If she had, the company's spies would have found out and her husband's job would have been in jeopardy.

Resentment burned like acid within the townspeople. They grew more bitter each time they passed the company store, saw its shelves heaped high with food and felt the pangs of hunger in their bellies. One day word spread that the store had been sold and the new owners were going to jack the prices higher. Muttering and swearing, an angry throng gathered in front of the store. Suddenly someone hurled a chunk of coal through its largest front window.

The sound of shattering glass was the signal which set off two hours of violence. The townspeople stampeded into the store, smashing and looting. They invaded all three stories of the building, acquiring food and clothing valued at $30,000. None of this was ever recovered. The items simply vanished, and the tight-lipped miners refused to discuss the incident with outsiders. The new owners of the store repudiated their purchase, forcing the company to stand the loss. When the miners heard the news, they hooted with glee.

Since his rise to the heights in Hollywood, Palance has told the store-riot story numerous times to close friends. However, when quizzed by reporters, he has declined to give details about his own role in the riot.

Palance, one of the toughest kids in a tough town, grew fast and learned fast. At the age of thirteen, he was six feet tall, a strong rangy youngster with a fiery temper. Interested in all sports, he enjoyed baseball the most. Because of his height and quick hands, he was a standout at first base and behind the plate. The kids of Lattimer scratched out their playing field along the sides of the coal slag piles. When the ball was knocked into the drainage ditch on the south side, all eighteen kids dived into the sooty water to retrieve it because it was the only ball they had.

During a close game one afternoon after school, young Palance—playing catcher—blocked the plate to prevent the tieing run. The runner was a youth four years his senior, a brawny, freckled redhead named Mike. As Mike slid toward the plate, Palance crouched low and upset Mike with a vicious shoulder block that knocked him sprawling on his tail in the black coal dust. Calmly Palance reached down and tagged him out. This made the redhead so mad he leaped to his feet cursing and swinging both fists.

Mike weighed twenty pounds more than Palance, who was all lanky arms and legs. But there was nothing awkward about the way Palance fought. He caught Mike's first punch on his forearm, let the next one slip harmlessly past his ear and then drove in his right. The other kids looked on with awe as Palance's fist hit Mike flush in the mouth, lifted him off his feet and sent him crashing to the ground, where he lay stunned for many moments before being revived.

Word of Palance's one-punch knockout spread throughout the region. It was by no means his first such brawl—he'd been scrapping on back lots for years just for the hell of it—but it brought him to the attention of men who arranged bouts at local smokers. Soon he was invited to participate in his first pro bout. He walked seven miles to the fight in a nearby town and battled to a draw with another tall teen-ager. Pocketing his 95-cent half of the purse, he walked back home again.

The money wasn't much, but even so it was double what he earned per hour laboring in the coal mines during summer vacation. After that he had a lot of bouts, winning most of them. When he told his parents he was thinking of quitting school to follow a boxing career, they were shocked.

"You stick to your books!" thundered his father. "We ain't going to have any dumbheads in this family!"

Palance obeyed, but continued to box occasionally for money. When he was seventeen, he weighed nearly two hundred pounds and was 6 feet 3½ inches tall. His grades in high school at the nearby city of Hazleton were B or better, and he went out for baseball, basketball and football as well as dramatics.

Given the leading role of an attorney in the senior play, he was smitten with his own performance until one of his sisters sent him the following note between acts: "You look terrible. Your socks are falling down."

Much more successful on the athletic fields, he was such a terror playing fullback for Hazleton High that he was named to the All-Regional team and offered twenty scholarships from leading universities, including Fordham and Notre Dame. He finally accepted Georgetown's offer as the most generous. He was, as the local paper said, "signed, sealed and delivered"—until an old friend, Mike Ronman, persuaded him to change his mind. Ronman (christened Zelezniak) was boxing coach at the University of North Carolina.

Blithely Palance went south. During his first scrimmage at North Carolina, he learned that college football was twice as vicious as high school ball. Playing on the freshman team against the varsity, he tried to tackle an onrushing halfback named George Snuffy Sternweiss, who gave him a high knee lift in the face. Sternweiss, later a second baseman for the New York Yankees, delivered the blow so crushingly that he broke Palance's nose. It was the first of five such breaks Palance was to suffer during his athletic career, changing his nose from a prominent, high-ridged model into a flattened wreck.

In his sophomore year, Palance broke his collarbone in a gridiron collision and was benched. Bored and restless, he decided to quit school. When he arrived back in Lattimer, his mother and father were astounded, then angry, finally tearful about his decision. To them a college degree was the key to an entire new world for the son on whom they had pinned such hopes.

But Palance refused to go back because a new ambition had erupted within him. While at North Carolina he had been on the boxing squad, acquiring more finesse with his hands than he'd ever believed possible. He was convinced that he could make more money in a year as a pro boxer than he'd earn in a lifetime as a college grad.

When his collarbone mended, Palance went to Louisville, Kentucky, and trained with Max Novich, who'd been on the boxing team with him at North Carolina. Two months later Palance had his first fight for real money—and won. The purse was $150, earned for just a few minutes' work, triumphant proof that he was on the right track.

He trained furiously. Sometimes he overtrained, but during the next two years he won nearly all his fights. His purses ranged from $200 to $400, but doctor bills, training fees and other expenses chewed up all his profits, keeping him perpetually bankrupt. His nose was broken four times in the ring, requiring expensive surgery. The last time it was flattened, he didn't bother to have it fixed. None of his injuries worried him particularly—until the night he caught that punch in the Adam's apple against Corky Kelly.

Abruptly his philosophy changed from supreme self-confidence to apprehension. For five days after his fight with Kelly he spat blood. He was unable to speak above a whisper and existed on soup because his throat could not tolerate solid foods. When his voice finally returned, it was changed from its usual rasp into a soft, hollow modulation. It was an improvement except in one respect. He had always loved to sing in a chesty baritone. Now he couldn't sing at all.

When he emerged from his Bronx hotel room after being holed up for a week, Palance had made his decision. To hell with boxing. The risks were too great for the financial return, and you had to be as lucky as Aladdin to get a crack at the big championship jackpots. He decided to join the Air Corps as a flier.

In those first months after Pearl Harbor, the nation was building its war machine at a frantic rate. Palance was rushed to an air base in Texas, but before his training began, he was given a second series of medical exams. When the chief physician heard the air whistling through Palance's flattened, twisted nostrils, he was aghast.

"Good Lord!" he exclaimed to an aide. "How did this man ever get in? He sounds like a tire with a fast leak!"

Palance was told that he could not receive final acceptance as a cadet unless he submitted to surgery. Within minutes after he agreed, he was on his way to the hospital where a team of surgeons rebuilt his nose.

When the final bandages were removed ten days later, Palance found that the doctors had given him a nose that was straight and fairly smooth. But from an aesthetic viewpoint it had a peculiar deficiency. It was entirely too small in comparison with his shaggy brows and formidable jaw. It looked as if the doctors had run out of material before finishing it, which was exactly what had happened. Palance's nose had been broken so many times there was not enough bone left to build it up to a normal size.

Palance received six quick weeks of cadet training in Texas, eight in Missouri, eight in Kansas and returned to Texas for final flight instruction crammed into a few more weeks. Twice he was threatened with washing out but came through each final check with a perfect flight. Then he had bad luck. He landed a trainer too hard, smashing a strut. He received a stiff punishment: twenty-five hours of extra marching on the parade ground.

Given one more chance, Palance came through with a flawless landing. He was given his wings and the rank of second lieutenant and sent to David Monathan Field at Tucson, Arizona, for advanced, pre-overseas training on four-motored B-24's, then among the biggest bombers in existence.

Early one morning in November, 1943, he took off toward the pink sunrise at the controls of a bomber, enjoying every moment of lifting the heavy bird into the air. When the plane was about a hundred feet up, the right outboard engine sputtered and died. It was the worst possible moment for such an emergency.

Palance tried to bring the nose level, but the plane went crazy, its port engines pulling it into a spin. A wingtip brushed the concrete landing strip and the plane crashed, crumpling the fuselage, one wing and the landing gear. It did not burn. But as it spun violently about, Palance's head whacked the instrument console. He and the co-pilot, the only other man aboard, were carried unconscious from the wreckage.

Palance spent two months in the hospital while the medics took endless X-ray pictures of his skull. "They seemed to think something was scrambled up," Palance recalled. "Maybe they were right. When I got out of the hospital, I took off in another B-24. I circled around a bit and everything felt fine. Then I started down for the landing. Right before my eyes, the landing strip moved over about a hundred yards—or seemed to. I yelled at the co-pilot and he took over the controls. And that was that."

Palance went back to the hospital for more tests. The doctors shook their heads. On April 2, 1944, a day less than two years after he had enlisted, Palance was mustered out on a medical discharge.

Bitter about his bad fortune, he went home for a few weeks. He worked at a succession of odd jobs and then decided he wanted to be a newspaper reporter. The following year he signed up for courses in journalism under the GI Bill at Stanford University in Palo Alto, California. One of his classes included instruction in all facets of radio work—writing, announcing, producing and acting.

Suddenly Palance discovered he was doing work that brought him enormous personal satisfaction as well as the thrill of unusual accomplishment. Thanks to Corky Kelly's throat blow, Palance's radio voice was exceptional—rich, soft and deep. Stimulated by the praise of his instructor and classmates, he tried out for a part in a college play called *My Indian Family*.

He found the stage even more fascinating than radio. His work was commended by Aline MacMahon, the star of the show and a veteran of Hollywood films and the stage. "Keep on with your acting," she told him. "Work hard and you'll more than get by."

The praise went to Palance's head. Impulsively he decided to quit college, although he needed only one ten-week biology course to obtain the B.A. degree so dearly desired by his parents. Determined to be an actor, he borrowed a hundred dollars from his Phi Beta Kappa roommate and took off for New York, egotistically certain that he could crack the big time on Broadway.

At first he had fantastic good luck. Three days after arriving in New York he heard that Robert Montgomery, ex-screen leading man turned play producer, was casting a stage production called *The Big Two*. With a group of other aspirants, Palance strode into Montgomery's office. Montgomery took one look at the aspirant's scarred face and broad shoulders and declared: "You're my man."

Palance became a husky Russian guard, speaking a few lines and staring about menacingly. But the play folded after a few performances—and Palance began a period of bleak near-starvation. Unable to snag any kind of steady acting work, he did odd jobs around New York during the next eighteen months—short-order cook, waiter and hot dog salesman. The work was menial, the pay was lousy but at least he got enough to eat.

One afternoon he tried selling ice cream bars from a pushcart at Idlewild (now Kennedy Airport). People came up to buy but turned away when they saw his grim, intense face. In an hour he made two sales. Disgusted with himself, he ate a dozen of the bars and turned the rest back in to the distributor, who made him pay for the missing ones. His financial score for the afternoon: Profits—None. Losses—$1.20.

Day after day Palance invaded as many Broadway producers' offices as he could. Finally he acquired a role as a circus strong man in a flopperoo called *Temporary Island,* which lasted seven nights.

After putting in a few weeks as a lifeguard at Jones Beach, he landed the role of Simon Peter in a modern religious play called *The Vigil.* It was a solemn, reverent turkey which collapsed after eleven performances, but Palance received his first good notices. Two critics referred to him as "dynamic."

His reviews attracted the attention of the road company producers of *A Streetcar Named Desire.* They signed him as Anthony Quinn's understudy in the role of Stanley Kowalski, the brooding Pole. His pay was $135 a week, more than double what his father earned in the mines. It was the best regular salary Palance had ever drawn, but there was an annoying drawback: Anthony Quinn was as healthy as a grizzly bear and Palance never got a chance to display his talent. After four months of inactivity, Palance became frustrated and depressed.

He quit in Chicago on a Saturday, arrived in New York jobless on a Sunday and on the same afternoon was hired for the leading role in the Broadway production of *Streetcar.* His good luck resulted from a misfortune which befell the play's star, Marlon Brando, who broke his nose in some offstage horseplay. Palance opened on Monday night.

During his first performance he acquired an intimate introduction to realistic acting. The script called for one of the actors to belt him in the mouth. At rehearsal the blow merely grazed Palance's cheek. But during the performance the other actor, nervous and tense, smashed him so hard that he loosened two of Palance's teeth. Palance reacted instinctively, as he had done so many times in the ring. He went into a crouch and started a haymaker toward the other man's jaw.

"Hold it!" shouted the director frantically from the wings.

Suddenly aware of where he was, Palance stopped the blow in midair. He shook his head to clear it and went on with his role. A few minutes later, still flustered, Palance grabbed one of the actresses harder than he intended. He was so big and his grip so fierce that the actress screamed in fright: "Let me go!"

Palance thought it was a new line put in by the New York company. He didn't know what to say in reply and froze for half a minute, forgetting all his lines. The other actors desperately fed him cues, trying to jar his memory. After what seemed an eternity, he recovered and finished strongly. He stayed in the role for a week, until Brando's return.

Next Palance was selected for the hero in *The Silver Tassie*, a drama by Sean O'Casey about a crippled athlete. His moody but aggressive performance was seen by scouts for Twentieth Century-Fox and he was put under contract for the film, *Panic in the Streets*, in which he portrayed a poisonous character named Blackie. This was the turning point of his career. He made Blackie so menacing and evil that he was quickly signed for two more villainous roles.

In *Shane*, a Western starring Alan Ladd, Palance played the part of Jack Wilson, a black-gloved, soft-voiced gunman who hungered to kill. Although he had only twelve lines to speak, Palance dominated the film so effectively with his chilling evilness that he received a nomination for an Academy Award. He received another nomination for his work in *Sudden Fear*, in which he portrayed a cruel, ambitious husband who would do anything—even murder—to get his way.

David Miller, director of the picture, took special pains with lights and camera to make Palance look handsome in the early reels. About the middle of the shooting, Palance heard Miller tell the cameraman: "From here on make him look awful. Shoot him as he really is."

After laboring five long years in New York to learn the acting trade, Palance was touted as Hollywood's newest "overnight sensation." In New York his stage salaries had been so haphazard he was in and out of debt with monotonous regularity. After two years in Hollywood his price per picture shot to $100,000 and he bought a $65,000 mansion in Beverly Hills.

Capitalizing on his ugliness, the studio's publicity mills began grinding out phony stories about how his features had been burned beyond recognition in his World War II plane crash and that Air Corps plastic surgeons had built him an entirely new face.

One official movie biography declared that, when he awoke in the Air Corps hospital and found his face destroyed, "he wanted to die until psychiatrists convinced him that life still offered him something special." It added that he had countless "delicate operations" and the "nightmare of losing one face and getting another had its disastrous effect on his personality, turning him into a strangely maladjusted man."

In interviews with the press, Palance angrily denied the studio allegations, declaring that he had never had plastic surgery or psychiatric treatment. His explanation that he had undergone simple nose operations to correct damage incurred in prizefighting was ignored by the studio publicity hounds, who continued to build him up as a sadistic character.

Meanwhile studio chiefs cast him in a flock of films in which he played an assortment of malicious, psychopathic evildoers, with camera angles chosen to emphasize his narrow, glittering eyes and the stark bones of his thin face. He portrayed Attila the Hun, Jack the Ripper, a murderous Apache, a gangster and such weirdies as Cagliostro, a deadly Italian alchemist, and Simon the Magician, who attempted to set up a cult in opposition to the disciples of Christ.

Television producers, however, saw other qualities in Palance. In CBS' Playhouse 90, he had his first major sympathetic role, that of Mountain McClintock, doomed prizefighter in *Requiem for a Heavyweight*. Drawing on his own experiences in the ring, Palance gave a performance so moodily tragic that he received an Emmy as television's best actor in 1956.

In another Playhouse 90 production, however, he did not fare as well. Cast as a dying film producer in F. Scott Fitzgerald's *The Last Tycoon*, Palance portrayed a soulful man of gentle manners and elegant clothes. The audience refused to accept Palance in a role with so little physical violence and the show's reviews were poor.

But Palance had developed such a taste for refinement

and restraint in his acting that he refused to do any more villainous roles. This precipitated rousing battles with his studios and personal representatives. Unable to get the parts he wanted, Palance told Hollywood to shove it, packed his bags and flew to Europe.

His abrupt move also had a second motivation: His marriage to redheaded actress Virginia Baker, whom he had wed in New York in 1949, was coming unglued at the seams and he wanted escape from domestic strife. In a divorce suit filed in Santa Monica in 1957, she charged that Palance, brooding about his failing career, drank to excess and beat her. The actor denied all the charges and filed a counter-suit.

Palance settled in the American-Swiss colony of Lausanne, Switzerland, and began looking about for sensitive, artistic roles. None were available to him, despite the fact that Europe was booming with film activity. Choking on his pride, he accepted the same melodramatic parts he had spurned in Hollywood.

He reconciled with his wife, who brought their three small children to Europe to visit him, but he refused to return to Hollywood. He made two pictures in Italy which he detested, battling temperamentally with the directors of both. After that he refused to work for eighteen months, waiting for better parts. None were offered.

Finally he was forced into such miserable epics as *Universal Judgment* and *Sword of the Conqueror*. The latter, released in September, 1962, was a gory Italian costume hodgepodge with an illogical story and remarkably poor dubbing. It was ridiculed by American critics. In 1963 Palance made *The Ghost at Noon*, a frothy farce with Brigitte Bardot, and then—totally disillusioned with Europe's film makers—he returned to California.

The lure which brought Palance back to Hollywood after a six-year absence was an offer to star in a major TV series and enjoy a percentage of its profits. The series, *The Greatest Show on Earth*, consisted of hour-long color dramas about circus life with Palance portraying Johnny Slate, tough, driving boss of the big top. When filming began, the show's producers and the ABC television network were certain it couldn't miss. But it turned out to be one of the biggest failures of the '63-'64 season.

Week after week, it was beset with critical story problems, caused partly by the fact that Palance was relegated to the sidelines while guest stars dominated the big scenes.

A few of the plots were dramatically excellent, but the majority were so dull and contrived that critics panned the series from coast to coast. Even worse were the show's financial woes. From the first week on, it catapulted ridiculously high over its budget, the thirty episodes eventually costing $1,100,000 more than anticipated. Palance came out of it very well financially, drawing a salary of over five thousand dollars a week, but the show's backers were plunged into a hole from which recovery was impossible.

While assembling the material for this article on Palance, I visited the Desilu Studios in Culver City, near Hollywood, to watch him work. By chance I arrived on the circus set the morning word was passed that the series was being cancelled. Gloom hung within the huge sound stage like a black thundercloud. Grips, electricians and other technicians stood around in small groups shaking their heads sadly.

While the cameras turned, Palance shouted orders through a megaphone at the circus' train crew, but his heart wasn't in it. When the scene ended, Palance stood by himself, tall and aloof, waiting for the cameras to be set up for the next shot. As I approached him, I remembered the warning one of his staff assistants had given me a few minutes earlier: "Jack's pretty glum this morning, so maybe you better not ask him any questions about the show being cancelled."

Palance smiled briefly at me. He looked every bit of his forty-four years, deep lines of tension and fatigue showing around his mouth and extremely deep-set eyes.

When I asked him a probing question about his boxing career, he shook his head, indicating coldly that he didn't want to talk about it any more.

"Why not?" I persisted.

"It's all history now," he said. "It doesn't mean anything any more."

"Are you ashamed of having been a boxer?"

"Of course not," he snapped. "Boxing was good for me. There were times when I was confused, when I didn't know why I was fighting. But for the most part it was a form of expression for me. I couldn't express myself mentally in those days, couldn't put my feelings into words. So I had to express myself physically. Boxing let me do that. Later I found other ways of expressing myself."

"I've heard that you were good," I said. "I've heard it

said that if your throat hadn't been smashed you might have been a top heavyweight."

He shook his head firmly. "Not a chance. I wasn't that good. I was just a club fighter. But one night, long after I quit fighting, I ran into a fellow who made me think I might have been a little better than I thought I was.

"It was the last place on earth I expected to meet another boxer. It was at the Metropolitan Opera in New York about eight years ago. While my wife and I were in the lobby during intermission, this fellow came up and stared at me. He was a middle-aged man but I could tell by the way he stood there, rocking back and forth a little, that he had been a fighter."

Palance demonstrated the man's stance, lifting his arms slightly like a boxer waiting for the bell to ring.

"The old pros always stand this way," he explained. "Instinct, I guess. Anyway, he looked me over carefully and he said: 'I saw you fight back in the forties. You were damned good. I would have liked to fight you myself.' Then he stuck out his hand and introduced himself. He was Gene Tunney."

Palance grinned with satisfaction. "I'd never met him before. And I never knew he watched any of my fights. If I'd known he was there I might have tried a lot harder."

After the *The Greatest Show on Earth* was finished, Jack Palance rested unhappily in his Beverly Hills mansion, devoting himself to his hobbies of reading classical literature and listening to recordings of classical music. When major film producers failed to beat a path to his door with offers of lucrative new roles, Palance decided to turn over a new leaf.

In a Hollywood trade paper, *The Reporter*, he revealed that he had directed the last episode of *The Greatest Show on Earth* as well as starring in it. He announced that it was his first attempt at directing—and his last. "Every actor should have a chance to direct," he said. "Just once. It will teach him to stick to his own trade, acting."

Declaring that he now had a better understanding of the problems of directors and producers, Palance declared candidly—and with surprising humility—that he had been unwise and immature in the past. He vowed to be more cooperative and less temperamental in his dealings with directors and producers.

His statements produced much head-shaking in the industry. The experts respected his efforts to change his stripes, but doubted that he would succeed. They were aware that Palance owed his success to the very elements of his personality that often made him so hard to live with on the set—his burning ego and explosive temperament, qualities which added strength and depth to his screen portrayals.

"Take those qualities from Palance," commented former Producer Robert Nesbitt, "and there would be nothing left. He would be just another ham actor going through the motions. He'll be far better off if he keeps on being the real Palance, hard to live with, hard to work with—but genuine."

Not all producers and directors would agree. Many who have worked with him have given in too easily to his demands, unwilling to risk a perilous temperamental outburst like the one Palance demonstrated in Santa Monica on September 6, 1957.

It happened in a corridor outside the courtroom where Mrs. Palance's suit for separate maintenance was being heard. Half a dozen photographers clustered near the doorway, hoping to get a picture of the actor when he arrived to give testimony.

Suddenly he stomped into the hallway, broad shoulders swinging, his legs taking long strides. The photographers turned and aimed their lenses at him.

Palance scowled, his big jaw set angrily and he released a torrent of obscenities.

"You dirty bastards!" he said. "I'll break those goddam cameras!"

Standing closest to Palance was 45-year-old George O'Day, a short, slight photographer for the Los Angeles *Herald-Express*. Palance glared at him and said: "You little ----! That goes for you too!"

O'Day waited until Palance had swept a few feet past him. Then he raised his camera and called: "Jack!"

Palance turned around. Seeing O'Day ready to shoot, he exploded with rage. In his right hand he carried a heavy bound script, more than two inches thick. As O'Day snapped his lens, Palance hurled the script. It sailed like a discus, striking O'Day in the chest and nearly knocking him off his feet.

"You son of a bitch!" shouted Palance. "I'll break every ----- bone in your body!"

Seizing O'Day by the lapels of his coat, he lifted him off his feet and jammed him up against the wall. But O'Day—eight inches shorter than his tall opponent and outweighed by sixty pounds—refused to be cowed.

Clutching his large Speed Graphic with both hands, he shoved it close to Palance's face and barked: "Let me go or I'll let you have this right in the kisser!"

Abruptly Palance realized how ludicrous the scene was. He lowered O'Day back to his feet. Then, without saying another word, he turned and strode into the courtroom.

Palance's quick moments of black fury later cost him $4,000—the amount he paid O'Day to settle the photographer's suit out of court.

The incident was not of major significance. It had no effect on Palance's career. But it showed what could happen to a proud ex-boxer after a few years of fighting tinsel tigers in the Hollywood jungle.

HOLLYWOOD MISFIT

• ARNOLD HANO

Somebody once called Marlon Brando the "prince of all screwballs . . . one of the foremost eccentrics of all time."

The eccentricity of Marlon Brando—like the oddness of painter Paul Gauguin or poet François Villon—is the insistence of an artist that he be judged not by his personal habits, but by his work. That his private life be his own.

Unfortunately, Brando has sometimes lived his private life so publicly and violently that the onlooker could hardly avoid noticing the only actor in the world at whom you must look down to verify that he is indeed wearing shoes.

Many film executives think Brando is the greatest actor in the world. Yet if he were to disappear tomorrow, he'd be equally remembered by movieland insiders as the oddball who came to Hollywood with one suit in his valise, and that with a hole in the knee and a rip in the seat. Just as Gauguin is remembered as the man who left his wife for the *wahines* of Tahiti, and Villon as the man who pimped when he was down and out.

With Brando it is worse. Neither Gauguin nor Villon were at the mercy of gossipists and their tens of millions of readers.

Like other misfits, Marlon Brando does not have the knack of accepting his lot, and yielding to it gracefully. When a simpering columnist asked Brando about his personal habits, he said he showered by spitting in the air and running under it. In an interview with Hedda Hopper, Brando's only contribution was two grunts.

Nor is Brando totally innocent. He has in the past gone out of his way to play the role of the oddball, the outsider. He walked a pet raccoon on a leash in Hollywood. He held a freshly laid egg while shaking hands with an important film executive. Straight-faced, he announced his engagement to Denise Darcel, whom he barely knew. He fell asleep while appearing on Wendy Barrie's TV show. (When he finally woke, and Miss Barrie asked him the title of his next movie, he mumbled: "I forget.")

This is Marlon Brando. A man who desperately wants to be left alone. A man who would very much like to be judged purely by his work—and then who will say airily of a past role that has been widely acclaimed: "It stinks."

Nor did it all begin with artistic success. There is a snapshot of Brando, aged thirteen, with his two sisters, Jocelyn and Frances. In the picture, Marlon and Frances are thumbing their noses at each other. All that has changed is that Brando's nose has since been broken, and his target is now society; the hand is still firmly in place.

Even before the snapshot, when Brando was a fifth-grader in Evanston, Illinois, he tied boyhood friend Wally Cox to a fencepost at night and left him there for hours.

And before that, Brando owned a pet chicken. When it died, the family respectfully buried the pet. Brando dug it up. The family buried it once more. Brando dug it up again.

The streak is long and wide and stubborn. Marlon

Brando almost graduated from two schools; twice he was expelled instead.

Brando once kept this writer waiting on the set for seven hours for an interview that had been scheduled by Paramount Pictures and confirmed by Brando's press agent and by the actor himself. Then sometime after midnight the actor said he was sorry, but it would have to wait for another time. This left the writer no choice but to motor home, fifty-five miles away, through a driving rain. (The next time Brando was as gracious as a man could possibly be, although his first words were: "Your fly is open," which surely is the epitome of a kettle calling a pot black.)

There is something inside the man that keeps derailing him. He means well. For a man who once earned the nickname of "The Slob," Brando can also be a man of fine manners and great kindness. Once he and a friend went to a play in Harlem. As Brando walked toward the entrance, an old woman asked the actor for a handout. The theater doorman rudely shoved the woman off. Brando whirled, grabbed the doorman by the lapels, and said with undisguised, thin-lipped menace: "Don't ever do that again!"

Yet during the shooting of a scene in *One-Eyed Jacks,* a stunt man dangled upside down by one leg while director Brando meditated on his next scene and forgot all about him until the man came close to passing out.

For a person who apparently does not give a fig for his public, his critics, and for many of his contemporaries in Hollywood, he is also painfully sensitive to criticism and broods over what is said of him in print. When this writer approached Brando for an interview for a national magazine three years ago, Brando and Paramount consented to the story, but only if it was agreed beforehand that nothing pertaining to Brando's personal life be discussed, that Brando would retain the right to censor the article in whole or in part, and that the writer could not turn around and sell an unauthorized article to a movie-fan magazine.

This is, of course, the price of fame, this thrusting of an individual into the public's eye, where every time he belches the echo finds its way into print. Other actors manage to live with it; some—probably because actors are usually frustrated people, and frustrated people like to talk—even enjoy discussing their private lives with interviewers. I sat in the dressing room of a star once while he and his wife discussed a trial separation in front of me; it was the first time I had ever seen either of them.

Not Brando. Yet he must have known—from the start —that thumbing his nose was going to get him more publicity than a dozen carefully arranged and hoked-up press-agent stunts. Back in the 1940's, when Brando appeared before Alfred Lunt and Lynn Fontanne to read for a possible part, the young actor turned tongue-tied, didn't know what to say.

"Just say anything," Lunt suggested kindly.

"Hickory-dickory-dock," Brando blurted, and walked out—certainly aware that his "exit" would travel the rounds of theatrical people.

Another time Brando read for a part in Noel Coward's *Present Laughter*. After his eye raced down a page of the frothy comedy, Brando threw the script to the floor and snarled at the playwright: "Don't you know there are people starving in the world?" Yet Brando surely knew not to expect social significance in a Coward play.

In Brando's brownstone apartment in Manhattan's west Fifties, where he lived at the time, a large sign was nailed to the wall: "YOU AIN'T LIVIN' IF YOU DON'T KNOW IT." Despite an addiction to such necessities as midnight bongo drums, tootling a recorder, and throwing paper bags of water down on passersby coming out of the jazz clubs, one wonders whether Brando really knew anything about livin', and that there really were people starving in the world.

Yet it must be emphasized: success did not spoil Marlon Brando. Whatever it is was always there.

The actor was born in Omaha, Nebraska, on April 3, 1924, the youngest of three children and the only son of Marlon Brando, Senior, and Dorothy Pennebaker Brando. The elder Brando was a successful executive of a chemical products company. Brando's mother was the artist of the family, a community-theater actress and director (who aspired to more than local stages, and who directed Henry Fonda's first stage role, in Omaha).

Brando's relationship with his mother may provide some insight into the actor—some understanding of why tragedy, or at least pathos, has triggered Brando's adult behavior.

Over sips of vodka in the Miyako Hotel in Kyoto,

Japan, during the shooting of *Sayonara* in 1957, Brando told author Truman Capote: "My mother was everything to me. A whole world. I tried so hard. I used to come home from school. There wouldn't be anybody home. Nothing in the icebox. Then the telephone would ring. Somebody calling from some bar. And they'd say, 'We've got a lady down here. You better come get her.'"

So Brando would bring his mother home. Then—again to Capote—Brando recounted another episode involving his mother: ". . . one day I didn't care any more. She was there. In a room. Holding on to me. And I let her fall. Because I couldn't take it any more—watch her breaking apart, in front of me, like a piece of porcelain. I stepped right over her. I walked right out. I was indifferent . . ."

Much of the anecdote rings discordantly, is not to be taken literally. For example, an empty icebox in a house of upper middle-class comfort—with at least two full-time servants!

When Brando was seventeen and in high school in Illinois, he poured a pint of hair tonic along a school corridor and doused a classroom wall with it. Then he printed a dirty word in the goo, put a match to the tonic and charred the epithet.

Expelled from high school, Brando was sent to Shattuck Military Academy in Minnesota, a place he has always referred to as "the asylum." Here Brando found himself antagonistic to the academy's regimented ways, symbolized by a church bell that rang every quarter-hour. One night Brando climbed the tower, removed the bell clapper, and buried it. He wasn't expelled for this prank, but when he emptied the contents of chamber pot from a dormitory window, coincidentally with someone's passing below, he was promptly ousted.

Brando was bailed out of this life by his father, who offered his son whatever money he would need to learn a profession. Nineteen-year-old Brando took the money and, in 1943, went to New York to enroll in the Dramatic Workshop of the New School for Social Research. There he studied acting under such talented people as Erwin Piscator and Stella Adler. Miss Adler, after a week, said "this puppy thing" might within a year be "the finest young actor in America."

After diverse parts in such plays as *I Remember Mama,* Maxwell Anderson's *Truckline Cafe,* and Shaw's *Candida* (Brando has always been an actor of extreme versatility, despite the rather widely-held contention that he can play only one note, and that in a mumble), Brando received word to try out for a role in a new Tennessee Williams play, *A Streetcar Named Desire*.

It is typical of Brando that he was without a dime in his jeans at the time and that he had to hitchhike to Williams' Cape Cod home to read for Elia Kazan, Williams, and producer Irene Selznick. He arrived at six in the morning, found the lights knocked out by a storm, fixed them himself. He also got the part, borrowed bus fare back to New York—and Brando, at a salary that soon reached $550 a week, was a zooming star. Coincidentally, he began to undergo psychoanalysis.

In this early period, Brando and his old buddy, Wally Cox, shared a Manhattan flat whose door was always open, and through which traipsed a bewildering stream of variegated characters on the fringe of show business, and other assorted down-and-outers. There was always something cooking, from fencing lessons to bongo-and-recorder sessions; in one corner there'd be a chess game, and in another a girl dancing with herself or a guy trying out his night-club act to a wall. And always, a phonograph blaring, or a radio, or both.

Once Cox and Brando decided to paint the flat. They did one wall, and then, as actress Shelley Winters recalls it, left the other walls undone so that for a year people had to stop over and around the debris of paints, brushes and canvas that mingled with fencing rapiers and Cox's silversmithing equipment and Brando's raccoon (who finally drove off Cox when he chewed out the seat of Wally's pants).

It was at this time that Brando also donned the black leather uniform of a delinquent motorcyclist, and his behavior started to become fairly steady copy. One day in March of 1949, Brando and his cycle were stopped by a policeman in Times Square. Not only did Brando have no license or registration on him, but when he searched his pockets for identification, out fell a sheaf of unanswered parking summonses. It was the first, but not the last trip Brando has made to court.

Romantically, Brando—whose sex appeal has always been so obvious that he was once described as a walking factory of male hormones—dated mostly non-show-biz girls, with a decided preference for hash-house waitresses and office secretaries. This also was not new; his grandmother had once reported that Marlon invariably brought home the cross-eyed girls back in Illinois.

Brando also began to show a taste for dark, exotic types—girls with Latin eyes and foreign accents. He has always held blondes in disdain.

But mainly the company Brando kept was more like a king's court or a mogul's gang of yes-men and hangers-on. The hanging-on was to Brando's liking; he was, as he himself put it, duke of his domain. As such, he gave advice freely. Once he told a friend: "Nobody should be poor. If I were you, I'd go out and steal."

Brando craved his court-jesters, his sycophants, his unquestioning admirers. Once he said: "If there are two hundred people in a room and one doesn't like me, I've got to get out." So maybe it has been fear all along, fear and a deep-seated inferiority complex, that has driven Brando on his lonely nonconformist road.

Love me, he may be screaming, love me the way I am; love me any way I am: dirty, rude, odd. Because if Brando could be accepted in cold-water flats amidst clutter and debris, if he could be accepted while belching and scratching his way through life, if people could like him despite insults and torn suits, then it was proof what a great guy he *really* was, down deep inside.

And while he tested his friends and coaxed them into his web, all of it made exciting copy; Brando was a legend in the making. One night, while doing *Streetcar Named Desire* on Broadway, Brando stepped to the lip of the stage and told a noisy female to keep quiet. During rehearsals, he would go down to a basement room below the stage and box with members of the cast and stagehands.

Brando, who stands five-foot-ten and weighs 170 pounds when he successfully diets, sometimes takes his boxing too seriously. In one sparring session, he had his nose broken. (The result, oddly, pleased producer Irene Selznick: "Before, he was just too beautiful. The broken nose gave him his sex appeal.")

Brando found his privacy disturbed by innumerable, probing interviewers, and to amuse himself, he said on different occasions that he had been born in Calcutta, Bombay, Rangoon, Bangkok and Mindanao. With considerable relish and a sense of the "theatrical," he told how he ate grasshopper legs and gazelle eyes. "The natives in the Belgian Congo," he exulted, "take the gazelle eyes and mash them into a paste. They're delicious."

More discerning reporters discovered, closer to the truth, that Brando's breakfast consisted of a raw egg or two sucked out of the shell and taken standing up to save time, washed down with juice.

But it wasn't until Brando made the plunge in 1949 and went to Hollywood with his single torn suit that the legends took on mammoth proportions. Brando's first film was *The Men,* a study of paraplegics. The actor entered a Veteran's Administration hospital outside Los Angeles for a few weeks to enable him to portray the role honestly.

One day, while in a wheelchair, Brando and a few of his paraplegic friends wheeled to a nearby bar for a quick one. (There is a usually accepted rumor that Brando neither drinks nor smokes; he does both, although on occasion he breaks the smoking habit briefly.) A female crackpot came over to the group—all of them real paraplegics, except Brando—and told them what a noble sacrifice they had made. She launched into an evangelistic song-and-dance, with attendant promised miracles in some vague future.

As she reached her crescendo, Brando suddenly started to grip the arms of his wheelchair with shaking hands, his eyes burning with fervor, sweat breaking out on his forehead. As the woman watched, open-mouthed, the actor tottered to his feet, then suddenly broke into a buck-and-wing. The woman screamed and fainted, and the paraplegics applauded madly.

Wherever he lived in and around Hollywood (Columnist Lee Belser once said that home, to Brando, "was not a palace, but just a place to hang his torn T-shirt"), the actor quickly got into the habit of greeting visitors in his underwear. This was Brando's great anti-Hollywood crusade—a crusade, incidentally that has been muted the past few years. Then it was a passionate battle between an actor described by Theodore Strauss as "part mud-spattered child, part genius . . . a harlequin who has not been housebroken," and the movie colony which Brando sneered at as a "cultural boneyard."

When a columnist gushed: "Why, you look just like everybody else!" Brando stalked to a corner of the room and stood on his head. He walked his pet raccoon, Russell, on a leash, and when asked what was next on the agenda, he'd drawl: "Next? I'm going down to the Ozarks, with Russell, and hide."

His brusqueness, which some translated as rudeness, was classic. He scratched whatever itched him whenever he felt like it. He picked his nose when talking with people he didn't like (and they were legion). When some fans stared at him in a restaurant, he picked up the salt and pepper shakers, held them to his eyes like binoculars, and stared back.

While officially engaged to Josanna Mariani-Berenger, nineteen-year-old daughter of a French fisherman, he was dating Rita Moreno. For one date with La Moreno, he arrived in his windbreaker; she was dressed to kill. For an appearance at an informal set party, he showed up in white tie and tails.

Sometimes he'd answer the phone in falsetto, pretending to be the maid. Other times he'd just let it ring.

But despite the high jinks, he had lapses of depression, showed evidence of acute sensitivity. He wept unashamedly during the movie *Wizard of Oz*, then dried his tears on the cheek of his date. One of the girls he squired at the time said later: "Why, he does things to you in public you wouldn't even expect in private!"

He painted black mustaches on statues in public parks. He rode his motorcycle all over town, and once to a bar in a disreputable section of east Los Angeles, where the cops showed up and insisted that Brando roll up his sleeve before he could convince them he wasn't on dope.

He drove his car at excessive speeds, squinting painfully through the windshield because he was and is nearsighted and had already mislaid or broken eight pairs of glasses. A friend spotted him racing down Hollywood Boulevard with his head hanging out the car window, mouth wide open, and the next day called Brando to ask if he had been ill. "No," Brando said happily, "I was drinking in the wind."

He took off for New York on a few occasions, once to study conversational French at the New School. This caused producer Stanley Kramer to say in astonishment: "Why, he doesn't even speak conversational English!" An executive at Fox toted up the items on the Brando dossier and said: "The only good thing you can say about this twerp is that he doesn't like marijuana."

In 1951, Brando went to Del Rio, Texas, to make *Viva Zapata!* He arrived, again, without a cent, outfitted in jeans, sneakers and toting the usual supply of T-shirts.

When Brando wasn't exploding firecrackers in hotel lobbies, doing Yoga exercises on hotel lawns, practicing running broad-jumps into swimming pools or taking walks between courses of meals, he was borrowing everything from money to dress shirts. (Brando scrupulously never forgets a debt.)

A battle. A raging one-man fight to maintain himself, to find himself, or to do something—anything—in the face of a film colony united against him.

But the films were made, and Brando the actor could do no wrong, although a tiny, stubborn, holdover group kept referring to a mumble (in parts that called for a mumble) and didn't realize there was no mumble when the role was Antony or Napoleon. And nobody ever could criticize Brando on the set. Always on time, always ready, never causing endless takes, a model of concentrated consecrated talent. Not yet thirty-one, he won an Academy Award in 1955 for his emoting in *On the Waterfront*, becoming the youngest actor ever to win an Oscar. Three other times he was nominated for the coveted award.

Behind it all, behind the snarling war and the clatter of his life and the pouring out of himself under paints and hot lights, something else was happening. The sporadic sessions of psychoanalysis, begun over five years earlier, had not seamed the jagged rips in Brando's psyche. The problem—whatever it was—worsened in 1953 when Brando's mother died; then the failure of that relationship became final and irrevocable.

About this time, Twentieth Century-Fox signed Brando for a role in *The Egyptian*. On the first day of shooting, early in 1954, with everybody on the lot waiting for the always prompt Brando, the producers received a wire from a New York psychiatrist, Dr. Bela Mittelmann. The telegram revealed that Brando was under the doctor's care back East, "a very sick and mentally confused boy."

Fox sued for two million dollars. The process server handed Brando the summons by announcing first through a closed door that he was a messenger who had come to tell the actor he had just been nominated for an Academy Award for his work as Antony. The case was later settled when Brando agreed to make *Desiree* for Fox, and Brando is said to have later exclaimed triumphantly: "I copped a medical plea!"

Yet despite Brando's sound artistic grounds for turning

down the role ("A camel opera," he called it. "Who can play opposite fifty thousand camels?"), Brando was in rough shape, a casualty in a war he had helped bring on, bucking America's greatest aristocracy, and aggravated by his own personal tragedies, unspoken then, unspoken today.

The analysis went on. Finally, in 1957, he said guardedly that the past eight years of his life had been a mess, but that the most recent two years were better, and that analysis had been of considerable help.

Brando was finally learning that his crusade would not change the movie colony; he was learning to live with and to adapt to the conditions of his life. And almost as though it had been Cinderella's tattered garb, the rudeness, and unkempt appearance, disappeared. Today, whatever unorthodoxy exists is usually under control, and purposeful.

On the set of *One-Eyed Jacks,* for example, young, untried actress Pina Pellicer was having trouble keeping a tentative, polite smile on her face in a scene in which she greeted Brando—a stranger—and said to him: "You are waiting for my father?"

In order to hold her smile, Brando—with the camera on the girl—said from offstage: "Yes, he went upstairs to sit on the toilet." It was not vulgarly said, but almost apologetically, and the smile on Miss Pellicer's face was exactly right.

Not that Brando today is over his miseries. His problem, if anything, seems deeper, more vital than the tomfoolery of painting mustaches on statues, or driving too fast. In short order, Brando has twice married, twice fathered sons, and twice been divorced. This is surely not the sign of growing equability. Yet it may be a sign of some maturity, this willingness, at last, to attempt to share his life with another person.

More than four years ago Brando discussed his need to be married: "You've got to have love," he said. "There's no other reason for living. Men are no different from mice. They're born to perform the same function. Procreate. What other reason is there for living except love?" He candidly admitted, "That has been my main trouble. My inability to love anyone."

On October 11, 1957, he married Anna Kashfi. Seven months later to the day, a son, Christian Devi, was born. The Brandos had, by that time, already broken up. Then in June of 1961, while engaged in a seemingly endless court wrangle with Miss Kashfi over custodial rights and back alimony, Brando revealed he had again married and again fathered a son and again been divorced—all within a year's time. This time the woman was Maria Louisa Castenada—a Latin actress known as Movita, almost ten years older than Brando.

Procreation, obviously, is not the answer for Brando. It hasn't worked. Marriage, for the actor, has just been another battlefield. And once again, the answer is not in Hollywood or Times Square, or on a hot speeding motor-cycle. Back from the past come the words of Brando's longest, oldest friend, Wally Cox.

"He always had to battle his way home," Cox recalls from their grade-school days in Illinois. "Brando would run along, poking an imaginary revolver at foes who lurked behind rocks, behind trees." And speaking of the countless times Brando has beaten Cox at chess: "He always had to win, at everything."

Perhaps when Brando learns—finally—you can't win at everything, there'll be some peace of mind. Meanwhile, it's been a war that only a brave and lonely man could have waged this long: cruel and sapping. And the feeling grows stronger that Brando will soon pocket for good that imaginary revolver, that the foes will disappear, and that he will have battled his way home, at last.

HOLLYWOOD SUICIDE

• TEDD THOMEY

Something disturbed her. She awoke with a start, her large eyes darting wildly around the hospital-like room.

She couldn't remember her name. Was she Frances Gumm or Judy Garland or three other people? And where was she? In a Los Angeles hospital or that other one in Boston?

She heard it again. The noise which had awakened her. The sound of someone snooping through her things, opening and closing drawers in the metal bureau on the other side of the room. Turning over in bed, she glanced nervously at the bureau and saw a woman in a white uniform lifting handkerchiefs and lingerie, searching for something she believed was hidden in the room.

"What are you doing?" she said.

The nurse did not reply or even bother to look at her.

"Why are you going through my things?" she asked, and now, recognizing the sound of her own voice—a famous voice known to millions of people—she remembered who she was. Judy Garland. She had been Judy Garland for years and years. And she was sick and very, very tired.

But she wasn't in a hospital. This place only looked like a hospital. It was really a sanitarium. And the woman who looked like a nurse was really a psychiatric technician. And she came snooping like this every morning at the intolerable hour of five o'clock, looking for hidden liquor or razor blades or dope. Which was ridiculous, of course, because patients had no way of getting their hands on such things.

"Go away," Judy said. "I'm so tired. Why won't you let me sleep?"

Ignoring her, the technician snooped through the remaining bureau drawers. Finding nothing, as usual, she turned and walked silently toward the door.

"Can't you even say good morning?" asked Judy. "Or even goodby?"

The technician shook her head primly and went out, closing the door soundlessly behind her.

The woman in the bed closed her eyes and tried to go back to sleep. But now she was too nervous and anxious. All her worries were reawakened, swimming about in her mind like blind fish at the black bottom of the sea. Was she crazy, as some people said? Was Judy Garland finally finished as a singer, actress, mother, wife? She had been in institutions like this before, but each time she had improved and gone back to what she loved most, singing before thousands of people who loved her as much as she loved them.

Would she be able to do that again? Would she again be able to earn a quarter of a million dollars a year, live like a queen in the finest hotels and apartments, her treasured voice making her the toast of New York, Hollywood and Europe? Or would she spend the rest of her days and nights in torment, locked away in institutions where doctors and technicians would struggle to keep her from taking her own life?

Hearing another sound, she opened her eyes and saw three doctors standing at the foot of her bed. How long had they been there? And why did people have to move so silently, so mysteriously in this hellish place?

"What time is it?" she asked. "Is it still morning?"

"Yes," said one of the doctors. "It's a little after nine. How are you feeling this morning?"

"Lousy."

"We're very sorry to hear that." The doctor pursed his lips sympathetically and consulted some papers in his hand. "We've been making a survey of your case, Miss Garland, and we'd like to ask you a few questions. Do you mind?"

"Go ahead."

"First, do you see things?"

"See things? What do you mean? What kind of things?"

"Well, little things—that crawl or fly?"

"What?"

She sat up angrily in bed and began shouting at the doctors. "How dare you come in here and ask me things like that! Stop treating me like a nut! I'm here for a rest! I'm exhausted! So get out, all three of you! Get out and let me rest!"

She pointed at the door. She knew she looked a fright, her hair disheveled, her face pale and puffy. And it was a mistake to throw a tantrum because it probably meant they would try to keep her here weeks and weeks longer. But she didn't care. She kept shouting until the three doctors retreated.

Then she fell back onto her blankets and wept without pause for more than an hour.

Similar incidents have occurred many times during the tumultuous life of Judy Garland, who was first placed in a sanitarium when she was twenty-five years old and an over-worked movie star. Now forty-two, and a veteran of endless trips in and out of various institutions, she is easily the film world's most celebrated, beloved and tormented personality.

For years her strange behavior patterns, including the allegedly prolonged use of drugs and booze, were kept secret by a conspiracy among her studios, ex-husbands and business associates. Finally the truth, perhaps igniting from spontaneous combustion like oily rags hidden in a closet, could no longer be concealed and Judy Garland was revealed as a hapless neurotic kept alive by therapy and pills.

Since her first nervous breakdown in 1947, Judy has been counted down and out and made more comebacks than Sugar Ray Robinson. Because her constant truancy caused film-makers to suffer grievous financial wounds in the Forties, she was fired regularly off the sets of multi-million dollar Hollywood films. Thanks to her brilliant talent, she was rehired as soon as she was well enough to stagger before the cameras. In the fifties, her tantrums and other personality quirks caused her to be fired by numerous night clubs and theaters throughout the world.

In 1963 she made one of her most spectacular comebacks when CBS—fully aware of the risks—signed her to a multi-million-dollar television contract calling for weekly hour-long shows. People inside and outside the industry declared that CBS must be out of its head to attempt such folly, pointing out that Miss Garland's frailties could never stand up under the pressures and punishments of an entire TV season. In Las Vegas where her peccadillos (such as skipping rehearsals, forgetting lyrics and collapsing on stage) were especially well known, thousands of dollars were wagered on her chances. Most bettors agreed that she would collapse by either her second or third show.

Shortly after she was signed, owners of CBS' affiliate stations throughout the country protested en masse. Hastily, CBS called a meeting in New York, inviting hundreds of station representatives to come by plane to view their new million-dollar baby in person and be convinced that she was as healthy as an Olympic distance runner.

The night before the meeting, Judy and her producer, George Schlatter, composed a special song parody designed to soothe the ruffled feathers of the affiliates. Stepping on stage in a Manhattan ballroom, Judy charmed the meeting by singing the following new words to the song *Call Me Irresponsible*:

"*Call me irresponsible, call me unreliable, but it's undeniably true—I'm irrevocably signed with you!*"

The station chiefs, so impressed by her beauty, slim new hundred-pound figure and wonderful voice, stood up and cheered.

For the first month or so of production Judy was sensational, making all rehearsals on time, staging shows which delighted her sponsors and ad agencies. The program failed to score well in the Neilsen ratings, however, and many newspaper critics were unkind. CBS panicked and began tampering with the show's format. Producer Schlatter and two writers were fired. Judy was ordered to act less nervous before the cameras and to quit fondling her guest stars affectionately on stage.

These new pressures upset Judy markedly. The first show taped under the altered format co-starred June Allyson, a high-spirited old pal who had worked with Judy years before in MGM musicals. For the program they sang tunes from such vintage movies as *Words and Music* and *Till the Clouds Roll By*. Perhaps the memories of the good old days at Metro affected both of them. According to several members of the cast, there was some drinking both before and after the taping.

The fun grew even more boisterous after the audience went home. A cake with sticky white frosting was rolled out to celebrate singer Mel Torme's thirty-eighth birthday. Miss Allyson seized the cake and pantomimed throwing it in his face. She chased him around the stage, cake cocked like a discus. Suddenly the cake slipped off the platter and crashed in a gooey mess on the floor.

Shrieking joyfully, Judy picked up a handful of white icing and threw it at Miss Allyson. The icing missed its target, splattering like a snowball on a backdrop. Miss Allyson, grinning, tossed a gob that stuck to the shoulder of Judy's dress. In return, she received a blob of frosting smack on her forehead and laughed as she caught falling crumbs on her outstretched tongue.

When the tape of the show was run the next day in CBS' private screening room, observers thought they noticed more slurred lines than usual as Judy spoke to the audience or traded chatter with Miss Allyson. Some of this was due, they knew, to the fact that Judy normally slurs some lines, a result of her tendency to be extremely keyed up for a performance. Partly for production reasons and partly because some portions of the show were quite slipshod, the director found it necessary to mix parts of the actual show with pieces of the taped dress rehearsal in order to come up with a full hour.

Asked whether drinking might have affected her performance, Judy laughed at the report. "I never in my life have had too much to drink," she said, "whether I'm working or not working. I really don't drink that much and neither does June." As for the icing-tossing incident, she admitted it occurred but dismissed it as "just silliness."

In the weeks afterward, Judy was noticeably more tense. The show's ratings, her morale, and that of her CBS co-workers, slipped badly. She was hours late for many rehearsals and skipped some entirely, resulting in bitterness among musicians and actors who were forced to cover up for her booboos.

"This is a disorganized operation," said one disgusted member of the production crew. "Nobody knows what they're doing. Every minute somebody comes up with a new revision in the script. Each revision is printed on a different colored paper. By the time we get to the end of a show, the script looks like a rainbow. Once we ran out of colors and had to start over again with white pages. It was madness!"

In January of 1964 the ax fell. CBS finally ran out of patience and fired Judy. Out of respect for her talent, the network permitted her to announce that she was discontinuing the show "in order to devote more time to my children." She promptly went into one of her celebrated deep blue funks. A few days later Judy's maid found her lying unconscious in the dressing room of her suite in New York's Sherry Netherlands Hotel. She was bleeding from a cut on the left side of her forehead and a puffy cut lip.

She was taken to Mt. Sinai Hospital where a physician said she had suffered a mild concussion, perhaps in a fall, but was regaining consciousness and would be all right. Asked whether Miss Garland had been drinking, the doctor declined comment.

The incident re-emphasized the remarkably complex "now I'm up, now I'm down" cycle of Judy Garland's career, stretching over nearly forty frenzied years in show business. She was born Frances Gumm on June 10, 1922, in Grand Rapids, Minnesota. Her father was Frank Avent Gumm, of Murfreesboro, Tennessee, a handsome 5-foot, 11-inch tenor who sang pop tunes with slides in movie houses. Her mother was Ethel Marian Milne, pit pianist in a small theater in Superior, Wisconsin. After their marriage, Frank and Ethel toured as a vaudeville song and dance act. Two daughters preceded Judy—Sue (who was to die a suicide) and Virginia.

Judy first joined the family on stage one Christmas Eve when she was three years old. Deciding to copy her sisters, she wandered from the wings and casually began singing *Jingle Bells*. The audience loved her and kept applauding through fifteen endless choruses. She finally had to be dragged off the stage, yelling, by her frantic mother. It was one of the family's finest hours in the theater, and they seldom reached such heights afterward. The five Gumms were so lousy that at times they were hit by pieces of cheese, gumdrops and paper wads hurled by disappointed audiences.

Judy was five years old when the family moved to the desolate, arid desert city of Lancaster, California, where Frank Gumm managed a movie house. Mrs. Gumm, determined that one or all of her daughters would succeed in show business, regularly hauled the three girls to nearby Los Angeles on week ends and sent them on vaudeville stages for as little as fifty cents per girl per performance.

For more than seven frustratingly unsuccessful years, Mrs. Gumm dragged Judy from theater to theater, studio to studio. Finally, in 1935—when she was thirteen—Judy got a contract at MGM. She was thick around the middle and healthy as a pony. She was not especially pretty, but she had big, pool-like brown eyes, a clean fresh charm and the stout torso it takes to blast out brassy songs. Perhaps because she was the baby of the family and badly spoiled, she became a problem child at MGM from the beginning, hating work and resenting authority.

Undoubtedly another factor which contributed to her moods and maladjustment was the death of her father, who succumbed suddenly from spinal meningitis three months after she obtained her first movie contract. Many years later she described her father's death as the most terrible thing that ever happened to her, saying:

"I adored him, but I wasn't as close to him as I wanted to be all my life. After he died so unexpectedly, I suffered dreadfully because I had never given him enough love and I could never make it up to him. I couldn't cry at his funeral, so I pretended to cry. I couldn't cry for eight days, and then I locked myself in the bathroom and cried for fourteen hours."

Judy's childhood had a strange, unreal quality. She grew up, literally, before the eyes of millions of spectators. When she was barely fifteen she became a major star in *Broadway Melody*. After that came *Love Finds Andy Hardy* with Mickey Rooney; *The Wizard of Oz,* in which she first sang

Over the Rainbow, and *Strike Up the Band.* She became an international institution—everybody's sugar girl.

MGM, having discovered and brought her up, felt the same paternal emotions as the movie fans, and some of the studio's foster-parents were as tactless as fathers often are. One incident may be cited as a shocker which could turn a delightful teen-ager into a neurotic problem child:

At fourteen, Judy was overworked and subjected to pressures which would have wracked the most mature adult. She made twelve major pictures in her teens. She was harassed by demands that she dance, cry and act before the cameras as well as do the one thing which came easily for her—sing. To supply energy for such supercharged demands, she stuffed herself with all the food she could find at every meal, sneaked double malteds between scenes—and swelled into an unphotogenic piece of blubber. An MGM executive ordered her to his office.

"You look like a hunchback," he told her sternly. "We love you, Judy, but you're so fat you look like a monster."

The child tried to smile through her tears, then ran. Hollywood veterans still regard that incident as the most brutal pronouncement a studio official ever made to a small girl. The timing was exceedingly unfortunate because at the time she was called a monster, she was violently in love with MGM's distinguished heartthrob, Clark Gable. The front office followed that error with a humiliating edict: No matter what Judy ordered for lunch, and no matter how hard she worked, she was to be given a small bowl of chicken soup . . . and nothing else.

A studio script girl, close to Judy during that period, recalled the soup treatment as torture for a teen-ager who burned up as much energy on the set as Judy did. "The kid was so hungry she cried into her soup," the woman said. "But she ate it. She was ashamed of herself. She felt ungainly and awkward. She was the loneliest child I ever saw. She made few friends her own age, partly because there were so few around the set."

The soup treatment at the age of fourteen was the beginning of Judy Garland's nightmarish dieting schedule. Three years later she became hooked on a sleeping pill-pep pill cycle which, combined with her dieting, all but destroyed her once rugged body. In an interview with a writer last year, she spoke bitterly about her frenzied days and nights as MGM's most overworked girl teen-ager.

"I had only one real friend in those days," she said.

"Mickey Rooney. And he was in the same crazy boat I was. When we were on production on *Babes in Arms,* they had us working endless days and nights in a wild effort to cut costs. They'd give us pep-up pills to keep us on our feet long after we were exhausted. Then they'd take us to the studio hospital and knock us cold with sleeping pills— Mickey sprawled out on one bed, me on another. Then, after four hours, they'd wake us up and give us the pep pills again, so we could work another seventy-two hours in a row. Half the time, Mickey and I were so worked up we felt like we were hanging upside down from the ceiling."

Judy admitted that her inability to sleep properly was not entirely MGM's fault. "All my life," she said, "I've never been able to get adjusted to nighttime sleeping. It began when I was just a kid working in theaters. Vaudeville was night work. Mom and Dad and us three girls would finish up at eleven or eleven-thirty at night and then we'd all go get something to eat to calm down. We'd get to bed about three in the morning and sleep very late, getting up at noon.

"When I got into the movies, I had to get up at five in the morning. I was supposed to go to bed at nine at night, but I just couldn't manage it. I was still on my old time-table, only I was getting to bed at three in the morning and being awakened at five. I'd arrive in make-up so drowsy that they practically had to paint eyeballs on my lids to make me look awake."

Judy's rebellion against assembly-line emoting inspired her abrupt elopement—at the age of nineteen—with composer David Rose in 1941. She was then at her loveliest, her face miraculously unmarked by the killing rigors of her film schedules, her figure slim, delightfully juvenile but nonetheless sexy.

As predicted, the marriage started to become unglued within a year and a half and ended in divorce after four years, with the blame placed on the professional conflicts of both partners. About the same time, Judy had a final parting from her mother, with whom she had bickered for years.

When she was twenty-one, unhappy Judy, living on coffee and cigarettes in an unsuccessful effort to trim off poundage, decided to solve her problems through psycho-analysis. This merely complicated her already wild daily schedule. She staggered out of bed an hour earlier every morning in order to be on her analyst's couch at six A.M.

After telling her troubles for fifty minutes to an elderly doctor, she dashed to MGM and worked until six P.M. Then she returned to the doctor's office for another hour of therapy before going home.

This $50-an-hour folly went on seven days a week for five years. It did the patient no good at all, because Judy was too self-conscious to tell the doctor the truth about herself and, instead, told him fanciful stories which she would make up as she went along.

Meanwhile her troubles at the studio multiplied like fruit flies. She was making five thousand dollars a week (and squandering most of it), but she was constantly so sleepy and hungry that she found it impossible to drag herself before the cameras on time. She held up productions, a cardinal sin in Hollywood. Incensed, MGM fired her from *The Barkleys of Broadway* and replaced her with Ginger Rogers. Judy wept for hours in her dressing room, complaining that no one loved her.

The following week she married director Vincente Minnelli. The marriage lasted through nearly six years of strife and monumental confusion on Judy's part. "She is constantly full of fears," Minnelli told studio friends. "I keep telling her to enjoy life, to enjoy being the great star she is. But she doesn't know how. She is a tormented woman."

One morning in 1947—when her marriage to Minnelli was in its second year—Judy woke up frightened and trembling in a small, strangely bare room. Slowly her memory returned and she realized she was in a Los Angeles sanitarium for a cure suggested by her doctor. Later that morning she heard peculiar screams coming from a nearby bungalow.

"Off with your heads," screeched a woman. "I'm Mary the Queen of Scots—and I say off with all your heads!"

When that voice stopped screaming, another replaced it, moaning: "I killed my babies. I don't know why, but I killed all my babies!"

The following day, when she was permitted to mingle with the other patients, Judy learned that her room was near locked Ward 10, which was filled with violently disturbed women. She asked to be moved to another part of the sanitarium where the patients were only mildly disturbed. Overcoming some of her self-consciousness, she made friends with some of them and discovered they were high-strung, sensitive people like herself who could not cope with the reality of their lives. Some were alcoholics; others had battled through narcotics cures.

After a month of rest, Judy calmed down sufficiently for MGM to put her back on the payroll. She went immediately into *Easter Parade*. The studio, unhappy because she had gained fifteen pounds while hospitalized, ordered her onto another crash diet. "Everything's going to be swell," studio officials told her. "When you finish *Easter Parade,* we'll let you have a nice long rest for six months."

The dieting and rigorous shooting schedule left Judy so tense and exhausted that when the picture was finished she was sent to another sanitarium. When she was released the studio reneged on its promise of a six-month vacation and put her to work in *Annie Get Your Gun*. MGM had purchased the stage property for her at a cost of $350,000. Judy, who had long coveted the part, was delighted and went to work enthusiastically.

During a grueling six-week session, she pre-recorded all the songs for the picture. Then at noon one day she fled from MGM, wailing that she could not go on. "I'm too tired!" she cried hysterically. "I'd like to sleep for a million years!" The studio tried a dozen stratagems in an effort to persuade her to return, but Judy remained adamant. She was suspended and replaced by Betty Hutton. MGM junked the songs Judy had recorded, and they immediately became collector's items, selling under the table for seventy-five and a hundred dollars.

Totally distraught, Judy went to her analyst. After several long, tearful sessions, she became despondent and told the doctor that she thought analysis was a waste of time. After remaining silent for nearly a minute, the doctor said thoughtfully:

"All right, Judy, if that's the way you feel, you should stop. But I want to tell you something important. I only give you six months to live."

His words struck her like a slap across the cheek. She began to weep.

"What do you mean?" she asked.

"Because you're suicidal," the doctor said. "Definitely."

It was the first time anyone had ever mentioned such a thing in her presence. She had never before thought of suicide. But after her visit to the doctor, the idea was often on her mind.

She became so distressed and nervous that hospitalization was again vital. Because she was flat broke, MGM agreed to pay all her bills at Boston's Peter Bent Brigham Hospital, provided she returned to work when she was well. She was so happy in the hospital that she remained eleven months, started to sleep regularly—and gained weight.

The studio called her back for *Summer Stock*. Startled by her plump figure, she was ordered to diet. Hysterics and delays piled up, but she managed to finish the picture. She went immediately into another, *Royal Wedding*. Part way through it, she again panicked and ran. Jane Powell was signed to finish the film, Judy was suspended and the studio gave stories to the newspapers implying that Judy was a nasty villainness who enjoyed torturing film executives at every opportunity.

Reading the headlines about herself in bed the next morning, Judy began screaming, "Lies, lies, lies!" She went into the bathroom, smashed a glass and drew a sharp fragment across her throat. Blood welled up. She returned to her bed, lay down and prepared to bleed to death.

Her maid came in, saw the wound—which was about a quarter-inch long—and dashed to a phone. A doctor and nurse arrived, followed by police and three dozen Hollywood reporters. In the mad weeks thereafter, MGM dissolved her long-term contract, at her request, and she pressed on with her divorce from Vincente Minnelli, getting custody of their five-year-old daughter, Liza. Her reputation for hysterics and production delays was now so widely known that no producer would consider her for a picture.

At this low point in her life, a new hero rode up on a white charger to save her. He was Sid Luft, a former test pilot for Douglas Aircraft who had become an independent promoter. A handsome, muscular fellow who exuded confidence, he had little money but was a clever operator. He offered Judy Garland two things she desperately needed—sympathy and a strong shoulder which she could drench with her tears.

Luft talked Roger Edens, an MGM lyricist, into writing a show for Judy. He offered the production to London's famed Palladium and the deal was snapped up. Judy opened there on April 10, 1951. She was so nervous she tripped and fell flat on her derrière before a distinguished opening night audience.

"Go on, Judy!" yelled the Londoners. "We love you!"

She continued in concert pitch, her voice never lustier, and scored a misty-eyed triumph. A few months afterward she brought vaudeville back to the Palace Theater in New

York. Again she was fat as a partridge, but when she sang
Over the Rainbow, Broadway gave Judy—then twenty-nine
years old—the kind of sentimental, sobbing welcome usually reserved for the aged great. It was probably the finest
personal triumph ever seen on an American vaudeville
stage.

Judy collapsed from overwork after six weeks. She rested
a few days, returned, and enjoyed a run of nineteen weeks,
breaking all Palace records. Night after night, people called
out the old refrain, "Judy, we love you!"

Suddenly she was a full blown legend. In cities across the
land Judy Garland cults sprang up, proclaiming her a
goddess who had risen to glory from a bed of pain and
woe. Sid and Judy brought the show to Los Angeles for
another tearful, audience-shouting triumph.

In the spring of 1952, after countless columns of specu-
lation had been printed about them, they were married in a
quick ceremony near San Francisco. It looked for sure now
as if Judy had lived up to her famed *Over the Rainbow*
song and had found, at last, career contentment and personal well being.

But a series of incidents involving her mother now began
to upset Judy. Her relations with her mother had been
boiling for many years, with Judy never able to forgive her
for squandering the earnings from her teen-aged years at
MGM. Her mother went into court and complained—
before reporters—that her famous and very rich daughter
would not support her. She took a job as a $60-a-week
clerk at Douglas Aircraft and some gossip columnists said
she did it merely to embarrass her daughter.

The Lufts' first child, Lorna, was born in December,
1952. The following month, Judy's mother—almost desti-
tute—dropped dead on a parking lot. The unsavory headlines which followed caused some who had said "We love
you, Judy" to decide they had been wrong about her. Judy
collapsed and returned to a sanitarium.

For two years she remained out of the public eye. Then
Warner Brothers decided to take a chance on her and
offered her *A Star Is Born.* Judy, who hadn't worked in a
film for over four years, was terrified and insisted that she
couldn't possibly do the part. "I'm washed up," she wailed
to Luft. "Finished! *Kaput.* I'll never act again!"

But Luft, knowing how badly they needed the money,
got her in shape and propelled her over to the sound stages

at Warner's. Judy did her best, but she was so jittery and sleepless that she delayed production. Luft then made a flabbergasting offer to the studio. "Judy's a night creature," he said. "She's at the peak of her talent after ten P.M. So why don't we film the picture at night?"

When they recovered from their shock, Warner Brothers agreed, realizing it was the only way to salvage the hundreds of thousands of dollars already spent on the picture.

Shooting went on all night, for weeks, with grips, cameramen and other technicians drawing fabulous salaries, paid at double and triple their normal union scale. The picture, originally budgeted at $3,000,000, cost a whopping $6,000,000 by the time it was in the can. But Warners got its money back when Judy's performance won an Academy Award nomination.

More concert tours followed. Again her fans loved her. She made outstanding appearances as a dramatic actress in such films as *Judgment at Nuremberg* and *A Child Is Waiting*. But being Judy Garland, a woman whose talent for fouling up her personal life is in exact proportion to her magnificent singing ability, she again went from triumph to tragedy. In a quavering voice she announced in a Santa Monica courtroom that she couldn't stand living another moment with her third husband.

"Sid Luft is a horrible man," she charged in her divorce suit. "He has beaten me with his fists. He has attempted to strangle me several times."

She demanded custody of their two small children and asked the court to restrain Luft from "harming me further or taking my children."

However, a few weeks later she admitted that she really didn't mean all those nasty things she said about Sid, adding that "we're back together again and everything is lovey-dovey." A few months later matters were upside down again when Judy once more filed suit for divorce. This suit also was permitted to lapse, making the Lufts champions in Hollywood's "on-again, off-again" marriage derby.

While singing in New York in 1960, Judy suffered another collapse. Her doctors at first thought it was the usual Garland swoon from fatigue, but closer examination revealed that her liver was badly damaged from an earlier bout with hepatitis. A specialist flew in from Chicago, pulled up a chair beside Judy's hospital bed and spoke to her in somber tones:

"Judy, I don't want to shock you too much, but I'm

going to be honest. You've got to change your whole way of living. You are going to be a semi-invalid. Your liver is so bad that you will *never* be able to sing again in clubs or theaters."

"Great," said Judy, sarcastically. "I've been working too damn hard anyway. I'd love a nice long rest."

"Aren't you shocked?" asked the doctor.

"Hell, no," she replied. "Nothing shocks me any more."

Later, she cried herself to sleep, aware that the end of her singing career—her source of real happiness—was a punishment worse than death. Terribly frightened, she followed her doctors' orders to the letter, stuffed herself with carbohydrates to build up her strength and shot up to 150 pounds. Because of her small, 4-foot, 11-inch frame, she looked like a grotesque balloon figure from Macy's Thanksgiving parade. But the diet which added all that weight saved her career. After six months her liver was regenerated enough so she could begin singing again.

That experience should have taught her a lesson. But, of course, it didn't. Two years later, having decided that life with Luft was again unbearable, she went to Lake Tahoe to establish residence for a divorce. Determined to regain her slim figure, she attempted a senseless fast. For thirty miserable days, she drank only tea, without cream or sugar. She ate no solid food, drank no other liquids and lost twenty-five pounds.

The result was a hellish kidney attack which felt like red hot pitchforks were being plunged into her back. Hospitalized, she again somehow survived. A few weeks later she opened at the Sahara in Las Vegas. Her act was so well received that she decided the time was now ripe for her to accept one of the generous offers which the TV networks had been waving under her pug nose for many years. She accepted CBS' King Croesus-like deal, an arrangement which—as indicated earlier—turned out to be one of the major disasters of her career.

Soon after that debacle, Judy Garland suffered a setback in court that seemed to darken the entire pattern of her life. Her marital battles with Sid Luft, now in their twelfth year but still unresolved, resulted in Luft going into court and publicly washing some of the dirtiest linen Hollywood had seen in years. Demanding custody of their children Luft charged that his wife was "an emotionally disturbed and unbalanced person" who had "attempted suicide more than twenty times."

In an affidavit Luft stated: "On at least three occasions during 1963 and on numerous previous occasions she has taken overdoses of barbiturates. On six occasions she has attempted suicide by slashing herself on her wrists, elbows or throat." (Later Luft trotted witnesses before the court who testified that Judy on many occasions spoke to the children in a loud, intoxicated voice. They said she consumed from two to four bottles of Liebfraumilch wine daily and once got so drunk that hotel employes saw her "running around without any clothes on.")

Judy, who was present when the affidavit was read, turned pale and the left the courtroom wearing the dazed expression of a sleepwalker. After that she seemed to say to hell with everything. Perhaps fearing that she had lost her children for good, she went abroad on a concert tour which produced one shocking incident after another.

In Melbourne, Australia, she was hooted off the stage before an angry audience of seven thousand, after arriving an hour late for the concert and then singing in a sour, un-Garland-like voice that sounded as if she had gargled with vinegar.

In Hong Kong a few days later, she received word that her sister Sue, age forty-nine, had—on her second attempt —succeeded in taking her own life via an overdose of nembutal.

This news hit Judy so hard that she suffered what was first reported to be a critical heart attack. The following day Mark Herron, identified as her traveling companion, told reporters that she had been in a coma for twelve hours after collapsing from "overexhaustion." He denied that she had taken sleeping pills, but was contradicted by a nurse who declared that Judy's illness was "some kind of poisoning."

Back in Hollywood, Judy's friends began asking: Who is this Mark Herron? Checking into his background, they learned that he was an obscure but handsome actor at least ten years younger than Judy.

After Judy was released from the Hong Kong hospital, she and Herron began enacting roles in a ludicrous, real-life farce. It began when Herron told reporters that he was no longer merely Judy's traveling companion. "I am her husband," he declared, adding that Judy had obtained a Mexican divorce from Luft. This news was greeted with jeers from Judy's California friends, who said she was still very much married to Luft.

"There has been no divorce," they said, "Mexican or otherwise. The matter is still unresolved in the Los Angeles courts."

Back in Hong Kong, Judy, wearing the beatific smile of a honeymooner, declared: "Certainly Mark and I are married. To make sure, we had two ceremonies, one aboard a Norwegian ship and the other in a Hong Kong hotel."

Herron, nodding blissfully, displayed two red papers with Chinese lettering which he said were the certificates of their two marriages.

In Tokyo a week later, Judy confessed sheepishly that she and Herron were not married. "But we are engaged," she added, "and we hope to be married—sometime."

Judy and Herron went on to England where, to the amazement of no one, she suffered two traumatic experiences within two days. First she was rushed to St. Stephens Hospital in London, bleeding from cuts on her wrists. The following night—defying her doctors' orders—she rose from her sickbed and staggered into the spotlight at the Palladium Theater.

She looked old and tired, her face bloated, dark bags beneath her eyes, her teeth tobacco-stained. But she proceeded to give a singing, weeping performance which critics described as the most fantastic they'd ever seen. "Thousands of staid Londoners cheered themselves hoarse," wrote John London in the Evening News. "I doubt whether, even in the long history of the Palladium, there has ever been anything to equal such a spontaneous outburst of affection."

That word "affection" is an important clue to explaining the recurring peculiar patterns of Judy Garland's life. Since her earliest years as a Hollywood teen-ager, she has sought affection like a baby craves sweets. A prominent Los Angeles psychiatrist, familiar with her history, offered the following analysis:

"Miss Garland is a child in the body of a forty-two-year-old woman. She will never grow up, nor will she ever be happy, no matter how great her professional success. Childlike she will go through the remainder of her life blaming everyone—her mother, her ex-husbands and her business managers—for her troubles. She will not place the blame where it rightly belongs, upon herself, because she will forever lack the maturity to see herself clearly.

"She is a perpetual teen-ager who must be given love not just every day or week, but every hour, every minute—

demanding such worship from her husbands, her children, her audiences. When there are loveless moments in her life, she becomes insecure, depressed and hates herself. It is then that she panics and anything may happen."

The doctor declined to predict what the future holds for Judy, but added ominously, "Statistics show that when a man or woman develops a lengthy pattern of repeated suicide attempts, eventually they succeed."

In the case of Judy Garland, a girl of enormous talent and infinite capacity for love, it is hoped that such will not be the end.

HOLLYWOOD SCOUNDREL

• *TEDD THOMEY*

David Niven once described his face as a cross between two pounds of halibut and an explosion in an old clothes closet. He was being unduly modest. The actor, although not handsome, is quite an elegant-looking gentleman. And he knows it.

There were times during World War II, however, when this needle-nosed, six-foot, two-inch Scotsman definitely resembled his own rude description of himself. One morning in April, 1945, during the bloody battle for Berlin, Lieutenant Colonel David Niven looked as if he might have gotten mixed up with an exploding hand grenade in a foxhole instead of a closet.

His once spotless uniform was rumpled, ripped and muddy from forty-eight hours of action with forward units of the British Army. His small mustache, usually as neatly trimmed as the hedges at Buckingham Palace, was straggly. He was in dire need of a haircut and a bath, and his thin, dirty face reflected the strain of six years in the major combat zones of Europe.

With another officer, Niven crouched behind an armored car hammering machine gun bullets into the headquarters building of Heinrich Himmler's SS police. Himmler and his top Nazi hatchetmen had fled many hours previously, but the brick building was being savagely defended by storm troopers firing rifles and burp guns from upper windows.

Niven, noted for his uncanny ability to appear cheerful no matter how rough things were, nudged his companion. Grinning like a schoolboy on a holiday, Niven pointed to a gigantic Nazi banner fastened to a ledge at the third-floor level and draped down the front of the headquarters building.

"Gad, what a beauty!" Niven said, shouting in order to be heard above the sound of the guns. "What a souvenir!"

Toward noon the sounds of gunfire diminished as the last of the building's defenders were slain or captured. Because of his rank, Lieutenant Colonel Niven was among the first staff officers to be told the building was secured. He dashed inside with a group of eager Tommies, who began searching for such Nazi souvenirs as Mauser rifles, steel helmets, Iron Crosses and flags. Although he knew there might still be snipers hidden in the upper parts of the building, Niven decided to risk a trip upstairs to find the banner he had noticed outside.

Other British soldiers had the same idea. Thanks to his long legs, which took the stairs three and four at a time, Niven was the first man to reach the third-floor level. He hunted through several Nazi offices before he found the one whose windows opened onto the ledge from which the great banner dangled.

Niven raised a window, bent down and unhooked a corner of the banner.

At that precise moment MGM studios, which had reluctantly granted him a wartime leave, came within an inch of losing one of its film stars.

Unknown to Niven, a Nazi soldier had concealed himself behind a desk in an adjacent office. The soldier, out of ammunition, leaped up and ran toward Niven with his bayonet extended.

Two shots were fired. As Niven whirled around, he saw the Nazi tumbling fatally wounded to the floor, having been shot by two British soldiers who had followed Niven upstairs.

When the Tommies explained what the German had been about to do, Niven expressed his gratitude to them for having saved his life. The two Tommies nodded and laughed. For a moment Niven failed to see what was so funny. Then realization dawned as he recalled how he had leaned out the window and bent down to unfasten the banner, his rear making a perfect target for the approaching bayonet.

He promptly joined in the laughter, his blue eyes twinkling as he remarked crisply: "My God, that was close, wasn't it? The bloody blighter nearly ran it up my ahss!"

Niven, who served with the British armed forces from 1939 to 1945, saw more combat during the war than any other actor. He made Commando raids into Norway and North Africa, was the second British soldier to enter Paris after the liberation and participated in the perilous crossing of Germany's Rhine River with an advance combat team.

He saw men blown in half by mortar shells and once came upon the remnants of an advancing Australian platoon which had been obliterated by 88-mm cannon fire from German tank destroyers. He returned home with a chestful of decorations, including the American Legion of Merit, and a trunkful of souvenirs, among them the huge Nazi banner from Himmler's headquarters.

The fact that Niven was able to serve with distinction came as a shock to his superior officers. When they permitted him to re-enter the British Army shortly after World War II broke out, they regarded him simply as a champagne-swizzling playboy seeking publicity. They were unimpressed with news stories which told how he had blithely given up a $2,000-a-week Hollywood salary in order to serve as a lieutenant earning a miniscule few shillings a day.

Their suspicions of Niven came from scrutinizing records of his service in the regular British Army, ten years previously. They found that he had, to put it mildly, flunked out. He had insulted a general and been placed under house arrest. Then he had made matters worse by getting drunk with the officer assigned to guard him. He had fled to London and then—to avoid a court-martial—had resigned his commission and lit out for Canada.

But in 1939–1940 England needed every trained officer she could find. Niven was restored to his rank as a second lieutenant and the brass began looking for a nice safe billet for him. They felt that the talents of the co-star of *Dawn Patrol* and *Wuthering Heights* could best be utilized by service in an entertainment unit. They were astonished when Niven reacted with outrage and insisted on combat duty.

He tried to get into the RAF but was rejected. "Couldn't pass the physical," he explained later. "They found a whimper in my ticker." Assigned to a rifle brigade, he served in a minor administrative post during the phony war in France in late 1939. Just before the devastating defeat of the British and French armies in 1940, he was returned to England and given an intriguing secret assignment.

At this point in the war, Adolf Hitler goosestepped proudly along the coast of France, shook his fist at the Channel and raved that England would be the next to fall. The British never doubted that he would invade. They also feared his invasion would be successful and speedily organized an underground guerrilla force designed to harass Germany's occupation troops. The underground was called Phantom Reconnaissance and consisted of Army units deployed in various disguises throughout the English countryside.

Niven became second in command of a Phantom unit consisting of 180 men and 16 officers who wandered about dressed as parsons, well-diggers and sheepherders. Disguised as a farmer, Niven often led parts of his unit on training forays into the forests and fields of northern England. During these expeditions, which lasted from ten days to two weeks, Niven and his men carried no army supplies, but lived off the land as they would have to do under the expected German occupation.

Roaming about like Robin Hood and his merry band, Niven and his gang raised general hell in the forests, exploding grenades in the streams to kill salmon and poaching for deer and pheasant on the estates of lords and earls.

When it became evident that Hitler was not going to invade England after all, the Phantom units were disbanded and Niven volunteered for duty in the Commandos. While awaiting his orders, he was transferred to temporary administrative duty at an RAF fighter station at Biggin Hill. The blitz was now in full swing, with German Stuka and Heinkel bombers filling the air over England every night. During a particularly heavy raid on the station, Niven jumped into a slit trench without realizing it was already occupied.

He landed on a white Pekinese which promptly bit him on the rear. When he yelped with pain, he discovered that the slit trench was also providing shelter for a lovely girl in a WAAF uniform. Her name was Primula Rollo and she angrily told Niven to stop assaulting her dog. When Niven tried to argue, she told him to shut up, pointing out politely that she—a cipher officer at the station—outranked him.

Niven, entranced with her beauty and fiery spirit, married her ten days later.

Primmy (his nickname for her) remained in London during Niven's service in the Commandos. She was bombed out of two houses but escaped unhurt with their two small children. Niven's first son, David, was born during a Nazi bombing raid. Minutes after the baby arrived, a bomb struck the hospital and killed a dozen children in a nearby ward.

Promoted to captain, Niven participated in several Commando raids, one of which was nearly a disaster. In 1942, the Commandos made landings on the Lofoten Islands off Norway, then occupied by Nazi troops. The Commandos landed at night in small boats, sabotaging power stations and bridges, and departing quickly before the Nazi soldiers could find them.

One night Niven, face blackened with charcoal to avoid reflecting light, was aboard a small boat which was leading four other landing craft toward one of the Lofoten Islands. The commander of the raiding group, a surly British major, gazed at the approaching shoreline through binoculars, looking for a certain farmhouse and barn. When he spotted the buildings, he told the boat pilot to head toward them. Their plan was to land near the farm, go inland a mile and blow up a stone bridge.

Niven examined the buildings through his binoculars and decided they were not the proper landmark. "That's the wrong farm," Niven told the major. "According to my map, we're too far south."

The major insisted angrily that he was right and called Niven an interfering fool. Meanwhile, the boats headed toward the beach and prepared to land. When they were a few hundred yards offshore, Niven spotted some German trucks, tents and ammunition carriers. He pointed them out to the major, who reacted with horror. He ordered the boats to turn around and head back out to sea.

The boats did not make a landing that night. Later it was determined that an entire German battalion was billeted at the spot the British major had chosen for his landing. If the small force of Commandos had gone ashore, they would have been wiped out.

Later in the war Niven, transferred back to the conventional army, landed at Normandy with the Allied invasion forces in 1944. He had several narrow escapes in the field, including being pinned down by mortar fire during the battle for Bastogne in Belgium.

Niven's morale hit bottom on a bleak, wet spring morning in 1945 when the Allied forces made ready to cross the heavily guarded Rhine River. Except for a few weeks off, when he made a film for the British War Office, Niven had seen seventy-two months of ceaseless service. He hadn't suffered a nick. But on that morning he had a premonition of death; he felt that he had been living on borrowed time and that his luck was about to run out.

Most men who go to war feel they will live through it, no matter how many others are killed. But Niven had no reason to believe in that fallacy. He had lost ancestors in other battles, at Waterloo, in the Crimea and in the Boer War. His father had been killed in action at the age of twenty-five in the Dardanelles during World War I.

Niven spent the last few minutes before the attack checking over his pistol, ammunition and other equipment. Suddenly a sergeant ran down the line of soldiers, distributing a load of mail which had just arrived. As men ripped open letters from home, their morale was boosted and they laughed and joked. Niven watched the sergeant tensely, hoping for letters from his wife and family.

"Here you are, Colonel," the sergeant said, thrusting an envelope into Niven's hand.

"Just this one?" Niven asked.

"That's all. Sorry, sir."

Niven tore it open without glancing at the outside. He pulled forth a sheet and read the following typewritten lines:

Lt. Col. David Niven
Army Field Post Office
Allied Expeditionary Force
Dear Sir:
   This is to inform you that we have absorbed the Leland Hayward Agency of which you were a client. Therefore we are now handling your business.
                              Sincerely yours,
                              Music Corporation of America

Niven was cheered enormously. The thought of death no longer chilled his heart. He was in safe hands. MCA had never lost a man and they weren't going to lose a certain colonel today, no matter how viciously the Germans battled to keep the Allies from crossing the Rhine.

MCA performed magnificently. Niven got through the day, and the rest of the war, without a scratch.

He was twenty-nine years old when the war started and thirty-five at its end. It cost him over a million dollars in lost film salaries, but this was not his chief regret. More than anything he lamented being deprived of his debonaire life in Hollywood, New York and London, where he had often been a more rakish scoundrel off the screen than he had ever been on it.

From his earliest days in Scotland, Niven had enjoyed a life full of misadventures, ranging from petty thievery and repeated whippings at boarding school to cutting up in the army, stealing food from restaurants and getting dangerously mixed up with Atlantic City gamblers and gangsters.

Born in Kirriemuir, Scotland, on March 1, 1910, he was christened James David Graham Niven. His father was a wealthy landowner who lived in a large country house staffed with footmen, butlers and gamekeepers. Niven inherited an appetite for mischief and mishaps from his father, who had an insatiable hunger for betting on thoroughbred horses. Before Niven was three years old, his father had lost his fortune and lands on the nags and the Nivens were forced to move from their great estate to a ramshackle cottage on the Isle of Wight.

A year later his father was killed in the war. Niven, his brother and two small sisters were raised by his mother and a stepfather whom he detested. Sent away to boarding school at Heatherdown, Niven became a lonely, rascally boy who was always in trouble.

One day he fell asleep while playing an organ accompaniment to a rousing anthem being sung by his classmates. As the organ's tones died to a wheeze, the headmaster awakened Niven by banging him on the head with a Bible. Niven leaped back into action, pumping the organ so hard he burst its bellows. For this misfortune he received a painful beating with a thin cane. Other infractions followed and he suffered eleven more canings.

Finally, school officials expelled him and he was sent to a private reformatory for wayward boys at Portsmouth.

Within a month he was sacked again, charged with being a bully and stealing candy and trinkets from stores. Sent to school at Stowe, he was quickly disgraced when the headmaster caught him cheating during an examination. But instead of caning him, this headmaster lectured him in kindly tones and straightened him out.

When he reached his mid-teens, Niven was a tall, slim youth whose good manners and bearing won him an appointment to Sandhurst, the West Point of England. But when he graduated as a second lieutenant a few years later, he was sick of military life, resented its inflexible discipline and bored with its centuries of stuffy tradition. He longed for adventure and escape. Sent to the island of Malta, he found the routine of the Highland Light Infantry even duller than that back at Sandhurst.

His search for entertainment led to one calamity after another. The weather at Malta was so hot and humid that Niven and another young officer rebelled against the heavy steel helmets they were required to wear. They sent to a London toy shop for two imitation helmets made from lightweight papier-mache. One day while they were on dress parade, a heavy rain fell, melting the paper hats. Like uncooked pizzas, they drooped down over the eyes of the two embarrassed young officers.

For that offense Niven was confined to quarters for three days. Shortly after his release, he committed another foolish *faux pas*. While walking to the parade ground in full uniform, he playfully thrust his officer's sword into a dummy used for bayonet practice. The blade snapped off about six inches from the hilt, leaving Niven with a dagger instead of a sword. There was no time to get another, and during parade ceremonies, the adjutant called out: "Officers, draw your swords!"

Dozens of blades flashed in the sunlight, but Niven didn't move. The adjutant noticed his peculiar hesitance and shouted: "Niven, I order you to draw your sword!"

Niven pulled out his blade, looking ludicrous as he stood stiffly at attention before the entire regiment, holding up his crazy-looking little dagger. The adjutant snarled sarcastically: "Stick an olive on that, Niven, and I'll send for a martini!"

Niven drew another three days in confinement. When his tour of duty ended at Malta, he was transferred to a post at Netheravon, England. He promptly began courting a beautiful girl in London, sixty miles away. Every evening he rushed to the city, spent a few hours with the girl and then caught the milk train back, dozing during the trip, arriving at the base just in time to make the six A.M. line-up on the parade ground.

Late one afternoon, General Bonham-Carter, commanding officer at Netheravon, called the officers together and began to lecture on the curving trajectory of machine gun bullets. Twenty-three-year-old Niven barely listened, his mind occupied with thoughts of a prettier set of curves in London. When General Carter finally completed his long talk, he asked, "Any questions, gentlemen?"

Lieutenant Niven raised his hand and said, "Yes, sir."

"Fine, Niven," said the general. "Speak right up."

"Could you tell me the time?" the impetuous youth asked. "I have to catch a train."

General Carter's jaw dropped. There was a tense silence while he stared malevolently at Niven.

"Stand up," said the general icily.

Niven rose and stood at attention.

"Consider yourself under arrest," barked the general. "Dismissed!"

Niven was marched off to his quarters and guarded by a young lieutenant who happened to be one of his closest friends. After a couple of hours of boredom, Niven invited his pal to have a nip of Scotch. They drained the bottle and then hatched a drunken escape plot. While his guard visited the men's room, Niven tied his bedsheets together into a rope and lowered himself out the window.

Niven drove a wobbly course to London. Sobering up, he realized with panic that he could be court-martialed and kicked out of the army in thorough disgrace. He consulted an old friend, Philip Astley, then married to screen star Madeleine Carroll. Astley urged him to take advantage of the rule permitting officers to resign during peacetime. Niven quickly wrote the following note to his commanding officer, Lieutenant Colonel Alex Telfer-Smollett:

"Dear Colonel: Request permission to resign commission. Love, Niven."

Colonel Smollett was so intrigued by Niven's unmilitary love note that he later framed it and kept it on the wall of his home in Scotland.

Niven did not wait for Smollett's reply. He sold his car, an old Bentley, to a newspaperman friend for enough cash to buy a steamer ticket, and within twenty-four hours was on his way to Canada. He arrived during the Depression in

May, 1933, so broke he had to take a job on a road construction gang in order to get money for food. After a week of that he became incapacitated with a throat infection. Desperately in need of funds while recuperating, he read a book on fox hunting which inspired him to try his hand at a bit of plagiarism. He copied several chapters from the book word for word, put his own name on the manuscript and sent it to a large Canadian newspaper.

Within a few days he received a check and a complimentary note from the editor requesting another article on the same subject. Niven was tempted but restrained himself. Before the article was published, he caught a train for New York where, although totally lacking in experience, he decided to become an actor.

During an Army leave in New York a few years before, Niven had become well-acquainted with heiress Barbara Hutton and her blue-chip friends in show business and financial circles. Renewing acquaintances, Niven cut a handsome figure about town. Despite his reverses, he had retained an excellent wardrobe, including tailored tweeds and two tuxedoes. His brilliant wit won him invitations to parties in New York's mansions and ritziest restaurants, where he hobknobbed with producers and theater owners. But none of them took him seriously when he hinted he was looking for work as an actor.

Borrowing small amounts from friends, he employed numerous schemes to maintain what appeared to be a rich man's life of ease. He rented a cheap room in a hotel on Lexington Avenue. Its front door was opposite the back door of the Waldorf. Every morning he left his hotel garbed in immaculate tweeds, crossed to the Waldorf and strolled through its posh lobbies. Sauntering out the Waldorf's front entrance, he received a salute from the doorman which never failed to lift his spirits.

Quite often, down to his last quarter, Niven would stroll into a restaurant and steal a fine breakfast, using an elaborate deception he worked out with an equally broke pal. Niven would sit by himself at a vacant table and order coffee and doughnuts. His friend sat at a table nearby, but they did not speak or look at one another. His friend stashed away a tremendous breakfast of steak, eggs, potatoes and toast. Upon finishing, both men asked for their checks at the same time and then secretly exchanged them. The friend paid Niven's paltry twenty-cent tab at the cashier's stand, then wandered outside and disappeared.

At that point Niven glanced at his check and called the waitress over. Very politely he said: "Miss, isn't there some mistake? You've charged me $2.25 for coffee and doughnuts."

The girl could see that he was still nibbling at part of a doughnut. Apologizing, she wrote him out a new check, commenting: "I'd like to get my hands on that other guy. The louse picked up your check."

"Yes, indeed," said Niven solemnly. "A scoundrel of the worst sort."

He paid his twenty cents, and met his friend at another restaurant a few blocks away. This time Niven enjoyed the feast. With his energy restored, he was prepared for a busy day of contacting friends who gave him leads to jobs in the theater. None of his contacts panned out, however, and he was reduced to finding other ways of scaring up money to live.

One evening Niven encountered two magnificent promoters named Douglas Hertz and Lefty Flynn. The three immediately discovered a common interest in making money as rapidly as possible. They dreamed up an outfit which they called The American Pony Express Racing Association, planning to organize teams of polo ponies and race them indoors on small tracks in auditoriums. The idea was so unusual it caught on. Soon Niven and his fellow promoters were selling stock to racing enthusiasts throughout New York and New Jersey.

With money from the stock sale, Niven, Hertz and Flynn bought a hundred pooped-out, old polo ponies and hired Indians and rodeo cowboys as jockeys. Opening night in Atlantic City's Municipal Auditorium was a tumultuous sellout, with standees lined up for a block outside. Wearing a magnificent red uniform and riding the best pony in the lot, Niven led the grand march into the arena while loudspeakers announced him as Captain David Niven, of the Royal Canadian Mounted Police. He smiled wryly to himself, aware that the Mounties might be out looking for him at that very moment, anxious to quiz him about the foxy way he had bamboozled a certain newspaper.

The next day Niven sat in his office, totaling the profits, happily certain that he and his partners were on their way to becoming racing tycoons overnight. Suddenly, five grim-faced men walked in without bothering to knock. Their hats were pulled down over their eyes and they wore long tight overcoats which bulged as though concealing pistols and revolvers. Their leader introduced himself.

Niven knew the name. The man was the overlord of Atlantic City's underworld. But the five tough guys looked so outlandish that he decided they were phonies participating in a plot cooked up by his pal Lefty Flynn, a masterful practical joker.

"Niven," said the gangster, "you got a damn good thing going here. Now here's the deal. We take over the popcorn, peanuts and hot dogs. We put in half a dozen of our bookies. Every night you tell us who's gonna win most of the races. In advance, naturally. So, naturally, you and your partners get cut in for a nice share of the action."

"Marvelous idea," replied Niven with an exaggerated sneer. "And here's what I want you chaps to do. You go to the grocery on the next corner. You buy a fresh pineapple. You cut off the top and hollow it out inside."

One of the hoods didn't like Niven's attitude. "Hey, boss," he scowled. "Dis here is a wise guy."

"Let him finish," snarled the boss.

"Thank you," said Niven crisply. "Then you bring the pineapple here. You write your crooked proposition on a piece of paper. You put the paper inside the pineapple. You put the top back on."

The boss stared at Niven as if he were an escapee from some limey booby hatch.

"Yeah," he said, "so I got this pineapple. So what do I do with it?"

When Niven told him, explaining explicitly where he should shove it, the boss' face turned fire-engine red. His henchmen swore and drew large and very real pistols from under their coats. One of the men started toward Niven, fist upraised.

Niven turned pale and his small mustache twitched. Realizing now that he had insulted the real gang boss, he expected to be shot or thrashed into a lifeless pulp.

But the boss called off his boys. Without another word, he turned and led them from the office. Later in the day, Niven and his partners were notified that all their local licenses and permits had been canceled. Having been operating on a shoestring, the partners knew they were whipped. They sold the polo ponies and sneaked out of town.

Still interested in an acting career, because it seemed like ridiculously easy work, Niven went to Hollywood. His contacts with the proper families in New York enabled him to meet equally influential people on the West Coast. During his first four months, he met scads of stars, directors and producers who enjoyed his charming company but offered him no jobs. Living as a house guest with a succession of friends, he kept his living expenses to near-zero, which was also the size of his bank account.

One day producer Edmund Goulding—whom Niven had met at a Beverly Hills party—called him over to MGM. "We're making a picture with Ruth Chatterton," said Goulding, "and I think you can do the part of her drunken brother."

Niven felt a touch of panic which caused him to tell Goulding the truth: "Gadzooks, Eddie, I've never acted in my life. I've just been putting on a big front."

"So what?" said Goulding. "Out here everybody puts on a big front. Let's make a test and see what you can do."

Niven got his brash self-confidence back and ad libbed his way through the screen test without a script or rehearsal. Goulding told him the test was so terrible he couldn't use him in the Chatterton picture. But Goulding also told him he showed promise and advised him to get an agent. Niven signed with Bill Hawks—and also borrowed two hundred dollars from him.

Shortly after this, Niven obtained his first acting role. He appeared as a sleeping Mexican in an early Hopalong Cassidy Western. His salary for the role was $3.50—the standard extra's rate in those Depression years. Meanwhile his original test was rerun a couple of times in MGM's projection rooms. Samuel Goldwyn happened to see it and recommended that Niven be sent to the Pasadena Playhouse to acquire acting polish.

The Englishman was given a minor walk-on part. On opening night he became totally unnerved when he peeped through the curtain and saw the first three rows crammed with Hollywood stars—all cocktail party acquaintances of his. He tried to calm down with a few jolts of Scotch. The result was chaos. He fumbled his lines, knocked over a chair and a lamp on stage—and was fired.

His next encounter with the Hollywood brass was more disastrous. He had met Douglas Fairbanks Sr. in London and been invited to have "lunch sometime in Hollywood." He rang up the great man and Fairbanks immediately invited him over for a steam bath. Broke as usual, Niven hadn't had any breakfast. He sat stark naked on a marble slab in the private steam bath and traded quips for 30 minutes with such giants of the film industry as Darryl Zanuck, Charlie Chaplin, Joe Schenck and Sid Grauman.

The sizzling heat and lack of food weakened Niven quickly. Fairbanks, under the impression that his guest was from a wealthy British family, asked him casually: "What are you going to do this year, Niven—the yacht circuit or the polo rounds?"

Before he could answer the question, Niven fainted. He was revived with a deluge of cold water and carried out. None of the tycoons offered him a job.

Despite Niven's alcoholic fiasco at the Pasadena Playhouse, Sam Goldwyn felt the tall, witty Scotsman deserved another chance. He gave Niven a bit player contract which paid $65 a week. It wasn't much but it was steady, and after that Niven's fortunes commenced to rise. The next year he was cast as one of Ruth Chatterton's lovers in *Dodsworth* at $150 a week and then signed for an even better part in a Ginger Rogers picture.

Niven now began to enjoy life as a fast-stepping Hollywood bachelor. He became the roommate of another gay dog, Errol Flynn, and they boozed it up at such a happy rate that they dubbed their beach apartment "Cirrhosis-by-the-Sea." Flynn's career as a swashbuckler was then moving into high gear. He suggested that Niven try out for the important supporting role of a young captain in Flynn's newest epic, *Charge of the Light Brigade.*

Unfortunately for Niven, there were a dozen top candidates for the job and the tryouts were conducted by Michael Curtiz, a tough-as-steel director who permitted no backtalk on the set. After listening to the first seven actors —all skilled pros—read their lines for the scene, Niven decided he didn't have a chance. When it was his turn, he strolled on stage wearing a to-hell-with-it-all expression.

"Where's your script?" demanded Curtiz.

"I know the part," said Niven.

"Where *is* your script?" repeated Curtiz.

"I left it in the makeup tent," said Niven.

"Run and get it," snapped Curtiz. "And I do mean run!"

It was a warm day and Niven's wool soldier's costume was hot and sticky. Angry and embarrassed, he boiled over and snapped back at Curtiz, saying, "You can damn well run and get it yourself!"

The cameraman choked, the assistant director paled and

Curtiz looked as if he'd been slapped in the face with a leather glove.

Niven, deciding he'd had it, started to walk off the set. But suddenly Curtiz began to laugh. "Dismiss the others," he roared. "Give the part to Mr. Smart Ass!"

After that Niven's career accelerated miraculously. In 1936, three years after coming to Hollywood, he starred in the comedy, *Thank You, Jeeves*. The following year he obtained the coveted role of Scotty, a doomed young pilot in *Dawn Patrol*, and casually stole that picture from Errol Flynn. From there he went on to *Wuthering Heights* and a flock of other hits, including *Bachelor Mother* in 1939, the last film he made before going off to war.

The David Niven who returned to Hollywood in 1946 was still a dashing character who found it easy to pick up his career. But he was different in several ways. He was more mature, there were permanent lines around his eyes and mouth and he was no longer a fast-living bachelor. Now a contented family man, he bought a handsome hilltop home in Pacific Palisades, overlooking the ocean, and sent for his pretty British wife Primmy and their two small sons, David Junior and Jamie.

A month after Primmy arrived from England, she and Niven spent an enjoyable weekend fishing off the coast with Clark Gable, Rex Harrison, Ida Lupino and Nigel Bruce. Afterward they went to Tyrone Power's house, where Power hosted a party honoring Primmy and welcoming her to this country. It was a warm, lazy evening in spring and someone suggested playing Sardines, a children's hide-and-go-seek game. The lights were turned off and all the participants scattered to look for hiding places.

Suddenly the game went from frolic to tragedy. Lovely Primmy—who had survived two bombings during the London blitz—opened what she thought was a door into a closet and tumbled headlong downstairs into the basement, suffering fatal injuries.

It was a long time before Niven was able to reassemble the broken pieces of his life. He submerged himself in his work and leaned heavily on his friends. Gradually things returned to normal. Two years later, Goldwyn sent him to England to make a picture with Sir Alexander Korda. Niven took his small boys along.

In London he met a gorgeous Swedish girl named Hjordis Tersmeden who reminded him of his lost wife. He fell in love again and married Hjordis two weeks after meeting her. She promptly transformed the Nivens back into a happy family unit.

Despite Hjordis' soothing influence, Niven's career went into a slump. His British picture, *Bonnie Prince Charlie,* in which he cavorted about in a blond wig and red kilts, was a flop. Returning to the United States, he severed his ties with MGM and began freelancing. His next effort was *Nina,* a Broadway play which he backed financially as well co-starred in with Gloria Swanson.

The play was a hilarious flop. On opening night Niven, a bit nervous, squeezed Miss Swanson too hard during a serious love scene. Her dress flew apart with a loud twanging sound and a piece of whalebone got stuck in Niven's long nose. First Niven giggled and then he laughed uproariously. So did the audience. In the *Herald Tribune* the next day, critic Walter Kerr wrote acidly: "Like the play, the clothes fell apart in the first act."

Niven lost so much money on *Nina* that he was now as flat broke as when he first landed in Hollywood in 1933. Undaunted, he obtained a starring role in the road company of the sexy play, *The Moon Is Blue.* He made such a hit he was signed for the screen version, which was a smash, grossing over $7,000,000. Having had the foresight to ask for a percentage of the film's profits, he was speedily restored to solvency.

More success followed. Mike Todd gave him the exhilarating role of dapper Phineas Fogg in his box-office blockbuster, *Around the World in 80 Days.* And then he obtained an un-Niven-like role in the film *Separate Tables.* The part called for him to portray a pathetic leech, a man who pretended to be a heroic major but who was in reality a molester of women. Niven's actor friends warned him that the role, radically different from anything he'd ever done, would put his career back on the skids.

But his performance was so electrifyingly evil that Niven won an Oscar as the top actor of 1958. On the night of the Oscar awards show, he was so nervous he had to take a swim in an ice-cold pool in order to calm down. Afterward, disdaining false modesty, he told a national television audience: "Dammit, I must say I wanted to win and I'm happy I did."

In the early fifties Niven tried his hand at live TV and found he detested it. "It's an actor's agony," he declared. "You go on overdressed, underpaid and under-rehearsed."

Deciding there was far more money to be made in the production end of TV, he joined with Dick Powell and Charles Boyer in a venture called Four Star Television. Although underfinanced in its infancy, Four Star soon zoomed to the top, producing such shows as *Zane Grey Theater, Richard Diamond, Private Eye; Alcoa* and *Goodyear Theaters, Trackdown, Mr. Adams and Eve* and *Burke's Law*.

During the next ten years, Four Star turned out thousands of TV dramas and comedies, helping to catapult Niven into the millionaire class.

Meanwhile Niven has all the work he can handle in major films produced in Hollywood and Europe, receiving salaries of $150,000 and $200,000 per production, plus an occasional juicy percentage. He bounces back and forth between his California home and a chalet in Switzerland which he describes as a "cuckoo clock on a hill." His film successes in recent years have included *The Guns of Navarone, Act of Mercy, The Captive City* and *Best of Enemies*.

Now fifty-six years old, Niven weighs a fairly trim 190 pounds and keeps the fat off his waistline by skiing and whacking tennis balls. With pouches under his eyes and deep creases beneath his jaw, he looks his age. His wavy hair is salted with gray and so thin in front that he wears a partial toupee before the cameras.

The rascal who once was nearly court-martialed, who lived like a parasite off his friends and stole breakfasts from restaurants, now enjoys club contacts in London with such uppercrust personalities as Prince Philip. His knack for doing witty, impulsive things keeps his tony friends in a constant titter.

For example, one day he went for a stroll along the English countryside with the wife of a noted diplomat. Suddenly her panties fell down. Niven didn't smile or make a comment. Gallantly he picked them up and stuffed them into his pocket.

Every Christmas since then, the diplomat's wife has received the same gift from Niven—a beautifully wrapped box containing a yard of elastic. Whenever they meet, he makes her laugh and blush by whispering: "Bloomers!"

Niven's friendship with Queen Elizabeth's husband is so chummy and casual that it recently provoked the following bit of nonsense:

While he was working in a London film studio, a janitor came up and said: "Mr. Niven, there's a bloke on the phone who says he's Prince Philip at Buckingham Palace and he wants to talk to you. Silly, what? Shall I tell him to ring off?"

"Of course not," said Niven.

He went to the phone. The caller was Prince Philip.

"Hello, David," he said. "Just wondered what you were doing."

"Nothing," said Niven.

"Same here," said Philip.

"Terribly boring, isn't it?" said Niven.

"Indeed," said the prince. "Well, I'll see you around. 'Bye, David."

" 'Bye, Philip."

They hung up. Niven strolled past the janitor—who regarded him with dumbstruck awe—and went back to work before the cameras.

VIOLENCE ADDICT

• *TEDD THOMEY*

All night long, actor George C. Scott dominated the theatrical party in midtown Manhattan. He was a big drinker, a loud talker and a showoff, but he seemed so fascinating—in a savage, destructive way—that the two dozen people there, even resentful other actors, found it difficult to keep their eyes off him.

This in itself was an achievement, because on that night in November, 1958, George C. Scott was the least known, least important actor in the room. If he had been wiser, and more sober, he would have kept his lip buttoned and listened respectfully to the conversation of the influential producers and directors who had scored major successes on Broadway.

But Scott could not keep his big trap shut any more than he could prevent the disaster about to befall him.

He was standing in the center of the living room, arguing with a middle-aged press agent. Scott's hand clutched a large glass of bourbon which he gulped with nervous intensity. It was his eighth or ninth drink, and he was drunker than anyone, including himself, realized. With peculiar logic he persisted in arguing that there was no need for publicity in the theater.

The press agent, a veteran of his trade, was a big-shouldered, graying man named Thurston. He became increasingly irritated by Scott's belligerent attitude and smart wisecracks.

"Hypocrisy and dishonesty!" rasped Scott. "That's all publicity is. No real actor needs it!"

Tilting his glass high, Scott drained it, then stared at Thurston with ill-disguised disgust.

"And I say you're full of crap!" retorted Thurston.

Those were stinging, insulting words. Thurston, who had also been drinking heavily, wouldn't have uttered them if he'd been better acquainted with Scott. All he knew about the actor was that he had a role in a foundering Broadway play, *Comes a Day*. If he'd been more alert, he would have read certain signs on Scott's hard face which indicated he was addicted to brutality and violence.

Scott's nose, twisted and scarred, protruded as a classic warning. It was a brawler's nose, broken five times during barroom fights while he served in the Marines. There was another scar at the corner of Scott's left eye, and two more ridges of heavy scar tissue were clearly evident on his blunt chin.

"What did you say?" demanded Scott, his voice harsh with rising fury.

"You're full of crap!" repeated Thurston, turning angrily as if to stride away.

Scott's arm shot out. He grabbed a handful of Thurston's shirtfront and silk tie. Thurston tried to break loose, but Scott's big hand held him too tightly.

Thurston struck heavily at Scott's arm. Then he landed a hard smash against Scott's thin-lipped mouth.

Scott might have been waiting for that. He grunted, a sound of satisfaction more than pain, dropped his whiskey glass on the rug and began swinging.

At first it seemed to be a fair match. Thurston was a large man, over 200 pounds. Scott was a six-footer, weighing 190. Scott hit Thurston a glancing blow on the shoulder and in return was banged solidly on the side of his head.

It was the last punch Thurston landed because after that Scott was all over him. Scott, younger, trimmer and better muscled, drove an enormous blow into Thurston's diaphragm. It knocked the wind out of the older man and left him goggle-eyed. As Thurston bent over, clutching his upper belly in agony, Scott delivered another punch. It was a blockbuster on the point of Thurston's jaw and it straightened him up momentarily like a puppet on a string. The sound of the blow, bone against bone, could be heard throughout the large apartment.

Women screamed. Two of the strongest, biggest men in the group tried to seize Scott, but he shook them off. He fought like a stuck bull, supercharged with drunken hatred. He hit Thurston again, although the press agent was defenseless, stumbling backward in a daze, hands dangling at his sides.

It took three men to stop the fight, but long after that Scott kept the place in an uproar. Even after he was overpowered and pinned to the floor, he kept struggling, kicking wildly at his captors and cursing them. When the police arrived, he started a new outburst, swinging his arms with frantic animal strength when the officers attempted to handcuff him.

Finally subdued, with his arms manacled behind him, he was escorted downstairs by four burly policemen and deposited in a patrol car.

When Scott awoke around dawn, he found himself in a drunk tank with a dozen other reeking, besotted men. It wasn't the first time he'd been jailed for drinking and fighting. Once he'd been brigged for boozing while in the Marines. But it was the first time he'd awakened in handcuffs and he felt deeply ashamed of himself.

Later in the morning, still manacled, he was taken before a magistrate. When Scott complained about the cuffs, an escorting officer told him gruffly: "They stay on, bud. After the rumpus you kicked up last night, we ain't taking any chances!"

Scott was stunned when he heard the charges against him, including felonious assault with intent to commit great bodily harm. Hazily he remembered how the party had started, but he had blacked out completely after that. He didn't recall the argument with Thurston or any of the other details of the brawl.

The proof of his misdeeds was present in the courtroom, however, in the bandaged, bruised person of Thurston. Fortunately for Scott, the press agent decided not to press the charges. The judge fined Scott twenty-five dollars for being drunk and disorderly and then gave him a tongue-lashing.

"Mr. Scott," said the judge, "I understand you're an actor. I've been told that you show considerable promise in the theatrical arts. So listen to my warning, young man. You are one of those cursed souls who *cannot* and *must not* drink. If you keep on, you will destroy not only your career, but yourself. You are either going to be a successful actor or a drunken idiot. Mr. Scott, the choice is up to you."

George C. Scott returned home a shaken man. He went into his bedroom and sat down on the bed, keeping his hands in his coat pockets so their alcoholic trembling would not be so noticeable. He wanted a drink. Wanted it so badly that his tongue prickled and burned with desire for the taste of whiskey. His throat felt swollen and dry and he knew, with a growing sense of urgency, that a few gurgles of liquor would soon calm those tortured tissues.

Instead, remembering the judge's warning words, he went into the bathroom and filled a glass with water. It tasted terrible, did nothing to ease the roaring demands within him, to depress the hangover pounding in his skull. As he opened the medicine cabinet door to get some aspirin, he caught a glimpse of his face in the mirror.

And he despised what he saw.

The evil, villainous face which stared back at him was bleary-eyed and unshaven, the skin pasty and unhealthy with premature lines around the eyes and mouth. It was a countenance which some day would be famed throughout the world for its unique portrayals of depravity and corruption in such films as *The Hustler*, *Dr. Strangelove* and *The Yellow Rolls Royce*.

But on that day in 1958 it was just the face of another shaky drunk. It was unique only because George Campbell Scott, then thirty-one years old, looked like a man of forty. For fourteen wild years, ever since he'd enlisted in the Marines at the age of seventeen, he'd been on one bender after another. It was alcohol which was responsible for quickening the ravages time had made on his hard face.

And it was alcohol that had ruined his two previous marriages, caused his closest friends to avoid him and cost him numerous vital acting jobs.

As he slammed the medicine cabinet door shut, Scott remembered another mirror and the violent episode of another night. It had happened a few months before at the home of an actor pal named Hank. Scott had been drinking steadily for two days before wandering up to Hank's apartment, where he'd downed several double martinis in a row. The ensuing reaction was part of a nightmarish pattern which had been occurring more frequently during his drinking bouts.

He had blacked out in Hank's front room.

When he awakened the next morning on Hank's davenport, there was broken glass on the rug—fragments from a large mirror which had been standing over the black tile fireplace. When he asked Hank how the mirror had broken, his friend was too embarrassed at first to tell him. But he grabbed Hank by the shoulder and shook the story out of him.

"You went out of your skull!" Hank said. "George, you scared the living hell out of me. I don't know who you thought I was, but you came at me with both fists swinging. You terrified me, yelling, 'Stand still, you bastard! I'm going to kill you!'"

"You're kidding," said Scott, but he knew in his heart that Hank was telling the truth.

Hank shook his head slowly. "George, I wish I was. You chased me all over the room, but you were so drunk you couldn't lay a finger on me. Then you saw your face in the mirror, and it was like a very bad scene from a Hollywood B movie. You snatched that tall vase off the mantel and you went after yourself in the mirror. You smashed it to a thousand pieces!"

The memory of his friend's words echoed in Scott's head, pulsating there with a mixture of hangover pain and memories of other drunken escapades in his life. Stumbling from the bathroom, he sank down heavily on the edge of his bed and stared at the wall. A word intruded into his confused thoughts. It was a loathsome word, one he tried to avoid with cowardly instincts each times its ugly meaning pushed itself into his consciousness.

Alcoholic.

The word had been intruding more frequently in recent months. And each time it came he shunned it because he could not admit to himself that he had sunk that low. But now it could no longer be dodged. *He was an alcoholic.* The evidence was everywhere about him: fingers which shook with an uncontrollable palsy . . . hangovers that never seemed to dissipate, their fumes beclouding all his waking and working hours . . . the desire for liquor which superseded all other hungers . . .

But worst of all were the blackouts. Such as the one last night involving the press agent, Thurston. It was terrifying to awaken afterward and not recall one detail of the terrible things people said he had done. In the past he had blacked out like that maybe once a year. But now the blackouts were coming oftener, sometimes twice a month, each more frightening than the previous one.

What was happening to him? And where would it lead? To a sanitarium to be dried out like other neurotic actors he'd known? Or would he plunge further, becoming a Skid Row bum, flopping in an alley somewhere, too far gone to brush the flies off his face?

That long afternoon in November eight years ago marked the low point of George C. Scott's life. It was inevitable that some day he would reach such a crossroads, because he had been heading for it since his earliest days in Detroit, Michigan, where he grew up. He had been a compulsive, headstrong boy, a battler always going all-out for the things he wanted.

From the time he was eight, when his mother died, he had hurled himself unsuccessfully against a never-ending flow of frustrations and failures. The shocking loss of his mother's love at that tender age made him suspicious of people and their motives. He was often a loner, withdrawn into himself, resisting the efforts of kindly grammar school teachers who, recognizing his intelligence, tried to help him.

Young Scott idolized his father, a well-to-do man who was benevolent and loving. But instead of being a source of happiness the boy's respect for his father became a monumental obstacle that would blight his life for decades.

The elder Scott was a powerfully successful, self-made industrial leader. Born in grinding poverty in a cabin in the hillbilly country of Virginia, Scott Senior had performed back-racking pick-and-shovel labor in coal mines and scratched for a living as a dirt farmer. Studying at night by firelight, like Abe Lincoln, he had educated himself, moved to Detroit and rose from salesman to executive vice president of the Ex-Cell-O Corporation.

In comparison, young Scott's early life was an idyllic combination of fine clothes, a large allowance and rich foods. But such luxuries were a supreme irritation to the boy. He felt that because he lacked hardships he should have progressed more rapidly than his father had done. He drove himself ceaselessly. But everything he did failed. His school grades did not measure up to his father's. When he reached high school, he went out for athletics, determined to win fame as a baseball star. He was pretty good, but never approached star status.

After graduating from high school, Scott enlisted eagerly in the Marines, hoping to become a decorated war hero, something his father had not accomplished. But when he finished his training in 1945, World War II was over and he was sent to Washington, D.C., for ceremonial duties. Day after day he found himself at Arlington National Cemetery, marching in solemn burial rites for heroes who had been killed at Saipan, Iwo Jima and Okinawa.

After his one hundredth such ceremony, Pfc. Scott couldn't take it any longer.

"My God!" he complained to a Marine buddy one day. "I'm having nightmares about these poor guys. I keep seeing graves and hearing taps in my sleep. If I don't do something pretty soon I'll go out of my — — mind!"

His buddy suggested two remedies: "See the chaplain— or get drunk!"

The thought of getting plastered seemed by far the most novel course. Until then the strongest thing Scott had tasted was beer, and not much of that. When his duties were over that evening, he and his pal hitchhiked into downtown Washington. They went into the first joint they saw and bellied up to the bar like a couple of cowhands in a John Wayne movie.

"Whiskey!" demanded Scott. "Straight!"

It burned in his throat, but he got it down without choking or coughing.

"More!" he grunted, flinging a five-dollar bill on the bartop.

Scott was barely past his eighteenth birthday. If the bartender thought the boy was underage, he kept his suspicions hidden, pouring drinks for the two Marines until the five spot changed owners.

After that Scott spent most of his free time in bars. Since

his funds were limited, he was forced to frequent the sleazier joints where the whiskey was raw, cheap and plentiful. By the time he was twenty, Sergeant Scott was a hardened carouser with a belly of steel. Sometimes he would drink all night without getting really drunk. Arriving back at the Marine base at dawn, he showered and shaved, reported to the drill field and marched his platoon all day without feeling particularly weary.

"I never had a hangover," Scott boasted to theatrical pals some years later. "I drank the worst rotgut known to man, but when it got inside me it turned mellow as butter."

It was during those years that Scott also discovered the pleasures of barroom brawling. He was now slightly over six feet tall, weighed 185, and had the heavy shoulders and well-muscled arms of a longshoreman. His first fist fight occurred in a bar one night after he and three other Marines had been to a movie featuring Robert Taylor and Ava Gardner. A fat, beer-guzzling sergeant-major began making remarks about Miss Gardner's performance.

"Worst damn actress I ever saw," commented the self-proclaimed drama critic. "Couldn't act her way out of a bundle of wet scivvy shirts."

Scott disagreed. "She's improving," he insisted. "She's better right now than half the broads in Hollywood!"

The sergeant-major made another crack about Ava Gardner, and then deliberately tipped over Scott's shot glass, which was half full of whiskey.

It was the signal for Scott to start swinging, and he didn't disappoint his Saturday night audience of Marines and sailors who roared for blood. There was no scientific boxing involved, as he well knew from having observed other brawlers. You simply stood toe to toe, slugged away with both fists, and the guy who lasted the longest was declared the winner. He hit the fat sergeant-major squarely on the nose, saw claret squirt, and then suffered a blow on his left eye that made it swell like a rotten potato.

The trouble with the fat sergeant-major was that he only looked fat. Underneath he was made of leather and brass, and he belted Scott all over the room. He broke the bridge of Scott's nose, twisted an ear into a soft pulp and sent him crashing twice to the floor with vicious forearm chops across the back of the neck.

"Jesus Christ!" muttered an impressed sailor. "Will you look at that!"

For the third time in three minutes, Scott dragged him-

self up from the floor. Acquiring new strength from somewhere, he flung himself upon the sergeant-major, fastening
both hands around his chunky throat.

The sergeant-major clubbed Scott on the back of the
head with both fists. But Scott was a clinging maniac who
couldn't be dislodged no matter what the other man did. In
ninety seconds, it was all over. Unable to breathe, the
sergeant-major toppled over backwards, his skull making a
magnificent clunk on the barroom floor. Scott rode him
down. He lifted the sergeant-major's limp head, clunked it
on the floor once more and then swayed victoriously to his
feet while the other servicemen whistled and applauded.

It was the first applause Scott ever earned. He discovered
that he had a voracious appetite for brawling. It seemed to
fill a need that lay somewhere within him. After a good
fight, no matter how bruised and bloody he was, he felt at
peace with the world. Sometimes he didn't drink for a
week or two after a brawl, being content to lie around the
Marine barracks, smoking and reading magazines and
books.

Many years later, when he was a struggling actor, he
confessed his problems to a psychiatrist and was told that
fighting and drinking were a kind of therapy for him. "You
are filled with self-hate," declared the doctor. "You hate
yourself because you consider yourself a miserable failure
compared to your father. You love your father, but you
also hate him for his successes. Your drinking and fighting
follow a consistent pattern of self-punishment. When you
get hurt in a fight, your subconscious needs are satisfied,
feeling you have been justly punished for your failures as
a person."

When his four-year Marine enlistment ended, Scott went
to Columbia, Missouri, and enrolled in the University of
Missouri's School of Journalism. He wanted to become a
newspaper reporter. At first he studied intensely, enjoying
the challenge of learning something new. But then he ran
into heavy disappointments. The deeper he delved into
journalism the more he realized he wasn't right for it. He
discovered that he detested interviewing people and was
embarrassed whenever he had to ask questions about their
work or personal life.

Confused and disillusioned, he yearned to try something
which would restore his confidence and high spirits. He
read an article in the campus newspaper telling of the need
for actors in a play, *The Winslow Boy*. He tried out and

obtained a tiny part. Inspired by the excitement on and around the stage, he signed up for roles in four more college plays. In one he spoke several lines of dialogue near the climax, receiving a tremendous burst of applause for a brief phrase which he delivered with stunning force.

That did it. He was solidly hooked, finding that two key words in a good play could be as stimulating as two jolts from a bottle of good bourbon. After that, letting his journalism courses slide, he drenched himself thoroughly in stage work of all kinds. He joined a theatrical company at nearby Stephens College for women, won several featured roles and met a beautiful sophomore actress named Carolyn Hughes. He fell in love with her. Like everything else he did, Scott went for her in a compulsive, willful way.

"Look, Carolyn baby," he told her one afternoon, "let's not kid around. Do you love me?"

"Of course, George!" was her reply.

They walked off the campus a few minutes later and never went back. They married and took acting jobs with stock companies in Toledo, Ohio, and Detroit. For the first few months of 1952, life was marvelous and George C. Scott, rising young actor and romantic bridegroom, had the world swinging by its tail. Then Carolyn became pregnant and suddenly there were no more acting jobs, not even with trashy road companies that paid leading men $35 a week.

At the age of twenty-six, Scott discovered once more that he was a monumental failure. He was a brand new father, deeply in debt—and had no job prospects whatsoever. Disgusted and discouraged, trying to hide from himself, he turned in his weakness to the most convenient solution: the bottle.

Carolyn couldn't stand the sight of him wallowing in self-pity. She walked out, taking the baby. The following year, 1954, they were divorced.

During the next twelve months, Scott bummed around the country. He hitchhiked, rode the rails, slept in flophouses and tried desperately to find acting jobs. The futility of his existence reached a climax one night in a fleabag hotel in Denver, where he was bedded down in a long, narrow, foul-smelling room with half a dozen other bums. He was weak and exhausted, having eaten nothing since breakfast when he'd had a cinnamon roll and coffee. He did, however, have the solace of a small bottle of cheap cooking burgundy which he'd earned by sweeping out a liquor store.

Lying on a filthy mattress, he was sipping from the bottle when a shadow loomed up beside his bunk.

"Gimme that!" said a rough voice.

A man's hand snatched away the bottle. When Scott, protesting, tried to sit up, a huge fist struck him on the forehead. For the next hour, Scott, semiconscious, lay on the floor, too weak to climb back into the bunk. Even more degrading, he was too weak to attack the thief who reclined nearby, killing Scott's bottle.

A few weeks later, with ten cents in his pocket, Scott arrived in Washington, D.C. Ignoring the sleazy haunts of his Marine Corps days, he used the dime to phone his sister, married to a building contractor. For the next few months, he lived in her house and worked in his brother-in-law's construction business. He drove a dirt truck, poured concrete, and was a general handyman. Regular meals and ample sleep put the bounce back in his step and his physical condition became better than it had been for years.

However, George C. Scott, the actor, could not possibly be satisfied with the dull, low station in life of George C. Scott, general handyman. He began to spend his evenings hanging around a semi-professional theatrical group in the Washington suburbs. Soon he was offered a good role in a strong, philosophical play by the Italian dramatist, Luigi Pirandello. Again he met a pretty actress, Pat Reed, and fell in love.

They were married—and the struggle began all over. Scott knew he was a great and talented actor; all he needed was the opportunity to convince the right theatrical people. He and his second bride moved to New York to be closer to the right people, who completely ignored him. Scott spent his nights working in a bank as the *ta-pocketa-pocketa* operator of an IBM proof machine. His salary was so insignificant he was forced to work in the daytime as a rug salesman. In his spare moments he hunted for acting jobs.

On two occasions directors turned him down for roles, saying: "Scott, it's that twisted nose of yours. You'll never be a leading man with all those lumps. Why don't you try plastic surgery?"

Scott shook his head proudly. "Not in a million years.

I earned this beak the hard way. I wouldn't change it even if God himself asked me!"

In October, 1957, Scott heard that director Stuart Vaughan was casting an off-Broadway production of *Richard III*. Scott wanted the role of Richard so badly he tensed up during his first audition. The lines he spoke were flat and meaningless. He asked for a second chance and the results were even worse.

Dejected and moody, Scott resorted to his usual remedy —a bottle. He went on a 24-hour bender and woke up the next morning in the damp garden of a friend's house. Hearing strange sniffing sounds, he lifted his heavy eyelids and stared into the curious eyes of his friend's two large police dogs.

Scott, disgusted with himself, dragged his weary body to a phone, called Vaughan and begged for a third chance. "That part's mine!" he declared hoarsely. "You've got to give it to me!"

Reluctantly the director agreed. Scott staggered home and downed great draughts of steaming black coffee. He stayed up all night reading soliloquies, practicing his phrasing and his Shakespearean gestures. When his wife insisted that he go to bed and rest, he thundered, "Damn it, no! I'm going to give it all I've got. If Vaughan turns me down, I'll give up acting once and for all. I'll go back to driving a dirt truck!"

In the morning Scott appeared at the theater cold sober, his whole appearance exuding great professional calm. Inside he was a trembling, nervous wreck, but no one suspected because he read for the role with a vigor and sensitivity seldom heard in an off-Broadway theater.

He got the part. It paid only forty-five dollars a week, but it was the turning point of his career. Sir Laurence Olivier's classic film version of *Richard III* was playing in New York's movie theaters at the same time. But many thought George C. Scott's Richard was better.

Thus one of Scott's battles ended, but the other didn't. His drinking became worse. The more successful he became, the more he drank. He needed liquor now to keep from tensing up before going on stage. Amazingly, he acted brilliantly even when he was so sodden with booze that he occasionally slurred a line or bumped into furniture. His performance in an off-Broadway production of *As You Like It* was so magnificent everyone knew he would soon make it big on Broadway itself.

Scott's drinking performance at home became so bad, however, that his second marriage failed. He was entering his blackout period now, with lapses of memory and acts of violence. During rehearsal one afternoon he flew into a drunken rage and tore up a backdrop painted to resemble a city park. It was an old piece of canvas which tore easily. He kicked at the painted shrubs and park benches until they were tattered rags.

Next he was starred in *Children of Darkness* with Colleen Dewhurst, a fiery actress impressed by Scott's acting genius and repulsed by his reputation as a drunkard. Nevertheless, she married him. At first his drinking bouts frightened her because she didn't know how to handle or help him. Eventually she learned that there was only one way to live with George C. Scott: He could not be pushed or coerced into laying off the liquor; she would have to wait patiently until he discovered for himself the harm he was doing—to her, as well as himself.

The decision was forced upon him far sooner than she dared hope. Scott's big opportunity came. He was cast in his first Broadway play, *Comes a Day* with Judith Anderson. He expected it to be a crashing success which would win him national acclaim. Instead it created hardly a stir and was destined to fold after a few weeks.

Once again Scott saw his hopes dashed. Knowing the play was doomed, he came onstage drunk nearly every night. This was the background for the Manhattan cocktail party where his brutal drunken attack on press agent Thurston led to Scott awakening manacled in jail. Added to his other humiliations was the fact that none of the cops or police station reporters recognized him as one of the featured players in a Broadway drama.

While Scott was at home that afternoon, suffering from a monstrous hangover and the even worse agony of admitting he was an alcoholic, the phone rang. In its way the ringing of that phone was as melodramatic as a plot twist in a story by de Maupassant or O. Henry. The caller was Scott's agent, and his voice displayed a note of restrained excitement.

"George," he said, "I've got news for you. I don't want you to get your hopes too high, because the deal isn't set yet. But here it is. Otto Preminger is considering you for a fat part in *Anatomy of a Murder*."

"What did you say?" exclaimed Scott.

"You heard me," was the reply. "One of Preminger's

story editors caught your performance in *Comes a Day*. He thought you were terrific. And he thinks you'll be terrific as the prosecuting attorney in *Anatomy*. If he can sell you to Otto, you're in!"

Three days later, Scott received another phone call. He was in! And this meant he could no longer postpone the biggest decision of his life. Otto Preminger was one of the most feared producer-directors on the coast, a martinet who permitted no alcoholic follies on his film sets. If Scott's drinking caused him to suffer blackouts in Hollywood, his work would suffer and Preminger would fire him.

There were two courses Scott could follow: He could continue boozing and his career would wobble hazily through its ups and downs; or he could quit the stuff cold turkey and make a run for stardom, huge salaries and top artistic fulfillment.

He decided to quit. Cold turkey, if he could.

It was rougher than he ever imagined anything could be. And there were bitter, miserable failures, because fourteen years of concentrated, devoted drinking could not be overcome overnight. More than once he slipped during the first drying-out weeks, sneaking a drink when his nerves cried out for release from the torment of long days and nights of tension. As he knew it would, one drink led to a second, then a third—and drunkenness.

He tried psychiatry. It didn't work. Then he went to a friend, a respected actor who was a reformed drunk and member of Alcoholics Anonymous. The friend took him to AA meetings and Scott began a process that patiently got him through one day, then two days, a week—and finally weeks of abstinence.

His third wife stuck by him during that arduous period, and Scott credited her influence with being as important as AA's. "Colleen was wonderful," he told writer Bill Davidson during an interview. "Not once did she push me or scold. But she wouldn't let me weaken. Whenever I found myself in a vast labyrinth of self-pity, she wouldn't let me take the easy way out. She never fell for my excuses, like, 'Be nice to me or I'll drink.' She was firm all the way."

When he reported for work two months later on Preminger's set, Scott was a model of sobriety. His portrayal of the icy-eyed, rasping-voiced prosecutor in *Anatomy of a Murder* was the finest part in the picture. It lifted him from acting anonymity to critical acclaim and a nomination in 1959 for an Oscar. Although he didn't win, his future was assured as scores of lucrative offers for new roles poured in from film and stage producers.

Topping them were deals involving long-term film contracts which would have made him a millionaire. Disdainfully Scott rejected them all. "I do not choose to make mediocre pictures," he said. "I want to be free to alternate between the best stage roles I can find and the best I can get in films. I won't make as much money—but I'll be my own man."

After that Scott revealed a prodigious capacity for overwork and an ability to lock horns with anybody or anything which he believed stood in his way. His rugged face, with its searching eyes, misshapen nose and angry mouth, was seen in a succession of remarkably powerful roles. He was the intense, vindictive judge advocate in *The Andersonville Trial*, a Broadway hit. Then he played the vicious, calculating gambler in Hollywood's *The Hustler*, and a stone-hearted police lieutenant in TV's *The Power and the Glory*. For his *Hustler* characterization he received his second Oscar nomination.

Scott immediately stunned the Academy of Motion Picture Arts and Sciences by rejecting the nomination. It was the first time in the 39-year history of the organization that such a thing had occurred. Insultingly outspoken, Scott revealed the reasons for his rejection, declaring: "The Academy structure is an orgy of advertising and publicity. It needs cleaning up. I have no respect for the Oscar awards."

Maintaining an iron self-discipline, Scott stayed off the booze for two, three, then four and five years. He and Colleen became the parents of two handsome children, Alex and Campbell. Scott—romping with the boys and teaching them baseball—gave the outward appearance of being a supremely happy family man. Whenever he developed a dry-mouthed hankering for a drink, he defeated the desire by (1) staying up all night with friends playing intense games of bridge or chess, or (2) exhausting himself with long sixteen- and eighteen-hour work days that drove him to bed for much-needed slumber.

In a 24-month period of furious activity, he appeared in two major films, *The List of Adrian Messenger* and *Dr. Strangelove;* starred in several major television dramas; did a summer season of Shakespeare in Central Park; acted in 17 one-hour episodes of his own CBS-TV series, *East Side, West Side,* and founded and helped finance The Theater of

Michigan. He sank $70,000 of his own money into the last activity, which was designed to produce plays in Detroit and then take them to Broadway.

He directed two of the plays, *General Seeger* and *Great Day in the Morning,* and suffered the indignity of seeing both flop. When he received the bad news that he had lost the entire $70,000 (his life savings), Scott swallowed dryly and cracked, "What the hell. I'll just have to go out and earn some more!"

He did. Having risen in five brief years from a lowly $45-a-week part-time actor to a star commanding $10,000 for a TV performance and $100,000 per major film, Scott found it easy to recoup his losses. Last year his TV work and performances in such films as *The Yellow Rolls Royce* and *The Bible* earned him an estimated quarter of a million dollars.

It appeared that George C. Scott had it made.

Then a shocking incident revealed that Scott—after resisting the temptations of the juice for seven long years —had fallen off the wagon with a crash that could be heard from London to New York.

The event had its beginning in the late summer of 1964 when Scott left his wife and children in Manhattan while he went to Rome to work in *The Bible.* It was an epic in which he labored for four and a half months, playing the role of Abraham. One of his co-stars was an actress he had idolized and fought for back in his Marine Corps days— Ava Gardner.

Soon after filming began, reports came from the set that Scott had fallen for Ava. There were also reports that much-married Ava, whose boyfriends in recent years had included young bullfighters as well as actors, was toying with the idea of adding Scott to her long list of conquests.

At first it seemed the wildest kind of a mismatch. Wasn't Ava, now an aging movie queen in her forties, at least five years older than 37-year-old Scott? And wasn't he supposed to be happily married to Colleen Dewhurst, who had helped rescue him from the sodden plight of alcoholism?

All was quiet until the shooting of the picture ended. Then, from London, came an Associated Press dispatch telling of a wild, drunken scene which had occurred in the posh Savoy Hotel, where both Scott and Miss Gardner were staying.

First the sounds of an argument were heard in Miss

Gardner's suite. Then there was a scream and a woman's voice, presumably Ava's, shouting, "No, George!"

When more noises erupted, including the shattering crash of a falling object, guests in nearby rooms notified the management. A small squad of hotel officials hurried to the actress' suite. They found Miss Gardner and Scott engaged in an angry, shouting dispute. The actor was glassy-eyed, red-faced and unable to walk without staggering.

Miss Gardner asked to have Scott ejected from her suite. Two of the biggest hotel officials, including the chief house detective, seized him firmly by the elbows and escorted him downstairs.

They took him outside where a trio of London policemen waited to make the arrest. Charging Scott with drunkenness, they haled him before a magistrate who released him on his own recognizance. The next day he was fined 10 shillings ($1.40).

The ugly scene in Ava's suite did not mean, however, that her romance with Scott had been broken off. Two weeks later columnists in New York and Hollywood reported that Scott was rushing eagerly ahead with plans to discard his wife and children in order to marry Ava.

If this were true—and Scott made no effort to deny the reports—it meant he was ready to add another wild chapter to his incredibly compulsive life.

Commented one of Scott's bridge-playing friends in Manhattan: "Ava will destroy him. In six months she'll have him back on the booze and climbing the walls."

Commented another friend: "Don't worry about George. He can take care of himself. He'll have Ava climbing the walls."

Whatever was in store for George C. Scott—whether he was to be rousingly drunk or icy-eyed sober—you could be sure of at least two things.

He wouldn't be dull. And he wouldn't be quiet.

WILD, WILD WORLD OF PETER O'TOOLE

• TEDD THOMEY

Poor as beggars, the O'Toole family wandered from city to city, from race track to race track. When the elder O'Toole returned after a good day at the track, the house was joyful and there was meat on the table. But when he lost, which was more likely, he came home in a black mood smelling of beer and ale. Dinner on those nights consisted of hard bread and a bit of fish.

On August 2, 1933, in Connemara, County Galway, Ireland, the O'Toole's were blessed with a baby christened Peter Seamus O'Toole by his Catholic parents. The father, Patrick Joseph O'Toole, was a bookie, poorly educated but smart, dogged most of the time by bad luck. His mother was a Scottish woman named Constance whom the son now refers to as a "saint."

Young Peter was educated sporadically in a succession of Catholic grammar schools. A bright pupil but unruly and stubborn, he was in continual trouble with his teachers, who were nuns and strict disciplinarians. Naturally left-handed, he was forced to write with his right hand. Whenever a nun caught him using his left hand, she whacked his knuckles sharply with a ruler. Today O'Toole's hand still has over thirty tiny white scars, each a reminder of a painful, stormy classroom scene.

One day the pupils in his second-grade class were told to draw horses. Peter finished his drawing before the others and sat idly behind his desk.

"Well," said the nun, looking down at his quickly scrawled animal, "why not draw something else—a saddle or perhaps a bridle?"

Within a few minutes she returned to see what he had drawn. Her face turned crimson. The horse now had a penis and was urinating strongly in the pasture.

With both hands, the nun began to whip the seven-year-old boy. Other nuns, hearing the clamor, rushed in, saw the drawing and were outraged. "Nasty boy!" they cried. "Nasty! Nasty!" All the nuns flailed their hands wildly at his cringing back, knocking him to the floor and not listening as he sobbed bewilderedly: "But, but . . . I was only drawing what I *saw* . . . only drawing what I *saw!*"

Such experiences embittered O'Toole not only against his teachers, but against the Catholic religion. At an early age he also acquired a disrespect for policemen.

When the O'Toole family moved from Ireland to Leeds, England, young Peter became lost one afternoon. He wandered about the city, gazing curiously at the strange buildings and streets, halting to watch a man paint a telephone pole green. When the painter walked away, leaving his equipment behind, Peter picked up the brush and finished daubing the pole, smearing a generous amount of green on his face and shirt. A policeman strolled up, grasped him firmly by the ear and marched him off to the station.

There a group of officers ridiculed the small Irish boy, teasing him about the green daubs on his nose and chin, and telling him frightening stories about how he would never see his parents again. "They were cruel about it," O'Toole recalls. "They were f—ing big nasties, and I never forgot their meanness. I hated them for it. . . "

His father's attitude toward the law did nothing to improve young Peter's opinion of policemen. Sometimes O'Toole senior would hide the boy beneath his overcoat and sneak him past the gate guards at the race tracks. One day his father bet so heavily on a losing nag that he did not have enough cash to pay his winning customers. Ten seconds after the race ended he closed up his bookie booth, grabbed Peter's hand and they scurried away.

A customer with a winning ticket saw them and shouted, "Stop that man!" Other customers took up the cry, pursuing Patrick O'Toole and his son around the stands toward shrubbery at the edge of the track. The two O'Tooles dived headlong into the thick branches, squirming and fighting their way through, ripping their jackets and trousers pockets in the process. They escaped, but Patrick O'Toole could not return to that particular track for a long time.

At the age of fourteen, Peter quit school for good and

went to work in a warehouse. After that he was employed as a copyboy and photographer's assistant at the Yorkshire *Evening News*. He liked the job very much until it occurred to him that newspapermen remain primarily on the sidelines of life recording the deeds of famous men, and very rarely become famous themselves. "I decided," he said, "that I very much wanted to be famous—so I resigned."

He tried his hand at a few amateur theatrical productions, impressed no one, and enlisted in the Royal Navy. He spent two years as an undistinguished signalman, developed a thorough disrespect for all things nautical and decided, on being discharged in 1954, that he would become a professional actor. He was twenty-one years old, tall as a lamppost and equally thin, and as cocky as a fighting rooster.

After squandering most of his service pay on ale, fish and chips and pretty girls, he spent twenty-three of his last thirty shillings for a theater ticket. He watched Sir Michael Redgrave play King Lear at Stratford-on-Avon and was so inspired that on the following day he hitchhiked to London.

Unshaven, badly in need of a bath, the scrawny Irishman strode into the famed Royal Academy of Dramatic Art and demanded an immediate audition. He wore a splotched green corduroy suit, sneakers and green socks. The academy's examiners were startled as much by his belligerent talent as they were by his clothes. After giving him intensive oral and written tests, they proclaimed him worthy of a scholarship.

" 'Tis me green socks that brought me luck!" crowed O'Toole. "I'll never change them!" (He wore the socks until their toes and heels were gaping holes, then bought an identical pair. To this day, he still wears green socks, even with tuxedoes.)

Graduating from the academy with honors two years later, he spurned a possible film contract and traveled instead to Bristol to gain additional basic technique with the Old Vic repertory company. One of his first acting chores was the portrayal of a Russian peasant in a Chekhov play. Describing the role some years later, O'Toole said:

"I was supposed to lumber onto the stage and say merely, 'Dr. Ostroff, the horses have arrived,' and then walk off. But I decided the part needed more imagination. So I played it with a slight limp, like Stalin's, and fixed my makeup like Stalin's. When I came on the stage, smoldering with resentment for the aristocracy, I heard a hush come over the audience. And then I ruined everything by blurting: 'Dr. Horsey, the Ostroffs have arrived!' "

Life with the Old Vic company was stimulating but financially disastrous. O'Toole's pay was a pitiful $22.40 a week, and for the first year of his stay in Bristol he had to mail more than half of that to a London landlord he had neglected to pay. Forced to scrimp on food, he had to live by his wits, cadging free dinners from friends until he wore out his welcome. Then he would employ his alternate food plan, which involved charming the waitresses in quiet little side street cafés.

Sitting down, he would order a cup of tea, all he could afford, and then begin chatting with the waitress. His system worked best on ugly girls who were as starved for flattery as he was for meat and potatoes.

"My, that's a lovely dress," he would begin. "Did you choose the material yourself?" If that didn't work, he would compliment the girl's hands, proclaiming her skin the fairest he'd seen in ages, asking: "What kind of soap do you use?" and then launching into a witty discussion of all the latest hand oils and creams.

Somewhere in the conversation he would mention casually and quite frankly that he was broke. At this point, the waitress seeing what he was up to, invariably reacted in one of two ways: (1) She would stamp away in a huff and ignore him until he paid for his tea and left; or (2) thrilled by his flattery, she would wink and say, "I'll see what I can do."

Usually the best the poor girl could do was a plate of spaghetti and tomato sauce, items which weren't watched too closely by the management. On rare occasions, O'Toole received a portion of steak or roast, but he suspected from their odd shapes that they were leftovers salvaged by the waitress from other plates.

During the next three and one-half years, O'Toole—existing like a threadbare refugee from a Charles Dickens novel—appeared in more than threescore roles at Bristol, ranging from Hamlet to comedy parts. In 1957 his first significant opportunity came when, despite the lack of a decent singing voice, he landed a small role in a musical in the West End, London's equivalent of Broadway. From then on, his luck bloomed handsomely and he acquired good dramatic roles.

In a play called *The Holiday*, he met a young doe-eyed Welsh actress named Sian Phillips. Aware that he had come straight from repertory theater, she knew without asking that he was bankrupt and began taking him out to dinner. Three months later they were married.

His next role, that of a loutish soldier in the play *The Long and The Short and The Tall,* won raves from London's normally ice-hearted critics. His notices produced a flock of generous movie offers, including *Lawrence of Arabia.* O'Toole, however, was a third choice for the role, producer Sam Spiegel having been turned down previously by Marlon Brando and Albert Finney, neither of whom relished the thought of roasting for ten months in the Jordanian wilderness.

For weeks before shooting on *Lawrence* began, director David Lean had heard rumors and stories about O'Toole's drinking sprees and casual abuse of his body through lack of sleep and proper meals. O'Toole had nearly lost the role at the outset when, during his first interview with producer Sam Spiegel, a fifth of whiskey had tumbled from his coat pocket. Spiegel had reacted explosively, shouting that he would not tolerate a drinker on his set. It had taken the director many long minutes to calm Spiegel and to convince him that O'Toole had promised to lay off the grog during working hours.

"His word is good," Lean had told the producer persuasively. "O'Toole may be a playboy off the set—but not in front of the cameras. He's a hard worker, dedicated to his craft."

O'Toole reported for work in *Lawrence* after having his nose resculptured by a plastic surgeon, who removed a bony prominence and gave him a proboscis which in profile resembles a sharp ski jump à la Bob Hope's. His salary for *Lawrence* in no way compared with the astronomical half-million-dollar fees he now commands for film performances. His *Lawrence* pay was between $60,000 and $75,000, an elegant sum for a former meal-scrounger, but mere pocket change for top actors and producers.

Aware that the role couldn't help but bring him worldwide attention, O'Toole accepted the first salary offer in a twinkling. But, for appearance's sake, he decided to hedge a bit. Nervy as a carnival barker, he told producer Spiegel bluntly: "I insist on a clause in the contract that will enable me to bring my wife to the desert once a month— at your expense."

Spiegel, who had refused such privileges to other members of the cast, including the temperamental Anthony Quinn, became furious.

"You ungrateful pup!" he stormed. "You're a complete unknown! What makes you think you rate such star treatment?"

"I *am* the star," replied O'Toole, refusing to be cowed. Finally Spiegel capitulated. Many months later, when his work in the picture showed all the earmarks of being spectacular, O'Toole made his admission: "Christ, I wanted this part so bad I would've worked for nothing. And without the clause, too!"

He deliberately made the comment within earshot of two of Spiegel's assistants, knowing what the effect would be when the pair carried the information back to their explosive boss.

Baal, written by the talented Bertol Brecht, was an outstanding London play, and O'Toole's first performance after *Lawrence.* For some reason O'Toole couldn't do it justice. His acting was flabby, weak, diffuse. For many nights, O'Toole was unable to sleep. His interest in the play dwindled and he gave up the role.

A year later, perched on a barstool in a Dublin tavern and tossing down scotch after scotch, O'Toole explained his failure to a group of acquaintances, including writer Gay Talese. *"Baal* was my first real artistic disaster," he said, "and it left me terror-stricken. I was a ship in a storm, wallowing without masts or rudder. 'You're in deep trouble, daddy,' I told myself, and I could feel that trouble all the way to my f---ing toes. It took me a long time to realize why. And then it dawned on me like a crack on the jaw. It was *Lawrence* that was still dragging me down. I was still so exhausted from that f---ing picture that I was emotionally bankrupt!"

Warming to his subject, and seeming to delight in carnivorous self-analysis, O'Toole pounded a fist hard against the scarred wood of the bar. "Lawrence!" he cried. "I became obsessed by that man, and it was bad for me. A true artist should be able to jump into a bucket of ---- and come out smelling of violets. I spent two years and three months making that picture, and it was two years, three months of thinking of nothing *but* Lawrence. I was him day after day, month after month, year after year, totally immersed, and it became bad for me, *personally*—and it killed my acting ability later . . ."

O'Toole shook his head slowly and then shuddered. "I'm

afraid *Lawrence* mutilated me for a while. Filming one character for that length of time was like a bath in acid. Christ, in one scene of the film I saw a close-up of my face when I was 27 years old and then—eight seconds later —there was another close-up of me when I was 29 years old! *Eight goddam seconds* and two years of my life had gone from me!" He paused, grimacing. "Oh, it's painful seeing it all there on the screen, solidified, embalmed. That's why I love the stage. It's art of the moment, making words into living flesh. It's more than mere behaviorism, which is what you get in the movies. For Christ's sake, what *are* movies anyway? Just f—ing moving photographs, that's all!"

In a monologue like that, O'Toole is often at his animated best, especially after sufficient scotch has stimulated his long, narrow frame. As he speaks, his intense eyes take on an incandescent light blue glow and his speech and mannerisms range in style from gutter profanities to the arch language of the drawing room. He is comfortable in any kind of company, a boisterous, fast-talking, adventuresome, compulsive, self-destructive, aggressive but likeable man who—at his present age of thirty-two—has already jammed a hundred years of furious action into his life.

Following his flop in *Baal*, O'Toole had a brief rest before starting *Becket*, a film in which he portrayed King Henry II. This time the critics were merciful, praising his intensive interpretation of the evil, scheming monarch. After banking his whopping big salary check, O'Toole declared that he intended to be merely a part-time film prostitute, alternating picture work with low-paying stage roles which supposedly would keep his theatrical honor untarnished.

He promptly poured his full energies into *Hamlet* for England's new National Theater, doing the uncut version which required nearly six hours of heavy emoting every night. Some of London's critics devoured him, finding fault with everything he did, lambasting the way he raced through certain scenes in an effort to trim the production's time to five hours.

O'Toole did his final *Hamlet* after midnight one night, stayed up until dawn swilling scotch and bourbon with friends and then dashed to the airport. Aching from eighteen inoculations against tropical diseases, he caught a plane for Hong Kong, where the first location shooting for *Lord*

Jim was to take place. Although exhausted from the flight, he was put to work within hours after his arrival, propelling a small boat in a scene which required him to paddle with the frenzy of a man possessed by demons. Such physical activity, combined with the heat and stench of the waterfront, caused him to dislike Hong Kong intensely. Referring to the city as a "miserable, stinking Manchester whore with slant eyes," he spent his off-camera hours lounging in bars and making caustic wisecracks about the British and Chinese residents.

To show his displeasure with the stuffy English management of the sedate hotel where he was staying, he trotted into its elegant main lobby one night pulling a ricksha. His passenger was the vehicle's grinning coolie driver.

Taking the coolie by the elbow, O'Toole led him into the bar and ordered two scotch and sodas.

"Mr. O'Toole!" demanded the hotel's horrified manager, "what *are* you doing?"

"Buying my colleague a drink," sang O'Toole happily, draping a friendly arm across the coolie's bare shoulder. "A bloke can work up a f---ing big thirst dragging around one of those f---ing rickshas!"

From Hong Kong, the *Lord Jim* company went into the jungles of Cambodia where O'Toole and other members of the crew came down with dysentery and heat rash that made clothing unbearable. O'Toole suffered dozens of bleeding bites on his arms and back from giant fleas which seemed as large as his fist. Then came the snakes, with a glitter-eyed curiosity about show business.

The first cobra to show up on the set slithered across the roof of a hut one evening and then dropped to the floor near three cute native actresses. As shrieking pandemonium broke out, a camera assistant rushed in and killed the snake with a clothes pole, stretching it out to its awesome seven-foot length. An hour later, an identical cobra was discovered on the roof, presumably the deceased reptile's loving mate. It, too, dropped off the roof, but eluded its pursuers and lurked in the shadows during the rest of the long night's jittery filming. When a script girl ventured into the ladies room the next morning, she found two snakes coiled up in friendly fashion inside the toilet bowl.

A couple of evenings later, O'Toole encountered a shiny black cobra while strolling down a jungle road. The snake reared up suddenly, hood spread, fangs bared. Both moved like lightning, O'Toole leaping backward like a long-legged hurdler, the cobra striking with angry frustration at the spot the actor had just vacated. "I took the coward's way out," said O'Toole. "I ran like hell all the way back to camp—and I thought that flaming reptile was behind me every step!"

He showed that he retains his childhood resentment toward policemen with a sarcastic comment regarding a Cambodia snake known as the two-step. "It's called that," he said, "because after it bites, you take two steps—and die. One day there was a tough, mean cop in a village where we were staying. While he was sitting on a stool, a two-step sidled up and wrapped itself around his foot. The snake showed a lovely flaming discretion. It didn't fang him, which merely proves that cops are lucky as well as nasty."

Almost as irritating as the snakes and insects was Cambodia's Crown Prince Sihanouk, whose political sympathies are aligned with Communist China. He arrived one day to tour the sets, but spent most of his time making insulting speeches about the British, calling them imperialists, warmongers and money grabbers. O'Toole shared the feelings of his fuming British co-workers, detesting the prince's slurs. But, unable to resist this opportunity to get in a dig at the Limeys, he stepped up to the prince and said with a broad grin: "Sir, I couldn't agree with you more. I happen to be Irish meself."

After three months in Cambodia, including a desperate week of seasickness during filming of additional boat scenes, O'Toole welcomed the chance to depart. "If I live to a thousand," he said bitterly, "I want nothing like Cambodia again. It was a bloody nightmare."

When he finished *Jim*, O'Toole's advisers warned him that the public was growing weary of seeing him in costume dramas. "Do something modern, masculine and gutty," they suggested. "Something in a ripped T-shirt à la Marlon Brando. Be a vicious S.O.B. who enjoys stubbing a fat cigar against a woman's leg." O'Toole, blithely determined to do what he pleased, listened with half an ear and signed for his first film comedy, *What's New Pussycat?* co-starring Peter Sellers.

The idea seemed clever, with O'Toole playing the part of a Parisian fashion editor offered bountiful amounts of luscious sex. Throughout the film he bedded or was about to bed such curvaceous treats as Romy Schneider, Paula Prentiss, Capucine and Ursula Andress. The latter two portrayed nymphomaniacs who stopped at nothing as they frantically schemed to maneuver O'Toole onto the nearest couch or sofa. However, the picture was a major disappointment to O'Toole's fans, who could not stomach the sight of their erstwhile two-fisted, swashbuckling hero padding coyly about in the guise of a fussy, prissy society dandy.

O'Toole dismissed the criticism by saying: "I did my damned best, as I always do. I'm an actor—the hardest working, bloodiest actor I know. I like to be where the action is, where things are humming, where I can shout at the sun and spit at the moon."

If film work grows dull at times, O'Toole can be found mixing into politics (he once marched in a London ban-the-bomb demonstration) or flying about the English countryside at the wheel of a snazzy, overpowered sports car. He considers himself an expert driver and perhaps he is. The British police have an entirely different opinion of his prowess, however, noting that he is hopelessly nearsighted and has been involved in numerous smashups.

In a three-month period in the early Sixties, when his acting fortunes were at a low ebb, he tried to release his frustrations on the highway. He was involved in four crackups during that frantic interval, crumpling so many fenders, headlights and radiators that a magistrate suspended his driving license for thirty days.

Although he is now wealthy enough to have a Rolls Royce, a collection of valuable art and a nineteen-room mansion in posh Hampstead, where he resides with his wife Sian and their two small children, O'Toole does his best to maintain the front of a carefree Irish roisterer.

He dresses in slovenly sport coats, and his shirtfronts are apt to be wrinkled and stained with drippings from ale glasses. He spends money whimsically, delighting in buying peculiar gifts for his wife (such as half a dozen oversize bras or a case of green beer), and in wagering heavily at the tracks where his father was once a bookie. When he has a day off, he sometimes hops aboard a plane for Ireland where his favorite betting place is the ten-pound window at the Punchtown race track on the outskirts of Dublin. His luck is usually as bad as his father's was before him, but afterwards he has a glorious time in the pubs, drinking with theatrical friends or with any stranger who has an honest brogue and wears a bit of green.

It is then, with his tongue loosened by alcohol, that

O'Toole the braggart comes forth, telling stories about his accomplishments which have a strong ring of truth, thanks to his actor's ability to make the most outrageous facts seem reasonable. He will start off with a modest account of how he memorized all the roles in all the works of Shakespeare in two weeks in order to get his first acting job with the Old Vic company. Then he will describe, gulp by gulp, how he once set a record at the Dirty Duck Pub by downing two and one-half pints of ale in forty seconds.

"Afterward," he adds, "I released a belch that knocked down the dart board and two tourists from Surrey."

Next he may impress the growing throng of bug-eyed listeners with a thrilling story of how he and his father once were chased by six angry police nasties at Punchtown. "My father," he says, "was a lovable, kind-hearted bookie who sometimes made miscalculations. He was, alas, no 'Wizard of Odds.'" O'Toole bows at the waist, pleased by the laughing response to his witticism.

"On that particular afternoon, Paddy, my father, was offering ten to one on a nag that should've been two to one at best. Bettors descended upon him in droves and soon his purse and pockets were bulging, fat as Mrs. O'Shaughnessy's sow. The nag's name was Conflict, well-chosen as it turned out. She won in a breeze, and fifty bettors showed up immediately, looking for Paddy O'Toole, who was, of course, nowhere to be found. This, as you might guess, stirred up one hell of a f---ing conflict . . ."

Again he bows, waiting for the laughter to subside.

"The bettors milled about like sheep at a shearing, screaming for the police. Two officers ran up at once. One of the bettors, wiser than the rest, pointed to a stable and screamed: *'Him and the boy run in there!'* Sure, and he was right, because there was Paddy O'Toole and his six-year-old son crouching in the shadows in a corner of the stable, hidden by a great and lovely pile of horse----.

"Well, they never would have seen us, except that Paddy, nervous as you might expect, dropped his purse. Loaded as it was with all that loot, it made a fearful f---ing noise, and they were on us in a flash." O'Toole shakes his head dolefully, but then his eyes brighten. "Paddy seized me by the scruff and we leaped through a window, landing in a yard where they were exercising the horses for the next race. Sure, and they were as lovely a flaming group of animals as you'll ever see."

O'Toole then launches into a dramatic description, with

quick gestures of his long thin arms, of how he and his father jumped upon the back of the nearest black mare. "She had legs like steel springs," he continues, "and in a twinkling we leaped over the gate—'twas easily six feet high—and were off down the road, galloping like the wind sweeping in from the coast of Killadoon. The police nasties came after us like madmen, six of them riding in three official cars, clanging their bells as if all of Ireland was on fire."

O'Toole downs the rest of his scotch, wipes his mouth, and his voice takes on new excitement as he tells how the three police cars chased the horse and its two frenzied riders from Dun Laoghaire to Bray and then to Kilcoole.

"We were doing fine," he says, "until we came to this dead end. One police car was rushing at us from the right, one on a road at the left and the other directly behind us. So Paddy did the only thing he could. He galloped the nag straight ahead through two wide open doors into a great building . . ."

O'Toole's voice is now very mournful. Pausing, he brushes at his blue eyes where genuine tears, big and glistening, are forming.

"Well—what happened?" someone asks, breathlessly.

And then O'Toole—relishing this opportunity to demonstrate the skills which now bring him a million dollars a year—delivers the tag line.

Laughter explodes through the pub as he declares with a sob: " 'Twas a factory for old broken-down horses. The nag, me father and I were all made into a big f---ing pot of glue!"